ICELAND'S
SECRET

Every owner of a physical copy of this edition of

ICELAND'S SECRET

can download the eBook for free direct from us at Harriman House, in a DRM-free format that can be read on any eReader, tablet or smartphone.

Simply head to:

ebooks.harriman-house.com/icelandssecret

to get your copy now.

ICELAND'S SECRET

The Untold Story of the World's Biggest Con

JARED BIBLER

HARRIMAN HOUSE LTD
3 Viceroy Court
Bedford Road
Petersfield
Hampshire
GU32 3LJ
GREAT BRITAIN
Tel: +44 (0)1730 233870

Email: enquiries@harriman-house.com
Website: harriman.house

First published in 2021.
Copyright © Jared Bibler.

Hardcover ISBN: 978-0-85719-899-0
eBook ISBN: 978-0-85719-900-3

British Library Cataloguing in Publication Data
A CIP catalogue record for this book can be obtained from the British Library.

CONTENTS

til þín, elskan mín

PROLOGUE

I COULD have driven to the *Fjármálaeftirlitið* (FME)—the financial supervisory authority of Iceland—from my home in about 12 minutes. Instead I am sitting in an old minibus with nine seats and no muffler and at the top of the hill I'll need to change to a bigger bus to get taken to my new office.

The whole trip will take almost an hour. The transfer point at Hamraborg looks like a big deal on the transit map: lots of bus routes converge here. In another country it would have a kiosk with hot coffee and someone selling newspapers. But here in Iceland it's merely a wind- and rain-swept hilltop, with schedules for the unreliable connections fastened haphazardly to streetlight poles.

Transferring passengers hold our bodies against a steady barrage of wind and icy droplets of rain, our expressions grim. No shelters. The city buses that pull up to the curbside are a hodgepodge of cast-offs from other Nordic countries, seemingly no two vehicles alike, all painted in various shades of yellow, and clearly never designed for the aggressive and unplanned system of speed bumps that plague suburban Reykjavík. Once inside the larger bus, the diesel-soaked air, fogged windows, and near-constant jostling induce nausea.

I try to ignore the immediate surroundings and focus on the day ahead. This is an important day for me. It is the first working day of April 2009, nearly six months to the day since the collapse of Iceland's banks, its economy, and nearly the nation.

As I look out the window of this old workhorse heading towards my new office, hearing the gnashing of the engine and the studded tires chewing Reykjavík's roadways beneath me, I feel grateful to have finally found paying work. But why did they choose me? Perhaps for the first time being an *útlendingur*—a foreigner—actually helped. I became an Icelandic citizen the year before, but nobody took *that* seriously. For most, I would remain a misfit. And maybe for this job they need someone who is a bit of an outsider.

Whatever the reason, I am grateful. The last few months have been tough. We have been running on fiscal fumes: only my fiancée Hulda's new job as office manager in a small law firm plus drawing down what was left of our meager savings allowed us to pay the bills each month. Slashed or zero incomes, frozen savings, a depleted stock market, ever-rising prices. The Icelandic crisis of 2008 was an earthquake that leveled the financial fortunes of a whole country.

The stock market has lost 97% of its value from its high in 2007, effectively a stunning reset of the whole market to zero. (By comparison the U.S. S&P 500 and German DAX indexes have each dropped around 55% in the same period: still big but not a wipeout.) The cause of the complete deletion of the Icelandic stock market is pretty clear: its value was more or less comprised of the shares of three collapsed banks. When these went bust, the entire market went with them. Unemployment has also surged in Iceland: from a handful of unemployed in 2007, by spring of 2009 the number of those without work has quintupled. (The U.S. media caterwauls about the terrible crisis in that country, where the number of unemployed doubled: a huge surge, to be sure, but nothing like five times.)[1]

I haven't worked for a paycheck the entire six months until this morning. Because I was the one to resign from the bank where I worked, rather than being fired, I haven't been eligible for unemployment benefits for most of the months I've been jobless. To keep myself from going crazy pacing our small apartment while Hulda worked and studied long days, I found unpaid employment at a start-up in January. I was developing a business plan for green

---

[1] Sources: Hagstofa Íslands, U.S. Bureau of Labor Statistics.

energy plants. But I worked for free, on a gentlemen's agreement that they'd pay me when they got funding. They weren't gentlemen.

We have been through the very darkest of winters. Hulda and I have taken a fine-tooth comb to our household finances and looked for ways to save every possible *króna* in order to keep ourselves afloat. Hence my bus ride this morning instead of a convenient trip by car: we are limiting ourselves to one tank of fuel per month. Our misery even reaches onto our plates: finding affordable food becomes an issue. Trying to get creative, I took a Sunday trip to Kólaportið, the weekend flea market and farmers' market in Reykjavík, where I picked up *bjúgur*, horsemeat sausages, and brought them home. These may very well constitute the cheapest edible protein in the Land. Hulda knew how to prepare them from her childhood: boiled in water. Once done, I tried to smile across the dinner table at her, but the smell, the taste, and especially the texture of the giant white gobs of horse-fat that popped out of the sliced casing were too much. For me, this is the sign that we have hit the bottom of the barrel.

The national political mood has also hit rock bottom during these past months. The politicians in power during the run-up to the crisis at first refused to step aside and call for new elections. The heads of the central bank and the FME itself similarly refused. But angry mobs gathered daily in the frigid cold of downtown Reykjavík all winter long. They banged loudly on pots and pans, carrying banners and chanting slogans in front of the *Alþingi* (parliament), every day for months. My friend Süßmann has his office in the old Apotek building overlooking this square. He's working to settle the estate of one of the banks with its foreign creditors, but his phone calls overseas are routinely interrupted by the clamor from the crowds.

One day he looked out the window to see that the national Christmas tree, a gift from Norway each year, was on fire. It did not last to see Christmas morning. Then, a New Year's TV broadcast, normally a staid roundtable discussion among a handful of top politicians, was interrupted when protesters clanged their way right into the live shoot. At last, we have new elections to look forward to at the end of the month[2] and hopefully a chance to start over for our tumultuous nation.

At this point, six months after the onset of the crisis, I would have taken any work at all. But this new opportunity is not just any job. Not only is the salary decent by post-crisis Icelandic standards, but this one feels like the chance to do something positive for my new country and for the people around us who have been suffering as much as us. I am going to be one of the few tasked with investigating the banking crisis, the very thing that plunged our nation into this black hole.

I am going to be an investigator for the FME, the financial supervisor of the Land.

A few days into my new job, a lawyer shows up at my desk. It's our first interaction and I am not sure if he's my teammate or my boss. I know he's the senior attorney on the team, but we both report to the same boss. So he can't delegate work to me. Or can he? The lawyers do seem to have the run of the place here. In Iceland there is often a near complete lack of organizational hierarchy, meaning most tasks are negotiated peer-to-peer. He looks at me jovially: "Jared, can you have a look at this? None of us really knows what to do with it."

I grab the document: just a couple of stapled pages under the letterhead of the Icelandic stock exchange and addressed to us, the FME. I puzzle over the subject line, turning it over to see a series of data tables. I look up and the lawyer has already disappeared. I take it apart line by line. In short, the stock exchange noticed some strange trading patterns in the three days right before the banks collapsed and thought that we, the market regulator, should be made aware of it.

I can check this out, I think. After all, I worked in a Wall Street back office, and then became a fund manager, so I've executed and settled some trades in my day. This material shouldn't prove too difficult to verify.

---

2   25 April 2009.

The letter runs to just three printed pages, including the tables. Short and sweet. Yet as I probe into the substance of it, the content hits me like a thunderbolt. This is absolutely wild; well beyond anything I have come across in my career. Even all the hijinks I tried to stop at Landsbanki, the ones that ultimately led me to resign, have nothing on this material. If this is even half true, it is completely nuts.

The document lays it all out in plain Icelandic. During three crucial days—the days immediately preceding the nation's collapse—the traders who buy and sell with the banks' own money bought nearly every single one of the banks' shares that crossed the public market. *At each bank!* Was this a coordinated effort to prop up the markets and make everyone think things were just fine? By that point it was far too late to stop the inevitable collapse, but that did not seem to matter to these guys. At a time when those three banks were running on fumes, barely able to pick up two *krónur* off the floor, they seem to be throwing everything they have left at buying up their own shares.

This activity is more than clearly illegal; it's beyond the pale. I can't believe these guys thought they would get away with it. Mumbling to myself in my cubicle, I pencil notes down the margins of the letter. Anyone with any knowledge at all of securities markets would be thunderstruck at the sight of this brazen buying. It's so destructive that it is hard to come up with a real-world analogy to explain it. It would be something like as bad as if a supermarket owner, seeing that nobody is buying his well-rotted tomatoes, hired dozens of actors to queue outside his store, buying up his produce with the store's own cash. But here we aren't talking about tomatoes, we are talking about the former high-flying blue-chip shares of Iceland, the three gleaming giant banks that made up nearly *all* of the value of the country's stock market. A market in which every one of us, rich and poor, had a good chunk of our retirement savings invested, via a legally mandated pension.

The letter raises far more questions for me than it answers. I list a few bullets for what I would like to understand better and walk down the hall to my new boss' office late that afternoon. Back in my

Wall Street days, a colleague would often remind us to "go to the videotape", by which he meant look at the actual data. Raw trades are what I really need to see. I realize halfway down the hallway that I have no idea how things work here. I just know that I am in possession of a potentially huge story.

Sigrún[3] is a careful woman who speaks in measured tones. In her fifties, always impeccably well dressed, she carries herself with confidence. She is in charge of all market regulation at the FME, and post-crisis, most of the investigations as well. She selected me for this new investigation role from nearly 200 applicants, so I know she has some confidence in me—and some expectations as well. I am happy to have found something so juicy so early in my new career as a regulator.

"Sigrún! I can't believe what I'm seeing here," I tell her. "I would like to see the detailed trading data. How can I get it?"

"We have a good relationship with the exchange," she replies, unmoved. "Just give them a ring."

At my desk I lift the phone and dial the contact on the letterhead and wait. The analysis is already a few months old but my counterpart remembers and says he can send some data related to these three trading days.

Then I wait. I go back to reading some auditor reports, thinking this request will take a few days. Within an hour, though, I get an email from the guy at the exchange. It has: guess what? An Excel file attached. Excel? *Really?* I think. I am not quite sure what I was expecting, but not a casual two-line email with an attached unlocked file filled with rows of trades. Maybe I shouldn't be surprised by this point; all of the Land seems to run on handmade Excel files.

I am by no means an expert user of this software. Most of my experience with spreadsheets comes from the bank: trying to analyze by how much we'd gouged our investors on a faulty price calculation,

3   The events described in this book are true to the best of the author's recollection and information. The following names have been changed and are fictive: Binni, Guðfinnur, Högni, Pétur, Siddi, Sigrún, Villi, and Waingro. Also changed from the original: Aurora Capital Management, Mike Shimrinmanson, and Zodiac Software.

or how many more days we had left until our pet hedge fund ran out of cash. So I'll need to figure out how to use Excel in a new way: to visualize trading flows across a whole market over many days. Studying the first graphs I generate, more than looking at rows of raw trades, helps me to begin to make sense of the story. I start with Kaupþing, the biggest Icelandic bank. Once I put the pictures up on one of my two screens, the pattern appears clearly for anyone to see.

The price barely moves over a whole day and the ID for the buyer is always the same, on each and every exchange trade. This market only had one buyer? Yes, just as the letter laid out. But I still don't believe my eyes. I call the stock exchange again.

"Is this everything? Are all the trades in the document you sent over?" I ask.

"Sure," the employee says.

"But there's only one guy at the bank buying everything."

"That's right," he replies, like nothing abnormal was happening.

This craziness can't have taken place for more than a few trading days. I make a new request the day after.

"I have a new inquiry," I tell my new friend at the stock market. He doesn't sound too delighted.

"Go ahead."

"I need two more weeks of trading data, starting mid-September, up until the three days before the collapse."

Bothered as he seems, he fills the new request pretty quickly. Upon opening the latest Excel file, I begin to understand how naïve I have been. I thought I would be able to catch the beginning of this pattern with only a few weeks' data. But all the trading days in September 2008 are near carbon copies of each other. The prop desk of Kaupþing would buy 90 to 100% of the market volume in KAUP shares all day and every day, gobbling up nearly every share that came across the exchange. And the same pattern holds for the other big banks, Landsbanki and Glitnir, in their own share issues.

Since the 1990s, many big banks developed prop desks, short for proprietary trading desks, and these three fast-growing Icelandic institutions wanted to be just like the big boys overseas. In a typical bank, these operations effectively served as in-house hedge funds, placing bets with the bank's own money. They tried to earn profits through both intraday trading and longer-term positions. What is jumping off the page at me here is that in each major Icelandic bank, the prop desk seemed to be taking a large and unannounced position in that bank's own shares. How could they justify this clearly manipulative behavior?

The raw data show that each Icelandic bank had one or two traders who had access to the bank's own funds and performed the same mission: keeping the share price of their own employer high. But something else strikes me as odd here: how did Nasdaq OMX, the stock exchange, not detect this earlier? And not raise an alarm with more eagerness? Why wait until months after the crisis and then send a letter focused on only the final three days? I can't help but wonder about this lack of prompt action. Did they just not see it? Did they not want to see it? I decide to keep hunting.

In my next conversation with the exchange I see the effect that my digging is starting to have. My 'friend' still answers my requests, but he seems more and more reluctant. He takes his time, doesn't always pick up the phone, responds laconically. I get the feeling my questions are making some members of the small Nasdaq outpost nervous. They don't try to discourage me, at least not explicitly. Nevertheless, the tone is changing. They seem to hope I'll find a different bone to chew on.

I need to keep up the charm offensive each time I place a call to the exchange. I next analyze all the way back to April 2008, a full six months before the crisis. But the daily buying by each bank is nearly the same over that whole period! So I go big, finally asking them to send a full five years of trading data. An Excel spreadsheet of gargantuan proportions, it is a file that my PC can barely open. Working inside it slows the machine to a crawl; these are nearly all the market trades done in Iceland over half a decade. Using my ever-improving Excel skills, I graph net purchases of shares by month as well as share price. And to my astonishment, I can trace the same pattern all the way back to the summer of 2004. This illegal buying has been going on in each of the three banks over the whole time I've been living in Iceland.

There are variations in the data, to be sure. During some relatively calmer periods, the banks' traders did not amass so many of their own shares. However, the overall picture is crystal clear: as soon as the stock price of any one bank declines even a little bit, the bank's prop desk pounces on it. The visuals make this trend obvious. There are almost no months in all those long years—the years of the 'Icelandic miracle', the years of Range Rovers, private jets, and Elton John being flown in to play a private birthday party—when these bank traders did not buy a substantial amount of the shares issued by their own employer.

Starting out at this job as a new investigator, I knew the expectation was that we might find a handful of rogue trades and money wires in the few weeks before each bank's collapse. We could dig into these few events, write reports, and then close the case files. But a years-long fraud perpetrated on the entire stock market of our proud nation is a much bigger discovery than anyone bargained for. I know now that I am on an important but precarious mission. Yet, in many ways, I still can't believe my eyes. It seems incredible that these three giant institutions would control the markets for their own shares for so many years without catching attention. And a bigger mystery is also becoming obvious: what did they do with all the shares once they'd bought them? We must have missed something. Something bigger than this trading pattern. We miscounted somewhere, we left something out.

These are the thoughts churning in my head as I ride the faded yellow bus back home in the bright light of an early spring evening at the conclusion of a roller-coaster first week at the FME.

The causes of the Icelandic financial crisis of 2006–08 are hardly understood and barely discussed either inside or outside the country even today. That is a mistake. This is a crisis that has clear relevance for every country that practices market capitalism. And these days, that's just about every country.

Iceland is a small nation, with only around 350,000 residents today. But it's still a country, with all of the trappings of larger places. Iceland is actually a perfect laboratory in which to view the forces at work in larger nations.

This crisis stands out in a couple of respects. First, by magnitude. The year 2008 saw a financial crisis spreading across nearly all of the Western world, but no country experienced the disaster the way Iceland did. Its three giant banks fell over in one week, quickly engulfing the whole economy. Icelanders who had savings in their stock portfolios had them no more: the stock market had lost all of its value. People who had their savings in cash fared no better: accounts and funds were frozen. Mortgage payments doubled almost overnight. The value of the currency dropped by half. The setback was not just huge, it was lasting; the country can still feel the crisis more than a decade later. The quick drop off in the currency kicked off a tourist invasion that, while initially providing a much-needed economic boost, has now reduced Iceland to a giant T-shirt shop. Meanwhile, those who lost their savings and their homes never got them back. Forced to start over from zero, many fled the country for better opportunities abroad.

Iceland also stands out in its response to this crisis. The magnitude of the crisis and the discontent of the Icelandic people were enough to trigger real, if short-lived, investigations into the responsibilities for the disaster. The financial supervisory authority, a special parliamentary commission, and the appointment of a special prosecutor whose team briefly counted over 100 staff made it possible to uncover at least some of the facts. These processes led to the criminal convictions of the heads of the three biggest banks, a handful of lower-level executives, and even the prime minister. This, again, is more than any other country managed to do after the 2008 financial crisis.

Was it enough? Have the lessons been properly learned? By no means. Despite the shocking depths of this crisis, today in Iceland almost nothing has changed in either the political or economic structures that underpin society. And the same can be said for the wider world as well.

The Icelandic crisis is a cautionary tale for the world, a saga of the high level of crime that follows unregulated Wild West capitalism. Don't think your own country is any better or worse than Iceland. This is the untold story of how it unfolded.

PART I—THE LAND

1

LAVA FIELDS

THE journey that took me to the heart of the biggest financial fraud in history began in a parking lot next to a lava field.

It's November 2003 and I am standing outside a perfectly clean office building perched in the middle of jagged fields of lava on the outskirts of the city of Reykjavík. The fresh Icelandic air is cold in a way that penetrates to my bones. Standing next to me is a soft-spoken shaven-headed Viking. We are looking north across the ragged black expanse at a blue monstrosity, Iceland's largest shopping mall. He's just walked me downstairs and outside. His next words are unexpected: "Well, if you want a job here, it's yours."

I don't know how to answer. I met Pétur the evening before in Vegamót, a downtown bar, on the advice of some new friends. We talked securities software for an hour. I explained the vagaries of trade settlements in the U.S. mortgage-backed market as well as the Japanese system of *jikko* before the conversation took a more personal turn. We realized we really got along. And then this morning he picked me up at my hotel and brought me here for a follow-up. His deputy, a hard-driving woman the same age as me, gave me a reasonable grilling, and then he good-copped her and showed me a presentation about his vision for his small software firm in a top-floor office. Now this: a job offer out of the blue.

In my surprise, I hesitate. It's true, I sent around 20 résumés out to companies in Iceland a few months before, a sort of Hail Mary pass to escape the increasingly oppressive world of mortgage-boom Wall Street where I'd been spending days, nights, and weekends for the better part of five years, but I never expected this kind of luck. Do I have a chance to uproot my life and move to Iceland? I'm suddenly scared.

So I tell him I will think it over and come back to him on Monday. It's a Saturday in November around noon. Which means the light is just about enough to see to walk in relative safety over the jagged rocks and pulverized black gravel that make up the parking lot. The Reykjavík sprawl does this, I'm learning: at its edges it stops abruptly and one is confronted with the harsh reality of life on the rock.

I make it to the mall entrance and my friend Heiða picks me up. It's my fourth time as a tourist in Iceland these past 18 months, and I have fallen in love with the place. I met Heiða and some of her friends on my first visit: a three-night stopover on my way home to Boston from Stockholm in May of 2002, courtesy of Icelandair's generous ticketing policies. The nearly endless light, the nearly endless late-night crowds on Laugavegur, and the nearly endless national soul all pretty much hooked me that first time.

Plus a drunken Icelandic sailor on shore leave came up to me in a bar, unbidden, took my hand in his coarse iron grip, and told me, "You are my brother. You are an Icelander."

Was he right? Could I really live here? Work here?

———

Nine months of wrangling with visas and paperwork later, it's the middle of August 2004 and I am finally in my first week of work at Zodiac, the small software company owned by Pétur. I wake up on the top floor of Heiða's family's house in Kópavogur. Last night I was up studying until midnight. My new Icelandic teacher handed me a CD yesterday and gave me her orders: "Listen to these dialogues and follow along in the book until you understand every word. *Every word.*"

I followed her instructions to the letter. At first the conversations were impenetrable. One has a family sitting around the breakfast table, and the little boy Guðni doesn't want to eat anything. He reluctantly agrees after his *pabbi* tells him: "*Fótboltamenn verða nú líka að borða!*"— footballers have to eat something too! Wrapping my head around these new words—and all the others too—took me hours. And I had to be up again at six.

My new life is chaos and confusion, with nothing solid to grab onto. After many months of waiting offshore for all the employment and visa paperwork to come through, I finally touched down in the Land on 9 August. I need to settle on a new apartment, and I am still awaiting a small shipment of housewares and my mom's old car from the States. So for a few weeks, my friend Heiða and her family have given me an extra room to stay in.

I come downstairs and Heiða's mom has already laid out breakfast. I am so happy to have these wonderful people to host me, but everything is so foreign. There are a bunch of things laid out in the middle of the table: something labeled *smjör*, cheese, sliced cucumbers, and other mysterious things in plastic tubs.[4] By watching the others, I learn I should toast a slice of bread and then put all of these things on top of it. Even the milk tastes different. There is nothing familiar here. The announcer on the radio is speaking ultra-fast. The language feels hermetic, despite the studying.

Thankfully, Heiða and her family all speak excellent English after having lived and worked for many years in southern Massachusetts. But one of the conditions Pétur laid out for hiring me was that I would become fluent in Icelandic as quickly as possible. Zodiac, his company, are even paying for part of my lessons.

I have to hurry from breakfast because another friend will drive me to the university for my morning language lesson and I have to walk to meet him at his house. It's cold and raining lightly—autumn

---

4 All of these items thoroughly encapsulated by one great Icelandic word: *álegg*.

weather for me, though ten days ago I was in the midst of a muggy Boston summer. We crawl through the Reykjavík morning traffic to the university, and I hope I won't be late again.

The lesson lasts from 8 to 10 and my teacher Guðrún, in her early 40s with short steely blond hair, is tough as nails. She's the best friend of Pétur's wife, thus the connection, but her work and passion is teaching Icelandic to foreigners. This is still a pretty new idea, as is the idea of emigrating to Iceland at all. Guðrún is the best teacher of the Icelandic language in the whole country, she hints. I believe her. She pushes me hard: we are doing a chapter or two of a basic textbook each day. (She wrote it.) Even the coffee breaks are no break: she flips through the morning paper, but stops at each headline and teaches me the words.

In one of the papers, the Icelandic banks are starting to advertise mortgages. To me this doesn't seem out of the ordinary at all, but she shakes her head disapprovingly. I can't figure out why: it's yet another way everything here feels upside-down.[5] My only reprieve is when we go outside so she can huddle for a cigarette against the leeward side of the drab grey university building. But then she piles on the homework. Each night I am pulling three or four hours.

After the lesson I need to take a taxi all the way back out to Kópavogur, to my new job. The work is not at all what I expected: programming in a new language, one I feel slow and dumb at. And it's hardcore programming. On the Street I'd been both an analyst and a coder. Here it's all coding, all the time: eight hours or more a day. Staring at a screen: the development environment, the bug reporting system. No phone calls from crazed NY guys to break things up.

I was warned that cars are super expensive in Iceland so I have schemed what I thought was a way around that. I bought my mom's trusty seven-year-old silver Toyota RAV4 and the day she handed

5   Much later I'll learn why she was so cynical: they were making this whole new book of business at a loss, and directly competing with the Icelandic government's Housing Finance Fund in doing so. Trying to force the government itself out of business?

me the keys, I drove it to the docks in Everett, Massachusetts for shipment up to the Land. It is a reliable car, four-wheel drive, perfect for the harsh reality of Icelandic driving that I already learned a bit about in my tourist days.

What I don't quite realize is *why* cars are so expensive in the Land. It has to do with a combination of import duties, value-added tax, and steep registration fees, all on top of the shipping costs themselves. Even importing the old car costs me about as much again as I've already paid to buy it. It's also a real hassle involving an opaque bureaucracy spread across three entities: the shipping company, Icelandic customs, and the registry of motor vehicles.

At the shipping company, I've been going back and forth with a young girl, perhaps 20, who runs my customs paperwork. Today is my fifth visit to Reykjavík harbor to sort out delivery since the car was unloaded ten days ago. This girl seems to be a summer intern, and to not really know the importation process at all. She gives me the title to the car but then calls me at work to ask that I bring it back in. As I see her interact with the other ladies there, I realize that nobody else in this office seems to have a firm grasp of how to import a vehicle either. It seems like the very first time anyone there has imported a car.

We go back and forth again, papers stapled and unstapled, the girl conferring with her co-workers at each step. I pay them a fee from my new Icelandic debit card. Then they run some numbers again and tell me they need to refund part of the fee. The final invoice has charges they can't really explain. I'm legitimately surprised when the girl at last tells me, "OK, your car is waiting for you."

I stand by the back door of the low-slung office building, almost more of a trailer. The door beeps open and I'm looking out at a sea of yet-to-be-processed vehicles, parked haphazardly in rows. Yellow shipping cranes tower over us, dwarfing the tiny office.

The dock worker who greets me on the other side of the door is young and brash. He thrills at driving his pickup truck too fast down the unfinished dirt roads of the loading area. We enter a labyrinth of cars, maybe a thousand at least, sitting out in the sun. We blast down a long row of vehicles, skidding to a stop behind my mom's familiar car. I smile to myself, sort of amazed to see it again after dropping it off an ocean away.

"Look at this piece of junk," the guy says. "You could at least have shipped a better car here from America. I thought you guys were supposed to be rich."

I am not really sure how to respond. But as I look around the vast lot it strikes me: all huge, expensive, brand new cars imported mostly from the U.S. by the looks of it. I see a dealer badge from a Long Island Jeep dealership on the car next to mine.

"I got to unload those Porsches up at the front last week," he says, gesturing at a 'king's row' of silver Carreras.

"Hey, I left my BMW back in the States," I say, rising to the bait. But since when is the trusty RAV4 considered a shitty car?

Status symbol or no, I'm happy to drive off the grubby lot on my own four wheels. *Ég á bíl!*—I have a car—and this will make all the difference in my new Icelandic life. Public transport in Iceland seems pretty abysmal, even after Boston (itself no Mecca). Out on the main road, an oncoming driver flashes me and I learn that Iceland is a headlights-always-on jurisdiction. One more stop: the inspection station, where I'll need to pay another giant fee. The inspector hands me a cordless drill and a piece of scrap wood and gestures at the floor. I kneel down on the rough concrete and drill my own mounting holes in brand-new TE-700 license plates that feature a bright blue and red Icelandic flag.

The comments of the young punk at the docks are running in my head as I roll around the streets of the capital enjoying my regained freedom. Everywhere I look now I see big, shiny, new SUVs and luxury cars. How do people afford these on an Icelandic salary?

My new street lies under the approach path for Reyjavík City airport and I see something I almost never saw back in my American life: a private jet streaking in to land nearly every time I go out for a walk. The incongruity isn't lost on me: I live in a neighborhood of modest fishermen's houses, brightly painted and clad in corrugated metal against the weather. Meanwhile cream-colored Gulfstreams slice the sky overhead at approach speed.

For a guy from New England, it feels a bit like living in a small Maine fishing town that has its own fleet of private aircraft. My Icelandic friends are surprised when I point out how strange I find it to see so many private jets, after so few in 30 years of living near one of America's wealthiest cities. They say: "Really? But in the movies you see them all the time!" Has Iceland succeeded in creating a Hollywood version of an economic paradise in the far reaches of the cold North Atlantic Ocean?

Iceland occupies one of the world's largest islands, a land a little bigger than the island of Ireland, and slightly smaller than England. In the U.S., its size is sometimes compared to the state of Kentucky— though I'm not sure how helpful that is. I prefer to think of the place as a floating New England.

It is a large land mass for such a small population, but most of the middle of the country is a high desert: windswept, uninhabitable, and largely impassable, thanks to one of the largest deforestations in human history. The population has always lived on farms and in fishing villages dotted around the green coastline, but in the last 120 years nearly two-thirds have streamed into Reykjavík and its suburbs. Before that time, there were almost no roads in the country and the chief method of transportation was by ship, circumnavigating the coastline, and by horseback on small paths inland.

Since World War II, Icelandic standards of living have shot through the roof, compared to the sod farmhouses and horse paths of centuries past. Today Iceland has a standard of living comparable with the rest of Europe, with a lot of that development made possible by the wealth of the seas. Iceland offers its residents a Nordic basket of social goods: universal health care, nine months of paid leave for both parents to share, and a decent education system that produces a claimed 100% literacy rate.

Once one drives away from the Reykjavík area, the country can feel to the uninitiated like a vast, empty, and unexplored land. I decide to take a long weekend road trip to the West Fjords, about five hours' drive from Reykjavík on a good day. One of my new friends cautions me about the wisdom of making such a journey. He warns me that the roads are not all paved and can suddenly become very slippery with rubble or slick with ice. He says that on many days of the year, much of that part of Iceland is impossible to access by road. And he calls me for updates a few times during the trip, to make sure I am OK.

I have purchased an Icelandic road atlas, which lists in detail the attractions on each little section of road. I am confused at first, because what the road atlas lists appears to my American eyes to be towns coming up. But actually each 'town' is just the name of a farm, and when I drive alongside, maybe that farm is only one building, and often that building is empty or even reduced to rubble after decades of absence. It is indicative of the Icelandic attitude toward places, even tiny clusters of buildings, that the word for town, *bær*, is the same as the word for farm. In a vast land with few inhabitants, every farm (and every farmer) takes on great importance.

October 2005 finds me on a Sunday drive around Reykjavík and some of the suburbs and I notice just how many new apartments and houses are being built on the outskirts. In the town of Hafnarfjörður, for example, a vast area next to the Haukur athletic complex is sprouting a completely new neighborhood, growing seemingly straight out of the lava. It doesn't look like anyone is living there yet, but seems as though it could support thousands of people. Outside of Njarðvík, close to the international airport, a sign proclaims a planned development of over 800 new apartments. The city is also expanding rapidly by the start of Route 1 at Heiðmörk. The sheer number of towering yellow cranes in these brand new neighborhoods is unlike anything I have seen anywhere else in the world.

I can't help but wonder who exactly is going to live in all of these new places. Sure, Iceland is experiencing a baby boom, but most of these little tykes aren't going to be able to sign a mortgage application anytime soon. The government also does not seem to be in a hurry to open the gates to lots of new immigrants. Could this be a speculative boom fueled by the Icelandic banks entering the mortgage market last year at cut rates, the thing that worried my teacher so much? House prices around the capital have hit record highs since then.

The combination of this building boom and the lofty stock market (the benchmark ICEX-15 index is up 37% this year alone) reminds me a lot of the good-old bubblicious days of the late 1990s in the U.S. It was a lovely time while it lasted—who can really say no to first-class flights to Asia and two-month bonuses?—but I remember how painful it was in the years following the bursting of the NASDAQ bubble.

What will happen to our little Icelandic economy if this bubble pops?

I go for my first solo meeting with a Zodiac Asset Manager client in early March 2006. I arrive at the main office of a savings bank in one of the drab industrial ghettos of Reykjavík and take an elevator up to the reception area. I have made real progress: speaking in Icelandic, I tell the receptionist my name, my company name, and the name of the person I am meeting, the head of wealth management. Understanding, she puts on her headset, calls upstairs and says, "Veistu hvar Jón er? Ég er með útlendingi hér."—"Do you know where John is? I have a foreigner here."

I understand her perfectly, but it seems like in the time between speaking to me and punching in the number she has forgotten I am even here. To me what she said feels like: "John! The foreigner is here to see you! Iceland's only foreigner!"

Later that same day we have a presentation at work on the growing equality of the sexes in Iceland on family matters. The presenter seems to take great pride in how family life is becoming more balanced in Iceland. He appears a fair-minded man. But at one point, to illustrate something, he says, "It's not as though we're all barbarians like in Turkey and Albania!"

Icelanders have a saying about the country: '*bezt í heimi*', meaning 'best in the world'. It is an expression that is often said tongue-in-cheek, with reference to Iceland's widely felt inferiority complex, but at another level there is almost always some genuine feeling behind it. In a historical sense, there are many reasons to be proud to be an Icelander.

Iceland was founded by disgruntled landholders from Norway, who bristled at the consolidation of the land under its first king and dreamed of a free place where they could farm to their hearts' content. These wealthy landowners fitted up longships, became known as Vikings, and began their migration west. The first settler arrived in Iceland around 874 AD. Previously, there had been no permanent human inhabitants in Iceland. Over the decades that followed, more farmers migrated west from Norway to this new promised land, often taking with them Celtic slaves captured in Ireland. (Explaining the presence of redheads and freckles in many Icelanders today.)

Just over 50 years later, in 930 AD, the need for some kind of government of this new land was evident, and the heads of each Icelandic estate began meeting once a year for several weeks in the height of summer in an assembly called the Alþing. This was effectively the first representative government since ancient times. This parliament has been meeting almost continually to this day.

A few centuries later, the early tales of settlement had grown into oral legends, and one man decided to write many of them down on parchment. These became the Icelandic sagas—an Icelandic word roughly equivalent to 'old saw'. Today most of what we know of Norse mythology is thanks to the work of one man, Snorri Sturluson, whose transcription of oral traditions onto sheepskin has survived the centuries. These sagas are the prose stories describing the settlement and early conflicts in Iceland, and they represent the oldest prose literature in the West. With our modern eyes, we expect them to read like novels, but the novel wasn't invented until more than 500 years later. Instead, they read as a straightforward recall of sometimes extraordinary events:

> "They ran to the door but there was no easy escape there, because of both the piled wood blocking the door and Egill

24

guarding it. He killed them in the doorway and just outside. It was only moments before the main room flared up and caved in. Everyone else was inside and trapped, while Egill went back to the woods and rejoined his companions."

The tone used to describe a vengeful murderous rampage can seem almost ho-hum to the modern reader, and therein lies a lot of the charm. These are great works of early literature.

Icelanders survived some horrible centuries of their own under Danish rule, subsisting on rotten grain sent over late by Danish ships in exchange for all the top-quality wool and fish they could hand over. Finally, in 1918, enough was enough: Iceland achieved home rule for the first time in more than 700 years. Then, in 1944, an occupied Denmark was unable to keep Iceland from achieving the full independence it had long sought.

Despite the best efforts of the Danes over the centuries, who mandated all official business be transacted in their guttural tongue, the Icelandic language survived mostly intact in its ancient form. The language itself is the western variant of Old Norse, and is from the Germanic family of languages, like English. Icelandic is in many ways a time capsule of the languages of that period, 1,200 years ago, and its grammar and vocabulary are very close to Old English. That modern Icelanders can read the old sagas and understand most of them with minimal footnotes is a tribute to the way a language can be preserved for a long time in isolation, and also a source of great pride for the country.

J.R.R. Tolkien, author of *The Lord of the Rings*, was an Oxford professor and scholar of Icelandic language and literature. He prescribed that any student of English literature who really wanted to understand 'the roots' should become fluent in Icelandic and read the sagas in their original form. As a native English speaker who has learned Icelandic, I tend to agree. The language is a giant, and I never learned English so well as when I began to learn Icelandic.

2

TEMBLORS

HAVE been living in Iceland around a year and a half by this point. During this time, the stock market, led by the shares of the three giant and ever-growing banks, has done nothing but go up. Two of my co-workers, both of whom sit out in the customer-facing area, are the biggest cheerleaders. The first is a mild-mannered old-school database guy, and whenever I go to visit his desk with a work question he's refreshing the numbers and wanting to talk shop. He evinces a quiet admiration for the new generation of leaders in Icelandic business. "These guys are geniuses," he says almost under his breath, explaining a private equity style sale-and-leaseback deal done to extract cash from one of the Icelandic home improvement chains. He seems to have an endless supply of whispered inside gossip and juicy tales from the world of high Icelandic finance, where I can tell he longs to be.

The second, Waingro, is far more unbridled in his enthusiasm. "Look at these banks, Jared!" he calls out to me from across the big open-plan room where he sits. His enthusiasm knows no bounds. "Yeah but what's the P/E ratio? What are these values based on?" I counter sometimes. "Who cares, Jared? It's gonna be great, Jared!"[6]

6   The main stock market index in Iceland increased in value by 330% from the beginning of January 2004 to July 2007 when it peaked. When I moved to Iceland in 2004 the market

I have been waiting for this stock market to have a correction since I arrived, and grow tired of being wrong when it rockets up again the next week. It seems to be going up in nearly a straight line, the main index more than doubling in value since my arrival. Every company on the exchange is going up, all the time, adding value steadily by close to 4% *a month*. I don't know enough to figure out what is behind this meteoric rise. And part of me is feeling dumb for missing out on the party, too.

So my academic curiosity kicks into overdrive when another friend sends me a link to a March 2006 report put out by Merrill Lynch credit analysts describing their questions on the sustainability of the Reykjavík financial sector: *Icelandic Banks: Not What You Are Thinking.*[7] The topmost headline already intrigues me: "We Are Only At the Beginning of the Icelandic Banks' Problems..." So I put my afternoon programming and bug-fixing on hold and start gobbling my way through the green-fringed PDF. Finally someone is putting solid facts around problems I had only intuited. Suddenly the world of the Icelandic banks seems far more suspicious to me. In fact, the story this report lays out reminds me of one of my favorite books of all time: *The Smartest Guys in the Room*, the leading book on the collapse of Enron.

The report equates Iceland to an emerging market. My knee-jerk reaction is to feel upset and to resist this depiction: how could this proud land, cradle of European parliamentary democracy, source of the West's oldest literature, and a current beacon of gender equality and gay rights be a developing nation? But a light bulb goes 'ping!' in my head. In an economic sense, of course it is true! Despite human development metrics like literacy, where Iceland leads the world, the economic system is young and fragile. Things start to click.[8]

---

had been returning 50 to 60% a year. Everybody was feeling rich. Nobody wanted to even hear about an investment that might return 'only' 10% or 20% a year.

7 notendur.hi.is/ajonsson/kennsla2006/Merrill%20Lynch%20-%20Icelandic%20Banks.pdf

8 A close look at Iceland's society and industry reveals a bit of a paradox for the country. The underpinnings of the economy are not what you might expect for a Western country with a high standard of living. Iceland's chief export for a long time was fish and fisheries products, only recently overtaken by tourism (as the country has been overtaken by

According to the Merrill report, both businesses and households in Iceland are borrowing at a rate much higher than the small economy can support. This borrowed cash is being used to pay for the good times I see all around me. And then on top of that, many Icelandic business deals are downright shady. The Merrill analysts relay the story of Íslandsbanki, the third of the three big banks, selling part of its Sjóvá insurance arm to a shell company called Þáttur, but then loaning the funds to that same company to pay for the sale. The loan was never repaid. Þáttur in turn owns Milestone which is a major shareholder in the bank that originated the deal. "Such arrangements do not at all appear to be unusual in the world of Icelandic finance," concludes the report dryly. One can almost hear the dripping London disdain.[9]

The Icelandic banks have been financing their tremendous growth mainly through borrowing from bigger banks in Europe. But the Europeans are growing weary of ever-higher towers of Icelandic debt, and so will make it harder for the local banks to borrow more. But the banks will need to do exactly this, because a lot of their debts are

tourists). The country also exports a lot of smelted aluminum products, as a way to export some of its energy. Fish, tourism, and heavy industrial products are not normally what one expects of a 'developed' economy, which might be expected to export its intellectual prowess in the form of high-value-added goods and services. Some of the lack of diversity of exports can be explained by the very small population. But in other ways there is a mismatch between these low-tech exports and the high level of literacy and (at least on paper) academic achievement of the population.

9   The Icelandic bankers and businessmen did a lot of deals, very fast, in those years. They seemingly never met a deal they did not like. The two most prominent banks, Kaupþing and Landsbanki, bought UK banks in order to expand into the UK. They acquired old London institutions, Heritable Bank and Singer & Friedlander. In the Singer & Friedlander deal, the story goes that Kaupþing purchased close to 20% in the London bank before even having a meeting about a potential merger. They seemed to have no interest in talking to the management of the bank they were buying to learn how they might work together. Tony Shearer, the CEO of Singer, resigned after the merger, saying the Kaupþing team were "not fit and proper people" to run the bank.

publications.parliament.uk/pa/cm200809/cmselect/cmtreasy/144/144w204.htm

news.bbc.co.uk/2/hi/business/7866729.stm

citywire.co.uk/new-model-adviser/news/young-inexperienced-and-in-debt-shearer-spells-out-his-concerns-about-kaupthing-directors/a328200

coming due soon, and the best way to pay off an old loan is to take a new one. Kaupþing alone, the biggest of the three, needs to 'roll' about US$8.6 billion in debt this year and next, a number on the same order as the annual production of the entirety of Iceland's economy.

On top of the problems with rolling over this vast debt, Merrill points to some other major issues. The Icelandic banks own huge stakes in companies listed on the Icelandic stock market, but they do not disclose these with any transparency. Maybe even worse is that two thirds of the value of the entire stock market is the shares of the banks themselves! If they ever get into trouble, they would bring the whole market down with them.

Icelandic finance is a complex arrangement of cross-shareholdings. One full page of the report is dedicated to a jaw-dropping diagram of these arrangements. The spider web of interdependent ownership makes the true risks baked into the system difficult to pinpoint. This picture alone makes me nervous about the true health of the Icelandic economy.

Finally, the analysts lay out the problems with the Icelandic banks and their mortgages to homeowners: the business they entered in August 2004 at the same time as I was struggling with my first Icelandic grammar homework. The problem is that Iceland already had a giant mortgage lender: the Icelandic government itself. Through the Housing Finance Fund (*Íbúðalánasjóður*), the government lends directly to individuals and families who want to buy a house. The presence of HFF in the mortgage market means that the banks must compete with the government itself when making mortgage loans. The banks hoped that the government would leave the mortgage business to them, but so far it has not. And since the HFF is government-backed, it can offer loans on terms that the banks can't match and remain profitable; they are losing money on their mortgage businesses while they hope for HFF to depart the market. On the Continent, mortgages are a steady source of solid income for banks. "Iceland is alone [in Europe] in having banks that have entered the [mortgage] market without really being able to make money from it." Again, that dry disdain.

Two weeks after Merrill, Danske Bank comes out with its own analysis, this one covering the Icelandic economy as a whole.[10] The Danes call the Icelandic economy the "most overheated" in the developed world, say "there has been a stunning expansion of debt, leverage and risk-taking that is almost without precedents [*sic*] anywhere in the world", and "Iceland looks worse on almost all measures than Thailand did before its crisis in 1997."

A negative ratings change by Fitch, followed by these piercing reports from Merrill and Danske, leads to a full-blown crisis in Icelandic finance. The Icelandic stock market drops sharply, losing more than 20% of its value from its peak in February 2006. Even the soaring Icelandic *króna* is not immune: our currency also drops like a rock, losing around 20% of its buying power in these few weeks. In this way the crisis of spring 2006 becomes real for me; suddenly my paycheck is worth only about 80% of what it had been the month before.

Waingro is unhappy with me. He jokingly accuses me of triggering the crisis by blogging about the Merrill publication on a tiny and barely read page I set up for family and friends. The Icelandic media are also unhappy. They seem to take their lead from bank spokespeople when reporting the story, circling the Icelandic wagons and downplaying the analysis. "Iceland is special," is a favorite trope, meaning: this is a system that works by different rules than other economies. "This report is based on outdated data," is another. And the classic, applied especially to the former colonial masters of Denmark: "These outlanders are just jealous of our success."

And at first they seem right: things somehow stabilize, then turn around again. By summer, both the stock market and the currency are off to the races again! Waingro is wheedling me at each new jump. I shake my head and bury it back in the bug reports.

---

10   notendur.hi.is/ajonsson/kennsla2006/Danske%20Bank%20-%20Geyser%20Crises%20
(Mars%202006).pdf

The International Monetary Fund comes out with a very critical report on Iceland's overheating economy that summer of 2006.[11] But with the stock market and Icelandic currency once more soaring, nobody seems to care. Its dire warnings are written in 'IMF speak', and that language does not translate well for the political and business elites of Iceland, who anyway do not want to hear the message. Icelandic is often far more blunt and literal than English, and the delicately phrased warnings in this report are not sharp enough for Icelandic ears. The text does not jump the gap linguistically and culturally, and nobody likes to spoil a good party anyway.

One feature of Icelandic society I am starting to really notice is the sense of egalitarianism. Because people make about the same money as each other, or think that they do, everyone feels entitled to have the same kind of life as his neighbor. But, probably owing to a long history of almost zero variety of consumer goods on offer, Icelanders are not that creative in their purchasing. If my neighbor gets a new silver Toyota Land Cruiser with a CD player and leather seats, that is a signal to me that I must also be able to afford such a thing. However, to show him that I am a little better than he is, I will buy the same silver Land Cruiser, but have one or two additional options, maybe heating in my leather seats and a CD changer instead.

I am also surprised about how closely compressed the salary band is for the average workers. Back in Boston, one person making double or triple what another makes is common, even while living in the same neighborhood. However, in Iceland, most people seem to make about the same amount. And people seem to feel like that is proper and fair.[12]

A few months later, in autumn, I am checking in for a flight on

11   www.imf.org/external/pubs/ft/scr/2006/cr06296.pdf
12   High tax rates further serve to compress take-home income. The top tax rate, which is now around 46%, kicks in on any income over about $86,000 a year. Below that the income tax rate is around 37%. There is also a value added tax (VAT) that for most goods and services stands at 24%. (2019 data.)

the cozy first floor of Keflavík International Airport, the main airport for the Land and part of a Cold War-era American military base: as a tribute to its roots, the bathroom sinks of the passenger terminal even feature disgusting American military-spec chlorinated water. In front of and behind me in the line is a very large and loud group of Icelanders checking in for the same flight to Boston.

On board I am seated next to two women I recognize from the check-in, and they tell me they are schoolteachers from the town of Keflavík, right next to the airport. The Icelandic currency has grown so strong that the school department of this little town can afford to send 30 or 40 teachers for an all-expenses weekend away. I feel the power of the *króna* too: when I return to Boston these days, things seem ridiculously cheap. I can take my parents and my brother and sister-in-law for a meal, throw in a huge tip, and the total cost will be less than a main course for just me in Reykjavík.

Inevitably, the strong currency makes us feel rich, and with this newfound wealth even somehow superior to the rest of the world. But there comes a downside: with most things being half as expensive outside Iceland as inside, every trip abroad becomes focused on shopping. Despite the buying power of the *króna* increasing so rapidly, within the Land prices are 'sticky': things in stores never get any cheaper. Probably this is due to the near total lack of competition in our small local market.

It is quite conceivable that the cost savings on a few large purchases can easily cover airfare and a hotel, making weekend shopping trips to the U.S. simple for Icelanders to justify. Aside from the cost advantages, a far broader selection awaits those who shop in America. With 1,000 Americans for every Icelander, this is not a surprise. So the pressure is on to use every trip abroad as a buying opportunity.

It has come to the point where I don't advertise my trips 'out' very much, but even so the requests inevitably begin to flood in from friends: iPods two and three at a time, kids' toys, anything they can think of. I'll get a phone call out of the blue: "So, I heard you are going to America next week?" This gets more and more annoying. And it carries the risk of big fines for me too: I am allowed back into

Iceland with only a couple hundred bucks worth of new merchandise. Everything above that I am supposed to declare and pay 24.5% value-added tax on all the new value these purchases add to the Land. But despite my pushback, the requests from my close friends keep coming. At one point I find myself waiting on a street corner in downtown Boston with a leg of Icelandic lamb, dropping it through the passenger window of a nearly rolling car and receiving in exchange a brown-paper-wrapped steering column for a 1998 Jeep Cherokee.

On this trip I have the usual list of items for myself and friends, and so rather than do something fun, I wheedle my brother into driving me over to the CambridgeSide Galleria one Wednesday morning. "If that's where you want to go," he shrugs as we head out to his car in the rain.

I haven't visited here since my college days, even living in Boston all those years in between. My local friends and I referred to the mall as the CambridgeSide Gonorrhea and made a point of avoiding it altogether. My brother parks in the empty garage underneath. At only ten in the morning, the place is just barely waking up. We get inside and find a ghost town there, too. Wanting to get in, get out, and get it over with, I start heading down my list: a few things for me, a lot more for my co-workers and friends.

We go into a CVS where I need to stock up on floss and shaving supplies: basic toiletries cost about 70% less than back in Iceland. Across the aisle from me I hear two ladies loudly puzzling over some cosmetics. It doesn't strike me as odd, and then I realize: I am only a couple miles from the Cambridge, Massachusetts hospital where I was born. But these women are having the discussion *in Icelandic*.

Then at the 'water massage' stand at the foot of an escalator, we see a curious man and woman staring at the machine, debating which one should go first. As we head up the escalator, I do a double take. They were also negotiating in Icelandic.

The third time it happens, inside a department store, I recognize the same two teachers from the airplane. "*Góðan daginn,*" I greet them and we get to talking. They tell me the whole school is here at CambridgeSide this morning. And in fact, it would appear that nearly 100% of the customers in the still-sleepy mall are hard-shopping Icelanders from Keflavík, up and out early in the rain to jam their suitcases full.

This expensive shopping center strikes me as an odd choice, as there are many better and cheaper places in and around Boston to buy all the stuff these teachers are hoarding. But Icelanders love to copy their countrymen exactly, and it turns out that the CambridgeSide Galleria has developed a kind of mystique back home in the Land. And hey: I'm here myself, right?

Anyway maybe it's not such an odd choice. Boston seems to have become the preferred shopping destination for Icelanders, offering slave-wage American prices just a short-hop five-hour flight away. One of the Icelandic tour companies even puts out a travel brochure laying out the best things to see in historic Boston, and near the top of that list is this mall. And despite the high prices here, most items still cost around half what they do back home. The whole mall is on sale! I join in the feeding frenzy myself, picking up a bunch of junk I don't need, like an inoperable Bluetooth headset for my phone.

These purchases add up in cost and weight. I spend most of the day before each night flight back to Iceland taking things out of boxes and blister packs and repacking them, trying to fit all this new merch into my allotted two suitcases. I get to the airport in Boston and see a fellow Icelander checking giant tires for an SUV as hold luggage. The Icelandair agent at Logan Airport simply slaps a KEF destination tag on each massive tire and sends them down the baggage belt. That guy maybe saves enough on those four tires to pay for his whole vacation.

Before Christmas, I read that the nightly Icelandair flight from Boston had just too much weight checked and the airline had to leave around 30 pieces of luggage behind in Beantown, taking them on a capacity available basis. It is hard to shake the feeling of unlimited money. Our currency has nearly doubled in value in just a few years. Each month I convert my salary to dollars and it's up a handful of per cent on the previous month. Give me another two years and I'll be making these trips by private jet!

———————

So why was the *króna* gaining so much on the dollar and the other major currencies of the world during the years of the Icelandic boom? In addition to the botched privatization of the banks, the Davíð Oddsson government also allowed the Icelandic currency to trade in international currency markets for the first time in April 2001.[13] Because Iceland has historically high inflation, and still does, the local currency must pay a higher yield. That means that even safe investments like government bonds must pay more interest than they would in countries with lower inflation.

The historic yield on the Icelandic currency is 10 to 20%. And financial markets try to capitalize on things like this: there is a thing called the carry trade where one can borrow cheap and invest rich. So you can borrow Japanese yen, or US dollars, or Swiss francs, and then buy Icelandic government bonds. You could borrow at a low interest rate in those days, maybe a couple of per cent, and buy Icelandic government bonds that were paying much more: maybe 10%. As an investor this is the equivalent of printing money. There were even savings products offered by Japanese banks to Japanese housewives where they could put their low-yielding yen into a domestic savings account and buy Icelandic *krónur* that way.

The carry trade works until it doesn't. It works until the higher-yielding currency that you bought crashes, losing value relative to the major currencies, and you're left holding the bag.

The carry trade was a source of enormous liquidity flowing into Iceland, beginning about 2002 and lasting through 2007. All that demand for Icelandic cash pushed up the price relative to other currencies, and the schoolteachers of Keflavík could afford to fly abroad just to go shopping.

---

13 The decision to float the Icelandic currency in the first place was part of a neoliberal economic program spearheaded by Prime Minister Davíð Oddsson. All of the easy money flowing into the country as a result fueled a banking and asset boom. Icelandic banks in those years were able to borrow seemingly as much as they wanted.

Davíð's privatization of the banks was classic crony capitalism. There was no competitive bidding process. The politicians who controlled the country handed out banks to their allies as favors, one major bank to each of the two political parties in power, with no serious bids from foreign institutions. This was a family affair.

3

THE GO-GO YEAR

THIS guy is just impeccably well dressed. I haven't ever seen a guy as 'metro'. Perfectly cut jeans, perfectly tucked-in shirt, perfectly coiffed hair piled up lovingly with mousse. His girlfriend, hanging from his arm as he shoots pool, is also perfect. When he opens his mouth, the Queen's English slides out, a faultless embodiment of centuries of casual global domination.

I am here for a summer billiards and darts party thrown by Heiða in her dad's garage. And for some reason, I didn't dress all that well this evening. This is a cardinal sin in the Land. No one leaves the house in less than his best, lest he stumble into an ex (a statistical probability in a population so small). Despite the wretchedness of this character in front of me, and the wretchedness of my own attire, I realize this is the kind of guy I'm going to have to make nice with if I ever want to leave behind the fixing of bugs in someone else's portfolio management software, and run real portfolios myself. Everything about this guy oozes successful banker.

I strike up a conversation with him. He answers in lukewarm tones at first, but then some kind of switch flips under the coiffure and he opens up. As his girlfriend looks on with a half-smile, he relates how he works in one of the Icelandic banks (of course) where they require his expertise in talking the way he talks, presumably to increase the bank's legitimacy with other similarly accented and coiffed Londoners.

I tell him I am supporting the Icelandic banks by developing asset management software. He barely tries to conceal his contempt. I push on, telling him I am looking to make a change, to get out of the back office and into the front of the house. And then, to my surprise, he offers to help.

"Sure mate, send me your CV, I'll see what I can do." He flicks his card out of his perfect wallet and holds it across to me. Maybe he's just trying to make his girlfriend believe he's sometimes nice. But, I'll take it.

I dash off a friendly email with my CV on Monday. He shoots back a one-liner. But a couple of days later, my little Nokia lights up. It's Landsbanki! The head of their asset management division wants me to come in for a meeting about a portfolio management position.

The team at the bank seems intrigued by the idea of hiring me. They grill me in the office of the head of asset management. They want to be sure that my desire to move from back-office software into fund management is serious. I spin a convincing yarn, even throwing some Dave Swensen portfolio construction theory into the mix.

I get the job offer just days after the one interview. And inexplicable stock market performance be damned: I am in! I am gonna be a rock star! Weekend trips to Cannes, here we come!

———

After starting at the bank, I am chatting across the trading desk with my new co-worker Fabio one Friday afternoon. I am a bit perplexed about how I came to land that first interview. Why did this dandy I'd met only once at a party help me out? Fabio was the one to whom he had sent my CV in the first place, and he tells me that the dandy is having a party at his place that weekend and wants us both to come. I take this as the opportunity to probe a little.

"I can't figure something out about that guy," I say.

"Hmmm?" asks Fabio across the desk.

"I mean, he seemed like such an asshole but then at the same time so willing to help me," I say. "I guess I totally misjudged him."

"Oh no: he's an asshole. He sent me your CV with a note, like: 'look at this loser I met at a party who thinks he can work in the big leagues'. He wanted me to interview you just so the two of us could laugh about you afterwards."

"Really?"

"Yeah, really. But then I had a look at your CV and it actually seemed OK."

———

The job starts out as wine and roses. Not just great parties, but engaging and challenging projects too! Applying the same mental horsepower as I had to coding software that few used or appreciated, I am seeing real results nearly every day from this new type of work. My first big task is creating the investment plan and marketing materials for a new fund of hedge funds that we sell to Icelandic institutional investors. The big pension funds of the Land have quite a lot of cash and would like to diversify a small fraction of their investment portfolios away from Icelandic stocks and bonds.

This turns into a perfect project for me. I am designing factsheets and presentations on the front side, and on the back side, creating a new process to filter the upwards of 9,000 hedge funds in the world. Our aim is to find hidden gems where we can place some of our fund's capital. I create a dossier on each good prospect we find, phoning the hedge fund managers for more detail, and planning site visits to New York and London to learn how they work and to decide if we will invest with them.

One March morning I come into the office and something is very odd: the glass door between our desks and the rest of the department is closed tight. I need to use my ID badge to beep myself through. I begin to prop the door open with the coat rack, as it always is. One of the journeymen fund managers is already in the office, sitting across the trading desk from the door. He shakes his head at me. "Don't do that now," he says.

"Why not?"

"FME is coming this morning." That's the financial regulator of the Land. And they will be in the office today, as everyone seems to know already. It's only now that I realize that this fancy electronic door that's always hidden behind a rack of heavy and expensive wool coats is supposed to be our 'Chinese wall', keeping our fund management dealings secret from the rest of the department.

Soon after, through the glass wall, I see two shy-looking ladies from the regulator chatting uncomfortably with one of the executives. They are ushered into a conference room and never make it back to our area. When I return from lunch, the secure door is once again ensconced behind its blanket of expensive overcoats.

Easter arrives fast this year. All of Iceland shuts down for five days of food and family. I go for a walk with my friend Waingro in the cool endless sunshine down by the creek in Kópavogur, after a big holiday dinner. "We made it, Jared," he says, "another winter is behind us." It is the first time I have heard an Icelander talk about the dark of winter in such honest terms. I feel relieved too. It seems all right to admit that now. But not too gleefully. In Iceland, the next winter always looms.

I come up the stairs in the old Landsbanki office building to the second floor, where the reception area is sandwiched between the stairs and a glass bridge connecting with the main bank buildings across Hafnarstræti, the most downtown of downtown 101 Reykjavík. An endless sun shines on this gorgeous late May day of 2007. The two gossipy reception ladies are seated behind their desk.

Standing near them, and turning to face me, is a beautiful Icelandic woman, with bright blue eyes and a face full of freckles. And I know this woman! It's Hulda from the old bank branch at the mall Smáralind. In my earliest days in the Land, she helped me set up my Icelandic bank accounts, and get my first credit card too. I liked talking to her so much that I once stopped in to see her at that same mall branch, with no goal other than to chat about summer vacation plans, always a safe topic in Iceland. I even asked her out to dinner once, by email—a horrendous mistake—and showed interest a couple of other times. She politely but steadfastly turned me down.

But here she is now, beaming at me with such a smile. Standing next to her is a woman I already know from the bank: the friendly Sigga, the person in charge of all employee union business. She's the one who helped me reserve a union summer house in the country a few weekends before.

"What are you doing here?" I ask the radiant Hulda.

"I'm going out for lunch with my mom," she says. Looking at her and Sigga, I can easily see now that they're mother and daughter. I smile at Sigga. "And what are you doing here?" Hulda asks me.

"I work here now!" I say. "Just on my way upstairs to the cafeteria."

Hulda volunteers that she now works just up the street at the RE/ MAX real estate office, then wishes me a nice lunch. The gossip-monger secretaries remain mute, but on high alert. As I walk up the stairs to the cafeteria, I feel four pairs of eyes burning into my back.

After lunch I look her up on the real estate broker's website. Many Icelandic companies put up photos and names of all their *starfsmenn* online. And sure enough she is among them, smiling out from the screen at me. I shoot a link to her profile across the trading desk to the journeyman asset manager. "Go for it Bibler!" he sends back.

A few days later, I stop in at RE/MAX at lunch, ostensibly to get some info on new apartments for sale in the building next to mine. Hulda is the only one there, typically dedicated to her work while the real estate agent tossers frolic at lunch. Her face brightens when she sees me. She finds the info in a file cabinet drawer and turns to hand it to me. It's now or never.

"So, how about a coffee with me sometime?" I blurt out.

She hesitates briefly. Then: "Sure. Why not?"

Five months later and Hulda and I have been together for nearly the whole time since that first coffee. Things happen fast in the Land.

I hear my two senior colleagues debating beyond my earshot. Something is up. Soon after they ask me if I want to go to Madrid with the department this year: a pretty fantastic invite. It turns out Landsbanki Asset Management invites all the Icelandic pension funds to an annual investment conference at some exotic locale. A long list of clients and selected employees make the cut, and it's a 'with *maki*' affair. That's Icelandic for spouse or partner, so Hulda is invited along too, for free.

She had planned to be away that weekend in Akureyri, north Iceland, where she is enrolled in a distance-learning degree program. She is very diligently working on her university classes alongside her full-time job, and these weekends away are some of her only face-to-face time with her professors. But she changes her plans to come along to Spain with me.

On the designated morning, we travel by luxury coach to Keflavík International Airport. Our plane is delayed so everyone drinks early-morning beers in the airport bar. Then we board an Icelandair 757—a plane set up for over 200 passengers—with just around 50 people. In Madrid it is already afternoon when we board another luxury coach, this one with an Icelandic-speaking guide who is proud to show us around his adopted city.

Bang in the city center is our five-star hotel. Could it be the best in all of Madrid? Our sales guy winks. We check into our rooms and go up to the roofdeck where he has rented the whole bar for us, with a magical view out over the warm city.

The investment conference starts early the following morning, but it turns out that I needn't have been nervous about giving my talk. We are in a windowless hotel function room with a captive audience of friendly Icelandic pension managers. The conference turns out to be more or less a six-hour shill for our own investment products. I give the presentation on our fund of hedge funds, the product I have helped develop from the beginning. Even the CEO of our bank, Sigurjón, is there. He has arrived by his own means (private jet, it's whispered) and his speech kicks off the day. A smattering of non-Landsbanki presenters during the event creates a veneer of a real, rather than captive, conference.

During the event, 'the wives' are sent off to learn how to make sangria and then to take a flamenco dance course. Followed, of course, by shopping. Hulda enjoys it but in retelling her day to me she rolls her eyes at the blatant sexism.

That evening we reconvene for more five-star food and a bar after that. Hulda and I go back to the hotel, but many others go to an after-party at a posh Madrid club where our sales guy flicks through a stack of €50 bills until the bouncers let the whole group past. Saturday we all take in a mandatory tour of the Landsbanki offices in Madrid—our bank now has offices in nearly every big European city—and then we have some free time for shopping and Picasso viewing: I really want to see *Guernica* and drag Hulda reluctantly along. In the evening, the bank has reserved all the tables in Madrid's prime flamenco restaurant. On Sunday it's back to the Land. Our chartered 757 has been waiting on the tarmac for us the whole time.

As I reflect on the whole surreal weekend back home, I realize just how beyond the pale it was. The bank spent easily upwards of €20,000 on each couple by my own guesstimate. The only point of the weekend was wining, dining, and partying—with a bit of sales sprinkled in. The weekend is named in a way so as to make it sound legit: *Landsbanki Investment Forum 2007.* All of our guests were decision makers at the Icelandic pension funds, and many of them represent public sector employees, employees who entrust these money managers to invest their retirement savings wisely. Would the pension fund managers ever disclose this windfall trip? I know what our sales guys would tell me: "Jared, all the banks are doing this. If we don't, we'll lose out."

I also get involved with something called the Landsbanki Currency Fund. Technically, I am listed as the manager although this is really a bureaucratic joke. The guy making all the investments for the fund is a lanky dude named Villi who sits upstairs at the currency desk. He has already worked on Wall Street and moved back to his native Iceland to ride the wave of the banking boom. Villi does a lot of macroeconomic reading. He will take a view, for example, that the Japanese yen is going to drop relative to the euro. Then he'll enter into a forward contract to deliver a given quantity of yen against euros in a month. If his bet turns out right, the yen will be cheaper to buy in the future and he'll be able to cover his contract with fewer euros, pocketing the difference as profit for the fund.

He seems to be pretty good at this. He creates foreign exchange pairs in ten or 15 combinations, and watches them all day, sharp-eyed, on massive trading screens.

Villi has already been running money like this for a while and has happy investors, but for internal political reasons his little operation is forced into the arms of asset management, where I work. Someone from Landsvaki, our management company, needs to be listed as the manager, and this falls to me. But I don't mind. It's a straightforward job and Villi is a good trader. He regularly stops by our office to shoot the global macroeconomic shizzle, and we trade ideas and war stories. I even decide to put a few of my own ISK in there and let them take a ride with Villi—best practice is for managers to have our own cash in the investments we market to others. Mainly I just take care of making sure the fund both has adequate collateral and that it can be easily marketed to new investors, with the same nice factsheet and promo materials I created for my other funds.

Because the fund is priced in local currency, ISK, its base return is very high. That is because the ISK is a historically weak and depreciating currency that must pay a high yield, even on something safe like a government bond, in order to attract investors. Since our underlying collateral is invested in ISK-denominated debt, the fund's performance as a whole benefits from this high double-digit return; the currency bets that Villi makes only serve to augment this return by several more percentage points. So the overall annual return is something like 15%.

Perceiving an opportunity, our sales guys decide they'd like to market this fund and its stunning return to yield-greedy Germans. But there is a problem with this logic: the German investors of course want to invest in their own currency, the euro. They wouldn't touch the Icelandic *króna* with a two-meter pole! And when we map out a putative EUR fund, most of the high return goes away: euro collateral like safe German government bonds has a much lower yield.

The sales guys still demand a new factsheet for a fund priced in EUR. I explain that we would need to use our base fund data but then layer on the effect of currency hedges and that most of the high yield will go away. So, without telling anyone, they go ahead and create a fake: take the legit document we already have, change ISK to EUR at the top, and send it off to Frankfurt.

The currency fund is a popular product, and it's priced so that new investors can come in and existing investors can redeem each week. Buying into the fund I get to watch our whole investment process: my own cash leaves my current account, shows up in the LCF main account, and then we use that new money to buy additional collateral and capitalize the fund's positions, allowing it to take on more risk.

Now that I have some of my own money at stake I am even more curious about the trading activity. I can see all the positions as Villi puts on or takes off currency pairs. So I'll pop in most days and look over all his trades. It's especially fun to watch the total value of the fund leap up when he has a good day; we have a little tool that shows the real-time value of all the fund's bets.

Sometimes I also check as our weekly trading gains get marked into a total value for the investment in my online banking, but there is something I can't figure out. The numbers don't really add up. I expect a certain end-of-week price based on what I know the fund holds, but the number I see in my own online statement is different, often a bit higher. It's strange. A few weeks go by like this and it bothers me more. I still can't explain it. So I call Villi and at the end of the trading day he comes down and we go over it together. He can't figure it out either. It's a big discrepancy.

A friendly woman who works in the back office of the bank is the one responsible for calculating the prices for all of our investment funds. This arrangement may sound OK on the surface, but it becomes quite odd considering that her boss, the head of back office, is married to the head of asset management, the boss of my boss. Knowledgeable investors normally demand that a completely separate and impartial third party put a price on opaque positions such as these; someone who is both an employee of the same firm and heir to a nasty nuptial conflict of interest probably would not qualify.

I call up the pricing lady and she agrees to come by. We sit together at my desk on an empty trading floor (everyone else is fishing, golfing, and boozing[14] by this point in the day) and go through my pricing model and then hers. And bingo! Her error jumps off the page at me. The fund pays out a performance fee periodically—when it has a good run, it pays some of the profits to Landsvaki, the asset management company—but she has left this fee amount in her price. Often this leads to an overvalue, where investors pay too much to come in, or profit too much as they exit.

Now we have a real problem, because it turns out she has had this bug in her spreadsheet since inception, well before I took over as manager. Over the next few days, we do a detailed week-by-week analysis on the published price versus the true fair price. The fund has been running for a few years already, and investors have been buying and selling steadily this whole time. There are some weeks where the price is correct, but about half of the time it is erroneous. Big money has both come in and flowed out, with investors sometimes overpaying or over-profiting by as much as 90 bips—close to one per cent.

I write up the analysis and take it to my managers. I propose that any investor who gained at the expense of the other fund unit-holders get to keep their gains, but that the bank make good its mistake for those customers who got screwed. We will need to contact dozens of customers and explain. I am not looking forward to this. I have no doubt upon whom the task will fall.

---

14 In that order.

But as it turns out, I needn't have worried at all! The bosses do not come back to me and when I bring it up again after ten days or so, I get: "We decided it's not really a big deal, only a few per cent here and there." Swept under the rug. Too bad, investors.

4

ROMANIAN DEVELOPMENTS

WE also manage a real-estate investment fund. Marketed as a high-risk, high-return vehicle, it allows the shareholders to get in on juicy property deals in the 'developing world' (Iceland excluded, of course). The fund launched and closed before I started, with some of the capital already deployed.

The fund is a cooperative venture with a firm called Askar Capital, one of the many Reykjavík investment companies that spring up during these years[15]. Askar claims special expertise in real estate, although around this time they also try to get us excited about their expertise in junk American subprime equity tranches offered by Bear Stearns.

When the big foreign money came into Iceland earlier in the decade, it began to inflate a vast bubble of anything and everything that a person could buy; things like local real estate and stocks mushroomed in value. But there is just not that much for sale in the tiny economy of Iceland. So a lot of this new money also flowed back offshore—for example, into property development in eastern Europe—via newly created investment companies. Askar was one of these.

---

15   Active 2007–10, Askar was technically designated an "investment bank" by the FME.

Fabio and I take a trip to Bucharest, where Askar has chartered a helicopter to fly us around and look at potential development sites. The Icelandic firm is putting big money into this country, which has been in the middle of a real estate boom for some years. Now they want to get us juiced up to invest even more alongside them. After seeing a couple of potential projects closer to the city center, we fly far out of Bucharest in a rattling chopper over forests, rivers, and dams. We land in a bright green field in the middle of nowhere, hot Romanian summer all around. It's a beautiful country and an expensive junket.

The most promising thing we see is a piece of formerly government-controlled land in an up-and-coming suburb of Bucharest. The proposal: knock down the old concrete building that sits there and throw up an office tower. The plot is situated kitty-corner from a tiny but allegedly trendy mall: could this be the CambridgeSide Galleria of Romania?

Askar says they have done the due diligence on the project, meaning they have dotted the i's and crossed the t's in a thorough feasibility and background check. They are partnered with a local developer, with whom they are already working on another project. They tell us the work is "shovel ready"; as soon as they have the cash from our fund they can rock and roll.

When we get back, Fabio discusses the trip with our boss and they agree to commit to the project. I am in the dark about this decision, but later find out that they've gone forward with it, and wired €5 million out of the fund to buy the land and start the project.

This is the smallest project our real estate fund takes on, and it seems to get lost in the shuffle. Each financial quarter we get a report from Askar on the progress of all the investments: in Turkey, Dubai, and now Romania. I've been assigned to generate an investor report on the back of this, and so I dutifully copy-paste, clean up the English, and get the document ready to go out to investors. I am curious about the one project I got to see in person, but the updates on 'my' office tower stay verbatim for two or three reporting quarters in a row. By this time the original timeline called for the new tower to be nearly finished.

I push on Fabio and the boss, who meet with Askar more often than I do. Nobody seems to know much about this investment. Finally in early 2008 they relent and let me do some digging. Our development partner in Romania meanwhile tells us there might be a buyer interested in our parcel, at a price around 10% higher than we paid, giving the fund some profit on the deal and letting us wire cash back to our investors and walk away.

Fabio and I take this back to our boss, advising that we move forward on soliciting a formal offer for the lot from this buyer.

"Absolutely not," he replies. "We won't even consider this."

"Why wouldn't we at least look to see if this is a serious offer?" I counter.

"Because 10% over eight months does not meet our return target for this fund." The Commandment has been handed down on a stone tablet. This topic is now closed.

So, we will need to continue our work with Askar to ensure a successful project during these increasingly shaky markets of 2008. And despite their claims of investing expertise, what Askar seems to be especially good at is ultra-high employee turnover. Each time we touch base on the outstanding projects, the last guy has left and we are dealing with a new project manager. I ask for an update on the Romanian project. They send me the same information they've been sending for half a year: the building permit has been issued and work will start soon. I call the new guy up. And it's Pétur, my old CEO from Zodiac! Apparently even he can be tempted away by the Dark Side.

"Hey, do you have a copy of this building permit?"

"Yeah, it's in the file," he says. "But it's in Romanian."

"That's OK, send it over," I say. "How about the old structure, what's the status there?"

"Oh that's already been demolished," he says. "They have started the foundation for the tower."

It takes a few more emails and a phone call, but finally they send me a PDF of the building permit. The file is a grainy one-pager, dated a few years in the past. This permit is not newly issued at all, the first warning sign. After all, our reports to investors have been trumpeting receipt of this document as the first real accomplishment. Even more oddly, when I translate the title of the document from Romanian, I don't get 'building permit' at all. It says "zoning certificate". This faded document turns out to merely be proof that the building site is zoned for industrial use. There is no mention of our project at all.

On top of that, Askar's reports of construction progress over the past months have been vague and contradictory. I email a friend who studies in Bucharest. I tell her if she wants to make a few bucks I'll send her out to the building site to report back on what's going on over there. She doesn't want money. She says she'd like to take a trip out there anyway. The next day, I get an email back from her and inside find four blurry Nokia phone camera photos. The site looks exactly as it did when I saw it nearly a year before: the old concrete building still stands, with some worn-down Ceaușescu-era cars parked in front. Nothing has happened.

Confronted, Askar's latest project team is forced to admit they have no idea what's going on. Pétur, who inherited this whole mess, seems embarrassed. Fabio and I have an easy time figuring out what's really happened: Askar has invested its own capital in a much bigger building site in Bucharest and the entirety of their thinly staffed efforts have been going into that. Trying to make lemonade, Askar circulates a new plan for our investment, one that calls for a 30-storey residential tower. They have chosen an even more grandiose project to try to meet the return targets of the fund in a market that gets weaker by the day.

Armed with the knowledge that Askar has been misleading us for a year, I draw up a comprehensive list of questions about the deal, and my boss sends me on a fact-finding trip to Bucharest. Our investment is a shambles. The land our fund bought is part of a larger parcel of government land arbitrarily cut in half. The old tower that we plan to knock down on our side of the lot is physically connected to another, lower structure, so that in order to build anything new, we first need to saw the second building in half! The Siamese twin is not an abandoned facility either, rather the headquarters of the national institute for nanotechnology research. I book a meeting with the head of the agency.

"You're the first person who's come and talked to me," he says, welcoming us into his spacious 1970s office. Together, we go over the project plans, which call for pilings to be driven deep into the ground in the construction of our fund-return-target-achieving skyscraper.

"But this will interfere with our delicate experiments," he says, over and over, like a mantra. The newest Askar shill, who looks like he'd much rather be out on the links, keeps intoning that there will be minimal disruption from this activity. But Mr. Nanotech has an ace up his sleeve: not only is our land industrial, and so unsuitable for either an office tower or a residential tower, but any change to this requires approval from a local official he happens to know well. There is no way we do any project without his green light.

Our local development partner is a gentle and soft-spoken man of about 30, heir to a wealthy Romanian family. We met on the first trip to Bucharest. Since then I have learned from the Askar boys that he studied theology and planned to become a priest. But something changed and he is entering the family business with this, his first-ever real estate development project. It also turns out that the other party in the land deal—the recipient of that €5m disbursement we made— is his own father. It seems like our office and/or residential tower may be a family test case: the first chance for the young seminarian to prove his business acumen to his dad.

And now the project is stuck. No way to get a permit to build anything at all on this half of a site, and no way to get out, either: that buyer from last winter is last winter's news, with Romanian real estate prices now in freefall. I solicit valuation estimates from two local estate agents, and as I feared the price per square meter is already well below our cost.

"If you want this project to succeed, why don't you have a guy down here full time to manage it?" asks Askar's Romanian man on the ground to me as we drive back downtown from the project site.

"I thought you were that guy," I tell him.

"No way, chief," he says. "I have too much to do on the big project."

5

AURORA

// "I NEED to trade!" The voice on the other end of the line sounds
a little manic. It belongs to a guy with a small office somewhere
nearby in downtown Reykjavík who is 'advising' one of our funds.
In fundspeak that means he is making the daily trading decisions
and we are stuck with the clean-up work. The Aurora fund itself
legally belongs to my employer, the captive money management arm
of Landsbanki. As the daily management of cash is grunt work that
nobody wants, it has landed on me, the lowest on the totem pole.

And the problem today, as the problem has been for weeks, is that
the €120m Aurora Capital Fund is fast running out of cash, and this
guy is on a buying bender. Every day he gets on the phone with his
brokers and tells them to buy more shares in the same three or four
names. We get the trade confirms by email and the fund needs to
have cash on hand three business days later to settle the trades. I've
called him to tell him he needs to stop buying or the fund won't have
the money to cover its obligations, and he is unhappy with me. He
needs to trade.

When people in our biz say 'trade' they usually mean 'buy and sell'.
But this guy can't seem to ever sell any shares. The only thing that
looks to make him happy is the idea of coming in and amassing some

more the next day. The shares are his precious children; how could he turn them out on the street?

This fund has been trouble from the get-go, but my bosses turn a deaf ear to any problems because it was forced on us by the CEO of the bank.

The bank's interest in playing host to Aurora actually seems to have been based on a misunderstanding. In the world of hedge funds, the 'prime broker' is the bank that holds custody of a fund's positions: shares, bonds, options. On the back of these valuable assets, the prime broker lends additional money, allowing the fund to lever up its balance sheet: to take on ownership of more assets than it has investor money to cover.

So Aurora had said it needed a prime broker, and the stockbrokers at Landsbanki had said "we'll do it!" They heard the words 'prime broker', thought it meant 'broker number one', and saw thousands of new trade executions, each one wrapped in their fat uncompetitive trading commissions, each commission feeding into their bonuses, each bonus feeding into their beer money. (Out in the real world, the name for this is the fund's 'executing broker', and a given fund may have several.)

Landsbanki has neither the skill nor the inclination to be a real prime broker. For trade settlement, we make use of the same rickety back-office software that my old employer Zodiac developed. It lacks even the most basic position-keeping functions: it can't tell you how much of anything you really hold at any point in time. The bank is also not set up to make a loan with stocks or bonds as collateral. Nor do our back office personnel seem equipped with the mental or systemic tools to settle a short sale, the very thing that puts the 'hedge' in hedge fund.

In order to manage the Aurora cash balance, I have to write my own position keeper. In a real bank the nuts and bolts of fund management, like cash provisioning, would be handled by automated systems, but here at Iceland's oldest bank we run everything on a series of home-grown spreadsheets. Microsoft Excel is the bubble gum and toothpicks of the financial world. My cash tracker is no exception.

In many markets and products, trades settle three business days after they are executed. Like when you buy a house or car, you sign a contract for the purchase and then on some agreed-upon later date you come with the money and take delivery of the valuable asset. It's no different with shares, but nobody in Iceland seems to really get this. Knowing the sum total of trades the fund does on any given day, I can see how much cash we will need to have on hand three days down the road.

Back before Christmas 2007, when I showed the empty suit who runs the fund management company the settlement report showing that the fund would be nearly out of money three days later, he asked incredulously, "How can you see the future, Jared?" He didn't believe me when I explained. "What if they sell something tomorrow?" he countered.

"Tomorrow would be too late because that cash wouldn't hit until the *following* day," I explained. "So for at least one overnight we'd be in trouble."

He was unconvinced, staring at me with owl eyes behind his large designer glasses.

In that case I had indeed seen the future, and the fund ran bone-dry as predicted. Still, nobody around me seemed curious to learn more of my black magic.

Now I hear it again on the phone. "I need to trade!" Half a year after the Christmas mess and this guy has exhausted all €60m of last-minute credit he got from a Swedish bank to save us from our Yuletide woes. Now we are back in the same situation: he doesn't slow down at all and just keeps buying. Every day, another couple hundred thousand euros of shopping spree to pay for. Finally the cash account of the fund is sitting at under €20,000. This time I decide to just let it ride and see what happens.

Bizarrely, the owner of the cash accounts for our giant investment funds is not us, the fund management company, but a branch office of Landsbanki at Laugavegur 77. This is a commercial and retail bank branch that serves the businesses on the main shopping street of our little capital city. I call up the account rep, an older-sounding lady.

"Are you the owner of this account number for Aurora Capital Fund?" I ask. I hear her punching it in.

"Yes..." she says hesitantly.

"Great, I wanted to let you know that in three days that account will be sitting at around negative €80,000."

"How do you know what will happen in three days?" She sounds bewildered.

I explain T+3 trade settlement to her as succinctly as I can. She doesn't seem to get it.

"Well, that can't be," she concludes. "That account cannot go negative."

"What will happen if it gets debited and it doesn't have the funds to cover?" I push.

"It can't happen."

We hang up. Three days later, I have successfully predicted the future for a second time: the account has indeed gone negative.

It's a euro-denominated account held within RB. *Reiknistofa Bankanna* is the master Icelandic account-keeping system shared by all the banks, and run out of an undisclosed location, rumored to be a garage somewhere in the 101. I log into this old mainframe greenscreen system to check the Aurora account balance versus my own spreadsheet. On this particular day I can see all the cash flows out to settle the very important 'I need to' trades. And the final balance has a minus sign in front of it. Otherwise, all appears normal.

Covering my ass, I copy the settled amounts and the final balance into an email and send it to my bosses, with another to the poor beleaguered account rep on Laugavegur. "Aurora is negative today, as I warned earlier in the week." But no response. They're all on vacation. July in Iceland and one finds oneself in a sort of land that time forgot. Nothing much at all happens.

I start to enjoy just letting it ride. I already know the next three days of cash activity and there is really nothing I can do to stop the account from going more deeply negative. I'm waiting for something to happen: some bank internal controller to call me screaming, someone to intervene. Someone to shut this insanity down.

But it just keeps on rolling. Days pass, then weeks. Each day the euro cash account ticks more and more into the red. I learn that this type of account was never designed to be negative at any time, so there is not even any penalty interest charged. We are in a sort of phantom zone; the fund is in effect getting an interest-free loan from the bank. At the conclusion of each day I dutifully send an email to my bosses: the head of alternative assets, the head of the fund management company, and the head of asset management himself.

Still nothing happens. The bosses keep ignoring my emails. But things in the account are becoming ridiculous. The negative balance that had started out as a mere €80,000 has blossomed and grown giant like a pumpkin plant in the endless light of Icelandic summer: it is now in excess of €6,200,000.

I decide to try one more thing. I call up an old friend from the Zodiac days who used to sit across from me and talk Björk and Sigur Rós. He now works in risk management at Landsbanki. I ask him to have lunch with me. I explain the situation to him. "That sounds like operational risk," he says. "We only really focus on trading risk."

"Who focuses on operational risk?" I ask.

"Nobody, really." He shrugs.

"Do me a favor," I say. I pass him a piece of paper with the Aurora euro cash account number on it. "Look this up in RB when you get back to your desk."

Later that day, I overhear my boss on the phone. He sounds defensive. He clicks off and leans across the desk. "Jared, that was the head of risk management. He wants to meet us about the Aurora cash stuff for some reason."

That meeting is enjoyable from start to finish. My boss claims that the large negative balance is nothing to really worry about. I parrot his statements, feigning nonchalance, the company man. Then I get to watch him get raked over the coals by the head of risk management, who gives us a couple of days to get the balance back above zero. That means my boss will have to call up Mr. 'I need to trade' and explain that he has to sell some positions. Or we will have to liquidate them ourselves, a prospect I have been relishing.

But this turns out to be far from the end of the drama. A few weeks after the fund's cash account is (surprisingly quickly) back to positive, I get an email from a partner of 'I need to trade'. He's actually the only one over there to whom I can relate as a human being. But this request is odd: "Please wire €5m to the below account in the name of Aurora Capital for participation in Shipping portfolio with [Mike Shimrinmanson]."[16]

I write back and explain that I need a little more information to put a wire through. And while he's at it, how about some documentation on this new investment Aurora is making? A contract, perhaps? The account turns out to be domiciled at a big Nordic bank, but in the name of a smaller investment firm. The Aurora guys offer zero detail on the investment itself.

This doesn't feel at all right to me. They want us to put through a naked cash wire worth millions and for a round-number amount, itself a red flag, to some guy's account in Norway?

Yes, they do. So I take it to my boss, the man with the skinny tie. I explain that I am not comfortable wiring out investor money against no paperwork. What's to say the Aurora 'advisers' aren't just taking the €5m for themselves by sending it to a friend? I stand next to him at his desk and explain the scenario. He taps through his inbox with a stone face. "Why do you always make problems, Jared?" he says. "Bring me solutions!"

But I persist. Why should we send millions to some joker's account? He finally looks up at me: "What bank holds the account?"

"Nordea," I say.

"Well, they're a reputable bank, we trade with them sometimes. I'm sure it's OK," he says, turning back to his inbox.

The depth of this man's arrogance seems to be matched only by his ignorance. Nordea is a bank many times larger than our own, and they maintain accounts for thousands of third parties: the fact that Landsbanki trades with the bank itself sometimes has no bearing on the prudence of making a money wire to the account of a random dude.

16 Name changed.

We do the wire. And then some time after that I get another email. They want to do another one. Of course! Why not? A second €5m... and then just a couple days after that a third! All told, €15m in cash straight out of our investment fund. Into the hands of: some Norwegian guy.

Around the same time, on 25 July 2008, the economy is starting to go off the rails in Iceland. A Merrill Lynch analyst points to super high credit derivative spreads as indicators that the market expects the Icelandic banks not to repay their debts. Asked about this, the Minister of Education and Culture, Þorgerður Katrín Gunnarsdóttir, comments on camera that maybe this analyst just needed some "continuing education".[17]

The many problems with Aurora have by now become legendary, at least within our small team. The fund had been kicked off and handed to us on the first day with 120 large, sitting in a cash account. The brokers upstairs had booked all the initial investors and that created an immediate problem. Aurora is, by law, a vehicle for professional investors only. To buy in one needs to meet any two out of the following three criteria: a lot of wealth, a lot of personal trades, or a lot of knowledge of markets. And the brokers had never bothered to check that their clients met the criteria.

In fact, a number of them don't, and can't. But I only hear whispers of this. I am not party to the shareholder list anyway, and don't care to be. But over the course of a year or more, I hear rumors that several of these individuals do not in fact satisfy these criteria. It's illegal to have them in the fund, but they've been with us this whole time.

I keep agitating our owl-eyed head of the fund management company: the one who was previously amazed by my fortune-telling powers. He seems to have the magic key to these secret investors. Finally, after more than a year he tells me in September 2008 that they are going to have to "exit" several of them, to the tune of millions of euros. He only discloses this because the fund needs to have enough cash on hand to make these large transfers.

These guys all bought into Aurora at the original price, €100 per share. But by this point in 2008, 'I need to trade' has lost massively. Shares are valued at only around €70, a 30% loss. The question is: how much to pay back these illegal investors as they exit the fund? Will they receive what they originally paid, or what their investments are now worth? It's a big difference: €100 versus €70. Based on the murmuring around the sales desk it seems pretty certain we will pay them out *all* their initial investment, or €100 per share, though owl-eyes will never give me a clean answer. The upshot is that we decided to steal millions belonging to legal investors to pay off other investors who never had a legitimate basis for being in the fund. And once again, as with the case of the currency fund pricing screw-up, the bank does not make good its mistake.

Then the biggest bomb hits. We learn that 'I need to trade' made a secret gigantic trade, priced in the tens of millions of euros, that he never reported to us. It's a long forward and we find out about it only when the counterparty demands settlement. (This is the second and unreported leg of the trade that magically solved our summer cash problems. Now that cash problem is back.) Finally, finally, and at long last my boss' boss (and best friend since kindergarten) is both furious and curious enough to take a gander at the same Aurora accounts that have become my daily grind. He comes in on a Sunday and calls my boss in as well. The first thing that jumps off the page at him are the three wires for exactly €5m each.

"What's this?" he says. "Why are these transfers?"

"No idea," shrugs my boss. "That looks like something Jared did."

I hear this story secondhand late Sunday afternoon. I'm fuming. I relay it all to Hulda, sitting together on her couch. We moved in together at the end of 2007, and by now she has heard the whole Aurora saga in near-daily briefings. I sleep fitfully that night, as I have for months, dreading the work week ahead.

Monday morning we're just waking up. Hulda has a strange but very clear expression when she turns to me. "I had a dream about your job," she says. "Don't let those assholes fire you. You should quit."

I've learned already that when my new fiancée says something with this quiet certainty, I need to listen. So I don't hesitate: I resign that week with effective date Friday, 30 September 2008. My contract stipulates three months of notice and I don't know if I'll be forced to work the entire period through year-end; the bosses are tight-lipped. The following Friday I am still reporting for work each day. By this time the word of my short-timer status has spread around the department. "Is today your last day?" co-workers ask, quietly, with raised eyebrows.

"I am not sure, they haven't told me," I reply.

That afternoon, I hear a rustle behind me. Our admin assistant is sneaking into the office kitchen with plastic sacks full of cakes from the best bakery in town. I catch her eye and she winks at me. Before long, the crows have descended on the desserts and soon it's an unauthorized but full-blown going away party for me. Sheepishly, my bosses shake my hand and wish me well. I am out the door.

The day of the cakes is Friday, 3 October 2008. The following Tuesday, 7 October 2008, Landsbanki collapses.

6

THE BIG ONE

I N the back of our Kópavogur apartment we have a little extra bedroom filled with odds and ends, including my old desktop Mac. I am glued to the computer screen, hitting refresh on the three primary Icelandic news sites in three different browser tabs all morning long. Events are moving fast. My knowledge of the Icelandic language is improving by leaps and bounds as I try to decode the utterances of our bankers and politicians.

The country's economy is unravelling before my eyes.

Last Friday we had cakes in the office. I was looking forward to a few months of casual job searching with full pay. Now five days later and my old employer has gone into receivership. I have no idea if they will even pay out my next month's salary.

In retrospect, the warning signs of the collapse were there for all to see, at least from my desk at the bank those final weeks. Lehman Brothers collapsed in the middle of September, spelling doom the world over. Three of the hedge funds I had chosen for our investors used Lehman as their prime broker and their assets were frozen. We had to price them at 0, as nobody was sure if they could get anything out of Lehman. There was a scramble to see which of our other investments could have ties to Lehman, so deep went that bank's tentacles in world finance. Then, the Landsbanki currency desk started offering annual interest of more than 10% on U.S. dollars and other hard currencies (versus closer to 0% out in the real world) that our funds placed with them for a few days or weeks. These super-high rates were paid via mispriced forward trades, a signal of just how desperate the bank was for hard cash. And on 29 September I had tried to book a large forward foreign exchange trade for Aurora between two hard currencies: euros and Canadian dollars. But none of the bigger European banks that would normally facilitate such a deal even wanted to trade with Landsbanki at this point, so we had to give up.

That Wednesday evening, we pay a visit to the home of some of our best friends, Waingro and Ella. What is normally a boisterous time becomes instead a conversation in hushed tones. We walk through the major recent events in detail: after the weekend's passage of the Emergency Law by Alþingi, the Icelandic Parliament, on Monday Glitnir collapsed and Tuesday was the turn of Landsbanki. "I just hope Kaupþing can hang on," Waingro says, shaking his head.

It is a wish that lasts only a few hours. The next day, Thursday, 9 October 2008, Kaupþing announces that it, too, is bankrupt.

In the famous words of Jim Cramer, I was still thinking "like an academic" in the weeks before the crisis. Feeling vindicated that my doubts about the Icelandic economy were going to be proven right. But when the crisis came, that feeling lasted all of an hour. Because this was hitting us all where it hurt: in our pay stubs and bank accounts.

Nearly all of our savings is sitting in a Landsbanki money market fund called *Peningabréf*. The name translates as 'money brief', signifying with as literal a name as possible a piece of paper that can be redeemed for money. But in this case it's been deemed unredeemable. The bank has frozen all the shares of this massive money market, the largest in the Land, without giving a date for when it will reopen access.

Back in September, Villi, the trader on the currency fund, and I tried to move the fund's collateral out of *Peningabréf* and into safer Icelandic government bonds, but were rebuffed by the head of asset management, the one who found the €5m money wires suspicious.

The two men had an altercation and security removed Villi from the office of the executive. I unsuccessfully tried the same thing with LARS, our fund of hedge funds, which kept its U.S. dollar cash in the same *Peningabréf* as well. The fact that our senior managers were doing everything to prevent a run on this supposedly safe investment made me realize, too late, that it might not be so safe at all.

In the end, the investors in both funds, but especially the currency fund, are forced to eat huge and completely avoidable losses as a result of this attempt to prop up the bank's own junk. It turns out that the *Peningabréf* was so full of bad debt that the managers who ran this massive money market fund maintained two sets of accounting books: one the value they showed to the public, and the second the fair market value, a far lower number.[18]

The week of the collapse I had ordered up some euro to pay a friend for some sports equipment he'd ordered for me from offshore. But the transfer from Icelandic *króna* to euro, something that would normally clear in milliseconds, is frozen seemingly mid-Landsbanki collapse. I've paid out the ISK but the euros didn't hit his account. I call the bank, which still employs nearly all those it did before its collapse, and ask when it will settle.

"We can't really say," says my former colleague. I call him back regularly, so my friend can get his money. After a few days, the bank changes the rate on the transfer, significantly to its advantage.

---

18 Each bank was surrounded by a satellite system of investment companies that bought up junk assets from the bank. These investment companies were financed by commercial paper that the banks purchased into their own money market funds. Many Icelanders, including us, invested in these supposedly safe money market funds. They were marketed as safe investments for retail clients, as good as a savings account. Customer service reps at the banks, like Hulda had been when I met her, were even offered bonuses for getting average Icelanders to move their savings into these funds. Of course, even these supposedly safe funds lost considerable value during the Icelandic financial crisis; in real terms they lost around 70% of their value and should have lost even more.

A lot of our personal savings were stuck in this intentionally mislabeled junk-bond fund. They mostly evaporated in the crisis. We finally gained access to our savings in Peningabréf, the "money market" fund, over the winter—but by that point the fund shares were mostly worthless.

"I've never heard of a bank changing the terms of a trading contract like this, after it was executed," I say.

"Me neither," he agrees. "But these aren't normal times." It's a question of take it or leave it, for me. Where else am I going to get hard currency versus ISK?

I spend my days pacing back and forth, waiting for the next piece of bad news to hit. The British, ostensibly a NATO ally of Iceland, have unilaterally listed the Republic of Iceland, the central bank of Iceland, and the Financial Supervisory Authority of Iceland as terrorist organizations on the website of Her Majesty's Treasury.[19] This news hits the Land like a bolt out of the blue: why do this? In a throwaway comment, Gordon Brown says it is to protect UK depositors' money. As a result of this action, all outstanding international payments to our country, money due us for exports we've already sent, are frozen, severely compounding the effects of the domestic crisis.

I stop in at the local branch of Landsbanki at Hamraborg and notice the place is jammed. Everyone is quiet, waiting for their number to be called, but I notice large amounts of cash going across the teller tables, in previously cashless Iceland. I call Hulda at work in a whisper. She agrees: clean out my checking account. If everyone

---

19 It is still not clear why the UK took this action. According to a 2018 report by the University of Iceland: "On 8 October, the British government froze all assets of Landsbanki under an Anti-Terrorism Act. On the Treasury's website, Landsbanki (and, briefly, the [central bank of Iceland] and other Icelandic institutions) was put on the same list as Al-Qaeda and the Talibans [sic]. The alleged purpose was to hinder money transfers to Iceland. But on 3 October a Supervisory Notice had been issued by the FSA to Landsbanki which hindered all money transfers out of the UK."

In other words, money wires were already frozen five days before, and the UK listed the nation of Iceland as a terrorist organization for other reasons. But why do this? The deeply researched report goes on to cite UK domestic political factors as the likely explanation. This action against Iceland was taken by two Scottish politicians, Gordon Brown, the UK prime minister, and Alistair Darling, the UK finance minister. At the same time, the two were organizing massive public bailouts of two large and unpopular Scottish banks, RBS and HBOS, and beating up on tiny Iceland perhaps provided a welcome distraction. But maybe even more importantly, both men stood publicly against Scottish independence, and it was thus in the interest of both to show how a small northern nation could struggle to prosper on its own. The public statements of each in subsequent years back up this theory. www.stjornarradid.is/lisalib/getfile.aspx?itemid=29cca5ac-c0c6-11e8-942c-005056bc530c

else is doing it, it only makes sense to join in. I plunge into the line, taking out much of the liquid ISK I still have in physical form. So this is what a run on the bank feels like. Living inside a real financial crash is now no longer academic for me: this is truly empirical and definitely frightening.

I feel constant nausea in the pit of my stomach these days. American friends and family, going through their own simultaneous miniature version of the same thing we are, are little help. When I try to explain how worried we are about food, about our monthly mortgage payment skyrocketing, they shut it down. "It's bad everywhere," they say, thinking they know.

But they don't know, because they don't know about *verðtrygging*. And this simple Icelandic word provides a great example of how language can shape thought. Translated literally to English, this comes out as 'price insurance', which sounds like a very good thing indeed. Who wouldn't love a little price insurance? Many Icelanders believe it to be good to this day. But it turns out to be Orwellian nomenclature. An accurate name would be 'inflation linking'. A never-debated clause slipped as a rider into a 1980s law in Iceland allows banks to charge not only the principal that a borrower borrows on a loan, but also to increase that principal balance so that it remains in line with inflation.

What this means in practice is that when one takes out a loan in Iceland, and this applies to mortgages as well as automobile loans, the borrower does not know the total amount she will be obligated to pay back. Instead, she is given an expected amortization schedule based on some guessed-at level of inflation over the term of the loan. This means that the principal balance owed ticks up each month according to the consumer inflation number from the preceding month.[20] For

---

20 These Icelandic mortgages could be compared to negative amortization loans, considered predatory in the United States, although the explicit link to an unknown future price series, consumer price inflation, gives them the added characteristic of a derivative. Packaging derivatives for retail sale to consumers is also contrary to EEA/Icelandic law, but nobody seems to mind.

Through the first months of the crisis, our mortgage payments steadily tick up and after half a year they are around 50% higher than they were at the banks' collapse, with each

holders of mortgages in Iceland—which is most households—this is a disaster. Not only does the total amount one owes always increase each month, but the monthly payments are adjusted ever upwards to reflect the new balance.

Taken economy-wide, and including the fact that much Icelandic corporate and government debt follows a similar paradigm, one can easily see how such a system builds inflation and inflation expectations into the entire economy. If each family's mortgage payments are ticking up each month, each parent will over time demand higher wages at work. In Iceland, unions are fortunately quite strong and bargain across entire sectors of the workforce. So, unions push up the wages which in turn increases the price of goods and services in Iceland, which inflates the prices of consumer goods, which then feeds into everybody's mortgage becoming more expensive. It is a vicious cycle, but of course ensures that the lenders in the economy, those who already have capital, not only make a real return on their money, but are completely insulated from the effects of inflation.

"You need to get out of here," Hulda says to me after a few days of sitting in our little office, refreshing the news websites. She has just started a new job at a small law firm, one of the premier debt collectors in the Land. "You had a hard few months at the bank. Why not take a week off and go somewhere else?"

Although it goes against all of my penurious instincts, she is right. Pacing around home and refreshing the news is doing me no good. So I decide to get away to France, as odd as it feels to be leaving. With Iceland and the world's economies collapsing, plane tickets out are now cheaper than I have ever seen. I should hopefully have a few more months of salary from the bank. And with my flight ticket receipt, I'll be able to buy hard currency from the bank; every foreign bill we own is a small insurance policy against a complete collapse of

---

new month promising an even higher bill. Our mortgage, like nearly every loan in Iceland, is linked in some way to the buying power of the sickly Icelandic *króna*. As the currency plummeted in value through the crisis, inflation shot through the roof. Inflation, which in most countries benefits borrowers, here in Iceland becomes an additional cross to be borne by the embattled everyman.

the ISK. The chance to hold paper euros is going to be well worth the cost of the whole trip! I spend all morning driving from branch to branch in Reykjavík, trying to show my flight ticket and buy a few hundred euros. But every place is clean out of foreign currency. Some of them even have resorted to posting handmade signs: "no €".

At least in France, I'll be able to take hard cash out of an ATM. I just hope our currency doesn't collapse much more in the meantime. During my few days there, I dutifully visit the machine each day and withdraw the max.

PART II—THE INVESTIGATION

7

TWO MONITORS AND
A TELEPHONE

THE headquarters of the FME are situated at the very edge of
Reykjavík, diagonally opposite Glæsibær, Iceland's first and saddest
shopping mall. The neighborhood is both far away from the beautiful
old center of the city and not close to Borgartún, an ugly strip near
the sea that the clueless have christened Iceland's Wall Street owing to
the location of Kaupþing's HQ. The big converted coach drops me at
a bleak bus shelter in front of the FME just before 8:30. I look up at
the white albatross of a building and feel a little proud. The bankers
still sit at their desks in shiny and eye-catching new buildings by the
sea or in glamorous old-world places downtown, but we regulators
call this dreary 1970s box home. Shabby chic.

As with most countries, the facilities allocated to the financial
authority tell you all you need to know about the value that society
places on effective market regulation. Iceland is no different. The
banks have the best locations, the nicest buildings, the sharpest-
dressed people. The regulator is pushed off to the side, a necessary
evil, insignificant at real prevention or enforcement. Never enough
resources, in number or skill, and not really taken seriously. Even

and maybe especially after the juggernaut of the Icelandic financial meltdown, this building feels forgotten. Although things are changing: the staff of FME is now around 50, up from 35 pre-crisis, counting external consultants. But it still feels like the real action is happening elsewhere: the three collapsed banks still have most of their 8,000 employees.[21]

These four floors above an Asian grocery store are going to be my workplace now. I walk around to the main entrance hidden down the side of the building. A small sign reads "reception area on 4th floor"; there isn't anyone to greet visitors. Pulling the door open for the first time, I feel anxiety and excitement too. Despite, or maybe because of, the odd location and the worn surroundings, I feel a sense of importance about what lies ahead.

My new office turns out to be on the top floor of the building in what had been the staff lunchroom a few weeks before. But, post-crisis, they needed more space—and here was a room. In Iceland, planning ahead is exceedingly rare. Making use of the resources right in front of one's nose is more common. And why would it be different here at the FME? Someone has dragged in cubicle walls that are propped up on stands, not even attached to or aligned with the floor. "There's nothing so permanent as something temporary" a wise machinist once explained to me. My desk lies there, empty. Blank. Just two dark monitors and a telephone.[22]

"Have a good start!" says the cheery HR lady who accompanies me to my desk, smiling. Icelanders seem to have the habit of wishing a good start to a new job. I find it very sweet. I haven't heard it before. In America, nobody expects anyone to have a good start. "There's a

21   If this ratio between staff at the Icelandic regulator and bank staff feels low, that's because it is. Iceland had roughly one regulator for every 230 bank employees at the end of 2007, whereas in London, one FSA staffer oversaw only around 50 bank employees at the same time. Sources: FSA Annual Report 2007, Statista.
22   The FME did not actually have any formal investigative or enforcement capability before I was hired. During the boom years the regulator had a staff of 35, but that was not just for bank enforcement, that was also to regulate all of the pension funds, and insurance companies, and investment funds, as well as the securities markets and the credit markets. The actual pre-crisis supervision team for the banks comprised just six or eight people.

reason it's called 'work',", my boss once advised me back in the Wall Street days. I am grateful for this new start, and for the welcoming parade of new co-workers stopping by my desk during these first days. Without fail, each asks me, "Nóg að gera?"—"Do you have enough to do?" When I assent, they smile and nod and walk away. Having enough to do seems to be the gold standard for Icelandic employment.

But actually, I don't really have enough to do at all. I end these conversations staring at my empty desk and feeling a bit lost. After six months with no real work, I am like a racehorse champing at the bit. I've already read all the welcome documents for working at the FME, and realized that my Icelandic language skills are about to get a whole lot better at this government job. But what's next? I want some action. I pace to the window and look out at Esja, the dark lady of a mountain that dominates the small Icelandic capital. "I guess it's up to me to make the action happen," I tell myself. I suddenly feel the weight of the whole of the crisis resting on my shoulders, an overwhelming sensation. Are they really relying on just me to investigate this whole huge mess? This world-scale banking crisis that set the whole country back a decade or two? That reduced us to eating horsemeat sausages and made me so desperate for a job that I even worked for free? Just me? Where should I start? How can I get this going?

I sit back at my desk and look across at the near-empty bookshelf where I have placed my FME employee handbook and some other first-day papers. I see a stack of reports that I must have missed. Maybe someone left them for me to read? I take them down and glance through them. Each is differently formatted and each bears the name of a different Big Four auditing firm: EY, KPMG, PwC. One of the reports consists of thick well-bound volumes, another appears to be just a few PowerPoint slides hastily stapled together. I know that about a month after the collapse, the FME requested these firms review any suspicious transactions during the last month of each bank's life. Each firm had to look at an institution that it did not previously audit. The idea being: maybe certain individuals in business or the government knew something was about to happen, and tried to do something illicit just before the collapse, like transfer some money offshore or sell some shares.

I am intrigued by the reports, and might as well dive into them. But it's going to be a tough slog. Had I any alternative reading material, I probably would have put these binders into my drawer. Each report is pages and pages long, all written in heavy-duty Icelandic. Not street Icelandic, not 'I'll take a lamb sub with everything' Icelandic. This is lawyer Icelandic, academic Icelandic, 'who can say for sure?' Icelandic. And no matter what flavor, this language has a grammar that seems to have been invented to avoid pinning any blame at all. In the sense of rough-and-ready vocabulary, Icelandic can seem very blunt, but when it comes to who did what and when, the Icelandic language offers an option that seems straight out of Zen Buddhism: the middle voice. This way of stringing words together can be so subtle that even the concept can hardly be translated or explained in other languages.

But I'll try. Here goes: even with a simple sentence, the reader of Icelandic can often have the surreal feeling that things have happened all by themselves with zero human involvement. The equivalent of the active-voice American-style sentence 'I made a mistake' is rarely heard in Icelandic. Even something more British like 'mistakes were made' is not heard too often. These forms assign or imply responsibility, respectively; even in the passive, second construction, mistakes were made *by someone*. Powerfully, the Icelandic language offers up a third, middle way of describing the making of a mistake as if it took place in a vacuum and never involved a living soul, the way electrons magically pop into and out of existence in the vastness of space. And Icelanders *love* this middle-voice grammar: even newspaper headlines and TV anchors use it often. With it, Icelandic politics and business can seem magical worlds, bereft of human influence.

The nearly Elvish auditor reports make copious use of this linguistic specialty, which in this context is utterly alien and perplexing to me. How can one investigate something and ignore the human actors at the core of it? The phrasing can make the reading, and along with it my work, frustrating and slow. But I'm digging deeply and carefully into this material in a way that will surely set the tone for the time to come. I find myself gravitating to the charts and tables, where my engineer's mind has always found more logic and comfort. Maybe I can start with some raw data and work my way out from there?

Delving into these auditor reports does have one merit: it gives me something to sink my teeth into while I get my bearings in the new organization. The financial statements of the banks quickly jump out at me. I've got cash flow and owner's equity fresh on my mind, as I am deep into preparation each evening for my second-level CFA exam in two months. I decide to see what the balance sheet of the largest bank, Kaupþing, has to show me. The last one available dates from June 2008, about three months before the collapse. Everything is stated in Icelandic *króna*, so all the numbers run to many digits. Even knowing this, they seem huge. Wanting to make a comparison with something out in the world, I look up the conversion rate for ISK to US dollar on that date and divide. When I see the result on my calculator screen I can't believe my eyes. It's just too big; even in dollars it runs to 11 digits. I do the calculation again, double-checking each figure as I press the keys slowly. But I get the same result.

My stomach lurches. This bank was stunningly huge: around $80bn in size at the time of its collapse, putting it in league with the very biggest bankruptcies in the world. I do some quick online searches for comparison, thinking first of Enron. That 2001 event caused ripples in international markets and media, the Big Five became the Big Four, books and movies were made, and it still ranks number seven on the all-time list of bankruptcies in the world's largest economy. And all by itself, the largest of the defunct Icelandic banks, our little Kaupþing, suffered a collapse about 30% larger than Enron's! Then I run the numbers for the three Icelandic banks together. Had they collapsed a few months earlier, this combined event would have been bigger than the largest bankruptcy in U.S. history. As it is, they are number three: eclipsed only by the recent Lehman Brothers and Washington Mutual collapses.

Seen another way, if we take the three Icelandic banks together we have something about the size of three Enrons. Imagine three such collapses in a single week in a country with 1/1000 the population of the USA. During the months between August and November 2008, unemployment in Iceland increased by nearly 5,000 people. This is the equivalent of five million Americans all losing their jobs at once.

These calculations and the comparisons leave me flabbergasted. I knew the collapse was big but I had no idea it was like this. I sit in my chair, empty desk and cubicle walls around me, overwhelmed by the task I am expected to face. How can I possibly begin to investigate something this big?

And just then, my colleague walks over to my desk with a three-page letter from the Icelandic Stock Exchange. Could this letter be the right place to begin?

8

THE BUYING MACHINE

A LL at once, I have a lot on my plate. The letter from the exchange, then all the Excel data jockeying I did with the trades they sent me, laid bare a years-long pattern of each of the three banks wantonly buying up its own shares. So that's a big lead, but a very basic question remains: where did all the shares vanish to? I am eager to explain this—without it, the buying behavior on its own does not add up. A big part of the story is still missing. I calculate that the biggest bank, Kaupþing, bought up around $1.25bn worth of its own equity on the Icelandic and Swedish markets in the year or so before it collapsed, out of a total market capitalization of around $5bn.[23] This means that these prop traders bought around a quarter of all the shares outstanding in their own bank! The two other banks seem to follow closely behind. I just can't figure out what they did with these shares after they amassed such a huge number of them.

I continue to run with the mystery of the disappearing shares. Where did they all go? Up until now, I have only analyzed the activity at the Icelandic stock exchange itself. I need to be able to see inside the banks. Each bank has its own internal trading systems. Trading

---

23 Market cap during these years is very tricky to state with certainty, as the value of the ISK versus the USD and other major currencies changed so rapidly as the crisis loomed.

desks, like the prop desk, keep their own books and records, called a trading book. So why not try to peek into those?

To gain access to these trading books, the banks themselves will have to provide us the information. This is an idea that won't please them. I will need to start formatting my own formal requests to each bank, and I am a bit daunted. I start by taking an existing request on another issue, a formal letter thick with Icelandic legalese, and copy-paste it. My request needs to be exact: dates, times, department names. I spend a whole afternoon on this first letter, one that requests copies of the trading books of Kaupþing, and then get a lawyer on the team to proofread it. The official FME document management system takes care of final formatting and printing on heavy paper. My new boss Sigrún and I both sign it, and then one of the secretaries in the pool downstairs calls up a courier to hand-deliver it to the bank. Then the wait begins. In these investigations, I am learning, there is always a wait. Standard practice is a seven-day deadline, one that Kaupþing will probably ignore.

And they do. More than a week has passed and I decide to change tack. Clearly, this bank is not eager to comply with information requests from us. It looks like they might simply leave an official letter unanswered and unacknowledged.

At the beginning of my job at *Fjármálaeftirlitið*, the agency issued me an ID badge with my photo on the front. I can use it to enter the building after hours, and we are supposed to wear them at all times at work. I also notice something special, though: on the back it reads "the holder of this badge is a representative of FME and entitled to all the powers given that agency under law 87/1998". These powers include showing up at any of our regulated entities, like the banks, even without warning, and asking for whatever information we need. We always cite this law when we write a formal request, but it seems quite rare that an FME employee takes advantage of what is written on the back of her badge.

So, with no information forthcoming, I go for the more radical approach: show up at the bank in person, unannounced, and demand

the data we need. Sigrún tells me to at least take a new copy of the
letter, reiterating the request, so I draft one up.

———————————

Kaupþing Bank stands by the sea. The ultra-modern headquarters
building—all black stone and mirrored-glass—is plopped next to
Höfði, the haunted old white house where Gorbachev and Reagan
met in 1986. Sacred ground. I park in the visitor spot and walk in,
heart pounding. At the lavish reception desk, I ask for the head of
internal audit, the woman tasked with fulfilling requests like the one
in my letter. Observing the dress and attitude of the receptionists here,
one would never know the bank had fallen into complete disgrace
only months before. Nor does the building show any signs of ruin:
a ten-meter waterfall runs down some kind of obelisk behind them.
I feel like a second-class citizen hailing from the linoleum world of
the FME.

The head of internal audit of course never agreed to a meeting,
and she is not pleased. But she shows up after a couple of minutes
and leads me to a conference room right off the lobby. I hand her my
second formal legal letter of request and reiterate our demand for the
bank's trading records, which I think will be the key to the biggest
puzzle I've ever confronted. She acts as if she wants the meeting to
be over as soon as possible. Her distaste for me is written in her face
and audible in her voice. For her the financial regulator is a tiny
nuisance to be borne, a gnat on her arm that she wants desperately
to swat away.

So she tries to get rid of me. She tells me they are still working
on the request and will have something for us "soon". But I remind
her that they are already past the deadline on the original letter. I am
happy to wait until she can provide us the information we need. Our
interaction has only the thinnest veneer of civility. In Iceland, after all,
the polite usually finish last.

It seems nobody from the FME has ever acted this way with her,
calmly insisting that a request be fulfilled. As much as she doesn't
like seeing me, the visit proves to be the right move: after only an

hour at the headquarters of Kaupþing, I am in possession of a sealed envelope containing the bank's written response and a USB key with electronic copies of the trading books.

The trip back to my office is even harder than the strained meeting with the internal auditor. I am really curious what I will find inside these trading books.

———

April is one of the most pleasant months in the Land, with the dark and depressing days of winter far in the rear-view mirror. At this time of the year, we get about 18 hours of light per day, so much light that we can't even make use of it all. Nevertheless it just keeps piling on: the days grow by one hour each week until next month. By early May there is finally so much light that from then until August is really just one long day: it never gets dark all summer. The winter struggle to survive, to get up and out of bed each dark morning, feels like something that happened to someone else.

Furthermore, my new job is proving even more engaging than I could have hoped.

My work is starting to take shape, with some tangible results appearing faster than I expected. The letter from the stock exchange laying out "suspicious trading behavior" plus the reams of data they've sent—and what I hope Kaupþing has provided—have certainly given me enough to sink my teeth into. But I still have a lot to learn about this new work environment: its habits, rules, and culture. I came into an organization staffed by very quiet people, even by Icelandic standards. These regulators do not enjoy conflict. They prefer to send a letter rather than go for a face-to-face meeting.

I am also still adjusting to the regimen of decrepit city buses that take me here to work. Those two hours each day give me plenty of time to ponder things like the name of our agency, *Fjármálaeftirlitið*. This word translates literally as 'The Oversight of Matters of Fees', with fees in this case meaning wealth. A studious friend explains that the word 'fee' in both English and Icelandic has an even older meaning: flock of sheep. After all, what's wealth to a Viking or an old English farmer but a flock of sheep? The nice but a bit jarring thing for me about this Icelandic language is that it's spoken only here, so proper names of places or government bureaus are often the most literal description, punctuated with a definite article. In the most basic sense, we the FME are the one and only overseers of all matters pertaining to flocks of sheep, and all forms of wealth derived therefrom.

This literalism sometimes creates awkward situations for me. Most Icelanders describe themselves professionally using whatever degree they received at university, regardless of their current job role or description: "Hi, I'm Jón, I'm an economist." Economics will follow Jón for the rest of his life, even if he is subsequently head of marketing. This manifests for me in my new investigative role when the boss introduces me inside and outside the FME as "Jared, a man who builds intricate machines". I graduated years ago as a mechanical engineer.

These university degree titles mark status in the Land, because a widespread fear of hierarchy means that the actual job titles conveyed by employers are often very stripped-down. Many professionals, like myself, receive the title *sérfræðingur*, 'possessor of special knowledge', a specialist.

So here I find myself, a *sérfraeðingur* at the regulator, and being very much a rookie at this institution, I wish to impress in this new role. Each day I make a habit of taking a late-afternoon walk down the hall to Sigrún's office, to keep her updated with the progress of the investigation and to keep myself steadily moving forward. She always looks happy to see me, and I manage to bring her a new development each day. I want to dig out and present her facts that matter. Not only because I am grateful for having this job. But also because, in this crisis that we Icelanders are living through each day, we all feel it in our gut: something is seriously and deeply rotten inside these banks. And if anyone is in a position to uncover whatever that is, it's me.

I get back to my desk from the meeting with the frosty Kaupþing staffer and fire up trusty Excel, opening a series of vast new chaotic spreadsheets from the guts of the biggest of the collapsed banks. To my surprise, though, it's not that difficult to decipher this stuff and it does not take long to confirm what we have seen from the stock exchange trading sheets. The gross numbers actually match up quite well; the bank's own trading records confirm the massive daily volumes. On the open market each day, the bank would buy and buy and buy. And then buy some more. Spending millions upon millions of ISK, keeping the Kaupþing share price from falling on the tiny stock market of Iceland each day, fueling water-cooler talk the Land over about the genius of this new breed of Icelandic banker, year after year.

The prop desk's trading books swell to bursting with the bank's own shares.

These trading records also provide me with the next desperately sought piece of the puzzle: at the end of each financial quarter, another desk at the bank—the brokerage desk—would buy the shares that the prop traders had spent the last three months accumulating. All of them. Even though that inventory could be worth two or three hundred million dollars, the brokers would swallow it all in one go, in just one or two trades.

Brokerage desks serve a very different purpose than prop desks: in a normal bank or brokerage firm a stockbroker takes customer orders ("buy me 1000 shares of IBM at market price, please"), executes that order on the open market, and delivers the shares to that customer against the money value of the trade.

We can finally see where all these shares went: how the prop desk unloaded the evidence of their dirty deeds. It was the bank's own brokers buying them. So that when quarter-end came, the shares were no longer legally in the hands of the bank itself. Keeping such huge share volumes on the bank's books, even intraday, without notifying the public, is illegal. But at least here the bank was in compliance with the law by the end of the quarter, by the time the sleepy auditors would come in and look over the numbers.

My gut tells me there must also be more to this story. For the ultimate collapse of these banks to be so devastating, there must have been a ticking time bomb buried deep inside.

9

SHARE LAUNDERING

NOTHING ever happens on time in Iceland, and that includes public transit. My commuting nightmare rolls on. The worst part is the connection I need to make on the way to work each morning. The shabby minibus that serves our little street is always a few minutes late, and the driver never seems happy to see me. After seesawing over five or ten speed bumps, we blast up the hill to the tune of rattling diesel exhaust. I look at my watch and wonder if we'll make it today. Fortunately, the connecting bus is often also late. I stand at the top of the hill at Hamraborg, exposed to sideways-blowing rain, watching down the off-ramp for the Number 2 to pull in from Hafnarfjörður. The number of Icelanders using public transportation has surged during the crisis, and I don't need the evening news to tell me that. A bus stop placed as an afterthought is now crowded each morning.

I walk across the rain-swept road to the office door, still in a bit of a funk from the queasy ride. At 8:30 a.m., the regulator remains quiet. Most employees don't show up until after 9:00. Climbing the stairs and thinking to myself that I'll have some nice quiet time to kick off the day, I bump into a colleague, Binni. He nods a curt greeting as he goes down the stairs past me. A new investigator like me, he started a week after I did. He's got carefully groomed hair, he's in decent shape and about the same age. More or less a typical thirtysomething Icelander. The only thing not typical: his near-permanent frown.

Up until now, our investigative paths have not crossed. Following different tracks, we are looking at different things. Binni keeps to himself most of the time. I have been so engrossed in the letter from the stock exchange and churning the raw trading data that followed, that I probably have not paid enough attention to my counterpart across the aisle. And we have not really bonded. I get the feeling that we have different perspectives on the banking collapse. I want to look back in time, to tell as complete a story as I can about how we got here. Binni, on the other hand, seems to hew closer to the bankers' perspective: the Icelandic financial system was going along just fine until the global financial crisis knocked it over. Everything I have seen makes me disagree with this view of events. To me, the Icelandic banks were always sandcastles. They were never built to last. Then a tsunami came along in October 2008 and wiped the beach clean.

Binni comes back in from outside, trailed by a cloud of cigarette fumes, and sits in his cubicle across from me. He clears his throat and sits back in his chair, a big auditor's report in hand. The surface of his desk is already covered with confidential pre-crisis documents from one of the banks. I can't help but think he is going too narrow, focusing in already on specific meetings and events without first knowing the bigger picture. I feel like we should be on a mission: to tell the information-starved Icelandic public, the people who ultimately pay our salaries, what exactly has happened to their savings and their pensions. I am really starting to put my heart and soul into this work. To me it looks like Binni is here just to collect a paycheck. And who can blame him? These days, collecting a regular paycheck in Iceland is lucky indeed.

———

Around this time, the American investigator William Black visits the FME. He gives us a speech in the cafeteria as we sit around formica tables.[24] He authored a book called *The Best Way To Rob A Bank is to Own One,* detailing his work to unravel the American savings and loan bust of the late 1980s. He and other U.S. investigators found big crime: thousands of indictments and dozens of convictions. It revs me up. Most of my fellow FME employees seem either shell-shocked or uncomprehending, but I am inspired by this brash-speaking guy. He tells us that we will need to work very hard. And he says that it will be the most enjoyable time of our careers. Other employees shrug as we walk back up the dingy stairwell to our offices, but I hold on to these two pieces of wisdom.

Many 'celebrities' of the finance world, like Bill Black, show their faces in Iceland around this time. Economists, analysts, professors: everyone wants to be here, to see with his own eyes the colossal damage of the biggest financial crisis in history. Paul Krugman, Joe Stiglitz: we witness a Nobel Prizewinners' ball on Icelandic evening television. Each esteemed guest presents his view about the state of the economy and what needs to be done going forward, before jetting off to some other country where parmesan cheese is still served.[25] For me, this stream of visitors serves as a reminder that those of us still here are doing very important work—the work of untangling the causes of this nightmare.

"Alright, Jared," my boss says, after carefully reading and examining my latest memo. "This is a good case. We have the two traders of

---

24 Once per week, on Thursday mornings, the FME provides breakfast for all the employees. We have to get in early, around 8:30, and there is usually also a presentation of some kind. The Icelanders call it breakfast, but to me these meals are always a mishmash of foods that I don't usually eat together. Vínarbrauð, the delectable Vienna bread breakfast pastry, has pride of place but then next to and surrounding it are plates of sliced bread, butter, ham, cheese, and potato salads full of vinegar. At the very end of the parade of food is a five-layer dark chocolate cake and next to that an industrial-grade steel bowl containing a small mountain of fresh whipped cream. We line up on both sides of the table and pile our plates high with all of these dishes.

25 The crash of the Icelandic *króna* during the crisis meant we could no longer import such niceties.

the biggest bank. Now we need to get this ready to send to the prosecutor."

"What about the head of the prop desk, the boss of these traders?" I ask, stunned that she would halt the investigation so quickly.

"What do you mean?"

"Aren't we going to investigate him?"

"Why would we do that?"

"Because he is responsible too! If he didn't know what was going on, it's negligence. If he did know, it's criminal."

She pauses and looks at me, genuinely puzzled. Icelanders don't seem to like the idea that a manager could be responsible for other people, for employees. I have had this insight at times in my two previous jobs here: Icelanders are not fond of the principle that one can lose his position for doing sloppy work. "I don't know if you could accuse him on that basis. But go ask the lawyers if you feel like it," she says.

Of course, I more than feel like it. It seems the natural thing to do. I couldn't have reconciled the idea of not pursuing it. I work it out so that I sit with a couple of our lawyers at the same lunch table. In an Icelandic government job, nobody has the money to eat outside work. Most government agencies in the Land do provide their employees with a subsidized hot meal of fish or meat, but not this one. At least we have a cafeteria: not the one that serves as my office, but a new one three floors down, a big open room with tables and newspapers. Icelanders love to flip through the paper while drinking their coffee and eating lunch, a level of relaxation and comfort at work I never experienced in Boston, San Francisco, or Salt Lake.

The row of windows looks out onto Suðurlandsbraut (Southlands-Boulevard), one of the busiest roads of the capital. The sounds of studded winter tires chewing grooves in the asphalt gives a special hum to the local traffic noise. The view past the cars and trucks becomes more appealing, opening out to a typical Icelandic vista of bright green, then blue sea, then the charcoal bulk of Esja, the mountain beyond. Almost everywhere one looks in Iceland is a majestic landscape like this. Trees can never grow very tall in the relentless wind, and this creates broad, clear, and often stunning sights. Inside, however, the atmosphere remains drab, with tables placed haphazardly in an ever-shifting, unplanned arrangement and without any decoration on the white plaster of the industrial walls.

So it is here that I sit down with the lawyers, bearing my own bowl of soup and plate of cheese, sliced bread, and *hangikjöt*, or smoked lamb, sliced thin. The same lunch every day. As Sigrún has warned me, our lawyers are indeed adamant that a bank boss cannot be held responsible for the actions of his team. Nonetheless I try to make a case of it as we sit around one of the big formica tables, slurping down our soup.

"Take a bus driver who goes for lunch with his boss. They drink beers and the boss can see that the driver is somewhat inebriated, yet ignores it. The driver gets back on the road after the meal and is then responsible for an accident, which ends in a kid being killed. Wouldn't the boss be held accountable?"

"Not really," says one of the lawyers, unconvinced by my example.

"What if the boss *bought* four beers for his employee at this lunch and watched him drink them? Would he be held accountable then?"

"No, I still don't think so," says the same attorney. "It is up to the driver to do his job properly."

This conclusion comes as a shock to me. What is the role of a boss? Why have managers or team leaders at all? I had run the bus-driver example past a lawyer friend in the U.S. just before the meeting as a sanity check. And he confirmed my view of things. The same friend probably would have shared my sense of shock as the lunchtime hypotheticals continued. These traders at Kaupþing sat at their desks and manipulated the share price every day for years. The penalty for market abuse like this is up to six years in prison.

"So, if they're found guilty, would these guys do six years for each trade, or for each day of manipulation?" I wonder aloud. "These are going to be some big sentences for these poor guys."

"Up to six years for market abuse," the second lawyer, on mute until now, responds.

"What do you mean, up to six years? Six years total, for everything? That's it?"

"What more do you want?"

"But these guys manipulated the market every day for years and they would only get up to six years? Don't these infractions stack up on each other?" I insist, naïvely. "It's multiple counts of the same crime, isn't it?"

"No, the crime is manipulation. One manipulation. No multiple counts of a crime, we don't do that here. That's an American thing," the other replies. They exchange bemused looks and then chuckle at whatever expression is on my face.

"Wow. I don't know what to say," I confess. "*Verði ykkur að góðu.*"[26] I get up to go back upstairs.

"Wait," one says. "You still have a chance to go after the boss of these guys. But only if you can show evidence that he knew what they were doing."

With this in mind—a tiny victory after a lunch of letdowns—I go directly back to Sigrún. She doesn't want to go any further with this case. I can sense her reluctance as I open the negotiation, a cartridge full of arguments ready to be fired.

"These two young traders spent a lot of Kaupþing money. How did they do that and nobody noticed?" I fire off. "Also, their boss, the head of the prop desk: he's responsible for the profit and loss on that trading. Is buying up their own shares really the best investment they can make? What kind of discussions did they have?" I know I am just adding to my own workload, but I am so curious about the kinds of emails that got sent back and forth at the prop desk. They couldn't have done this much manipulative buying each day and never talked about it. Right?

Sigrún sighs and waves her hand. It's a green light; she'll sign a request letter once I've drafted it. However, it's also clear I won't get any help screening through any emails we get. Binni and I have made some progress in our working relationship recently, but I know

26 Roughly, *Bon appetit!* We don't seem to have a good translation for this in English, as I guess nobody in England ever expected to enjoy a meal.

there's no way he'll agree to help me on this one either. He's already made comments like, "All these graphs and charts you're making, you really think there's a case there?" He also seems dead-set against the idea of looking at anyone's emails. ("What do you think you'll find?") He's much more a fan of sticking to the official documents, like minutes of bank committee meetings. He's straight, by the book. I am ready to pull at any thread that will enlighten me on what looks to be a giant years-long illegal operation.

I get the request letter sent off the same day, asking for full email extracts of the two prop traders, their boss, his boss, and the boss of that guy as well. I add the fifth name at the last minute, guessing that knowledge of the multi-billion-dollar scheme might not be confined to such low levels. Instead of giving the bank seven days to respond, we tell them to respond *án tafar*: without delay. But, and no surprise here, they do delay. They don't even acknowledge the request for a couple days. When I follow the letter up with a phone call, I get passed around between departments. Tired of waiting, frustrated by their lack of accountability, I opt for a change of strategy and some fresh Icelandic air. I decide to go back down there in person.

Thinking I will be better off accompanied, I decide to take an IT colleague along. A heavy-set ultra-laid-back dude in his late 30s, Siddi in fact represents the entirety of the IT department of the FME and is more used to upgrading Windows and programming desk phones than conducting forensic email retrievals. He looks excited to join me, like he might in fact relish the opportunity to help twist an arm or two in order to get what we need.

We drive down to the harbor, toward the gleaming Kaupþing headquarters with the ten-meter waterfall inside. Surprised for a second time, and certainly no more welcoming than the first, the head of internal audit tells us that the request for the emails is out of her hands; but that we can "rest assured" that the bank's IT department is already "working on it".

"Good, so we will just wait here until you are ready to hand them over," I say to her, smiling. She is not smiling. She looks at us through her glasses with cold blue eyes. I keep grinning.

Perhaps the resolution behind my expression helps. I can see how bank employees neither respect nor fear those of us from the regulator, and this attitude makes me all the more convinced that we have to keep pushing. We sit across from her while she makes a call to the bank's IT department, located in some remote hellhole at the suburban ghetto edge of Rey-K City.

From the way the conversation is going on her end, it becomes obvious to us that in fact nothing has been done yet. She turns to us with the awkward look of someone caught in her own deception.

"They will start immediately," she promises.

"We have time," I reply. "Actually, we will wait as long as necessary." I'm now convinced I can't go away and trust them to comply. I feel my colleague's mounting excitement about the whole subdued battle. The bank, on the other hand, wants to get rid of us as fast as possible. No one likes to have the regulator in their house.

"They are working on the extracts now," she says. "Your colleague can go there if he likes and watch them. But nothing will happen in this office in any case."

As it happens, the email extracts run very quickly. My IT friend makes several trips to the hellhole on the outskirts of town and keeps me posted on the return from each triumphant visit. The next day he calls me down to his office and shows me a big black hard drive containing five years of employees' emails in .pst files.

"Which tool do we use to access these?" I ask.

"Tool?" he says. "The guys on the third floor just used their Outlooks to read them."

I have heard that the investment funds regulation team had conducted email searches recently, working on some other post-crisis investigations. I had no idea they used Outlook for this purpose.

"But that's crazy," I say. "Their personal Outlook account? Then they might just forward or reply to one of these bankers' emails by accident from their official work email?"

"That's what they did," he shrugs, with an I-just-work-here expression.

I ask him for a dedicated computer and an installation of Outlook that I can use for reading these emails. He's proud when he tells me that in fact he has plenty of old hardware around his office. (Such abundance is never to be taken for granted in the Land.) We make a copy so that the original hard drive from Kaupþing can be evidence-bagged and sealed away. And soon I am digging into this mess, with Bill Gates' pride and joy as my search tool. I quickly figure out that the search feature in the old program is beyond useless: when I look for a common keyword, like 'trade', I get just a handful of hits, whereas just by scrolling through a folder I can find thousands of such mails extant. As a search tool, Outlook is junk.

Reluctantly, I decide that first morning that the most bulletproof way is to go by hand, reading each and every email in chronological order until I find what I am looking for. I open promising folders and arrow-down through emails very fast, maybe one or two seconds to read each mail, but there are thousands of messages to get through. I feel like I have come back from vacation to an overflowing inbox, and I am trying to find the important messages, only here I've come back from five people's vacations and they've been away five years. Worse, when one employee sends another a mail, I end up running across it twice, or even more times if it is sent to a group. It takes me days of squinting, headaches, and creepy dreams, but in this endless interlinked mailbox I finally find the missing piece.

At the end of quarter, the head of prop trading was worried about how many of the bank's own shares his 'boys' had accumulated on the open market. He didn't want all of those shares sitting on his own trading book. And legitimately so: the amount easily crossed the legal limit.[27] At the end of some reporting quarters in 2008, the value of its own shares held by the bank was worth hundreds of millions of dollars.

So the prop desk head would then get in touch with his boss (the head of treasury) or his boss' boss (the CEO of the Icelandic business unit) to ask what to do with this shameful portfolio. The more senior

27 In fact the bank had been over the legal limit for much of the financial quarter and just never bothered to report it; the managers apparently decided it was only worth following the law when quarter-end came and they were being checked.

executive suggested to speak with the head of the brokerage desk, who would make a "package": the brokers would buy the whole block of shares from the prop desk. Hundreds of millions in one or a handful of trades. I have seen these big movements already in the trading books, but here it is being discussed between real people.

The value of these big trades was of course already cast. The traders marked them at the last market price, the same market price set by these same men in their diligent trade-by-trade manipulation of the public stock markets. And herein lay the genius of the whole scheme. From Abu Dhabi to Zanzibar, the market price of a thing is the 'real' price, so he who controls the market, controls the value.

The emails I had carefully tracked down were the missing link, the evidence that this buying of shares wasn't an isolated action carried out by two rogue traders. It was systematic and coordinated. None of my colleagues at the FME could argue otherwise anymore.

I find something else, too. Wanting to expand their footprint in Scandinavia, Kaupþing had hired an experienced banker to oversee their operations in the region. An outsider. Within weeks of his employment, he had caught wind of the massive trafficking the bank was doing in its own shares. So he drafted an email about this and sent it to the most senior Kaupþing executives in Iceland. He told them he had serious reservations about what they were doing, that if the undeclared share-buying came to light it could sink them all. Not happy with the low-key response to that mail, he reached out to a senior partner at a prestigious London law firm. The lawyer emailed back several strongly worded paragraphs pointing out both the illegality of such actions, and the reputational consequences if they were discovered. The outsider forwarded the legal opinion to the top execs in Iceland and advised that Kaupþing needed to cease such purchases immediately. It was the General Counsel of Kaupþing who answered the mail on behalf of the other executives. He said that if Kaupþing stopped buying up its own shares on the Icelandic market, "the market will lose its trust in us". The outsider departed the bank soon after.

In the end, showing the complicity of these very senior Kaupþing managers through their own words becomes remarkably easy. The emails, once I find them, are simple and straightforward: these are not sophisticated schemes at all. The hard part is not to speak about the discovery, the manipulations, the glorious details of this case with Hulda or anyone outside. At dinner she sees my eyes sparkling. I know she can tell that we made a breakthrough and any other conversations stall. "I'm doing something big," I finally let drop as we wash the dishes. "I know," she smiles. It looks like it is tougher for me to keep my silence than it is for her not to be able to hear the story. "Go get 'em, babe," she says. These bankers, the ones who screwed us out of our future, and the whole country too, she doesn't need to add.

Everybody tells me that these days.

10

OUT THE BACK DOOR

MY personal situation has admittedly improved over the last few weeks. Feeling more and more prosperous, I am back to driving. Many days now I swap Strætó, the Reykjavík bus, for my trusty silver RAV4, RZzy. I drop Hulda off at work and then continue on to my office. No more long bus tours of the rainy Reykjavík sprawl for me. Each morning, mine is seemingly the first car in the lot. And each evening one of the last to leave. But I give myself enough time for my daily swim, a healthy habit I have picked up in the Land. These days, the after-work plunge into warm geothermal water remains a life saver, especially when the investigations get stressful. That, plus another new habit: lunchtime yoga.

Summer, though, is when you really don't want to be working in Iceland. The light never disappears. At six, usually the time when I pack and go home, I have almost the equivalent of a full workday of light remaining for evening activities. Most of my co-workers are away on long holidays, which I can't seem to let myself join. The FME gave me a week off in early June for my second CFA exam and then I took another one in early July but I just can't imagine myself stopping for too long in the middle of this investigation. I am too immersed in it. I realize that any forward progress on this case pretty much depends on me alone, and this motivates me to keep going when almost everyone else in the country is off at a summerhouse. Anyway, compared to my old life on Wall Street, life in Iceland is more or less a permanent vacation! If I need a break, I can use one of the many swimming pools that dot the Reykjavík neighborhoods.

The open questions from work often follow me right into the open-air hot tubs, and these days I'm thinking: what were the Kaupþing boys doing with all of these shares they were buying up?

If I look at just the last year of the bank's life, for example, more than a quarter of all the Kaupþing shares outstanding flowed through the bank's own proprietary trading desk, grabbed directly off the exchange in this unprecedented one-sided buying operation. That means roughly a quarter of all the extant Kaupþing shares had crossed the market during these few months, and they were purchased in turn by the bank. But what became of them? The management had to do something with them because if they had declared the buying publicly, then even the sleepy regulator and ho-hum auditors of Iceland would have probably felt the need to ask some questions.

In a normal buy-back scheme, the bought-up shares are retired, meaning the total number of shares outstanding is reduced, and the remaining owners of the company each sit with a larger fraction of ownership. Kaupþing couldn't declare these massive daily buys of their own equity, so the idea of retiring those shares outright couldn't work either, as then they'd have to go public with the fact of the large purchases. The only option remaining was to hide the shares somehow, in a way that the public couldn't easily detect. But how? What was this back door?

I know from my trading analysis that the brokers got stuck with the shares. But the brokers' own trading books are also supposed to be flat at the end of each trading day. After all, a broker is not holding positions either, just buying and selling to fulfill orders from his customers. And more or less, the Kaupþing brokers did do this: the same day as the broker gobbled down huge slugs of the bank's own shares internally from the prop traders, he would pass them out to clients. In huge amounts. One of them purchased around a million dollars' worth of shares at once. A private person, in that case. A lot of the time, though, the buyers were companies, in deals much bigger than just a million bucks.

It's effectively a one-way conveyor belt moving shares off the public market to the Kaupþing prop desk to the brokers to their clients. I sketch out a big diagram with arrows showing this conveyor belt and how it operated over five years. I haven't paid much attention to the ultimate clients, but something about them nags at me.

The intense working summer helps me consolidate all the bits and pieces of the case into the beginnings of a report. And then, at the end of July, I get an unexpected insight. Home from work on a Friday evening, kicked back on the sofa, I skim the day's news online while Hulda cooks dinner. One story jumps out at me: a new website, called WikiLeaks, has a link to a confidential document from inside Kaupþing Bank, and the Icelandic newspaper *Fréttablaðið* has written a short piece on it. I have never heard of WikiLeaks—it appears to be like a Wikipedia for leaked information—and I am fascinated by what I am able to pull up on my laptop: it's the "large exposure report" for Kaupþing, the same bank I am investigating, made just weeks before its collapse.

I hear my fiancée saying something to me in the background. Her words float in the room but never make it all the way to my brain. What I have in front of my eyes is just too compelling. And very long. I am scrolling and scrolling. The leaked document is a slide deck prepared for senior management and never intended to be shown outside the bank, and it details each of the "large exposures": the outstanding loans made by Kaupþing for more than €45m. The slides are black and bold on a masters-of-the-universe PowerPoint template and then in an English riddled with middle-school mistakes, some poor grunts at the bank have set out the facts. The name of a big borrower heads each slide, then under that are the exotic names of his companies, the activities of his companies (usually 'investment'), the risks (many), and the collateral (very little).[28]

28 wikileaks.org/wiki/Financial_collapse:_Confidential_exposure_analysis_of_205_companies_each_owing_above_EUR45M_to_Icelandic_bank_Kaupthing,_26_Sep_2008

By now I am out on the back deck, in the sunshine, scrolling the screen and taking notes. There is just too much here; this is a treasure trove of atrocious banking. And finally, as Hulda is on the verge of pulling me by the arm inside to the dinner table, I realize what I am really looking at. Here lies the missing piece. The piece that completes the puzzle; the answer to the question. Where did all those shares go? *Here they are.* This is the back door: these loans and funny companies are the hiding place.

It is a eureka moment. Until now I could perceive only half of the mechanism. Suddenly, the whole machinery, all the cogs, wheels, gears, and pinions are visible. And billions of Icelandic *krónur* flowed through the whole thing.

Back at work on Monday morning, I walk across to Binni to show him a printout of the leaked slide deck. It brings together both of our investigations. It shows that all of the largest borrowers from Kaupþing were also giant shareholders of the same bank: Kaupþing was dumping its junk shares on its own clients and lending them the money to take them off its hands! For a commercial bank, the loans it has made are its gems, its valuable property, investments it has carefully selected to earn back interest. Whereas the bulk of this Kaupþing loan book was built around hiding its own shares, the same ones it had been buying to keep the price from falling.

"This is our missing link!" I say, a bit excited.

"Show me," he replies unmoved. Then he casts a sidelong glance at my printout. "But we had this presentation a long time ago," he says.

"How come you didn't show this to me?"

"Didn't think it mattered so much. This is the loan piece, and you were working on some trading stuff."

I stare at him aghast. He turns back to his work. After a few minutes, he comes over to my desk with a file.

"Look at that—it's what I presented to our board."

Inside the file is Binni's report on one of the funny companies from the PowerPoint, Holt Investment Limited. This is nowhere near the biggest crooked loan deal laid out in that slideshow, but it's of decent size. Cross-referencing with the trade data, I see that this company spent about $250m buying shares in Kaupþing Bank from the bank's own brokers in February and September of 2008. To pay the money it owed on the trades, the company took out "VIP loans" from Kaupþing that Binni discovered and documented in his case file. Was there any collateral for these giant loans? Was there some real estate behind it? Some other companies maybe? Nope, the collateral for the giant loans was merely the value of the bank's own shares themselves.[29]

Now that I understand the way loans formed such a core piece of the share-laundering scheme, I can begin to see a far bigger picture. I could already see the corrosive effect of the daily manipulation on our little stock market, but now I am beginning to grasp the follow-on corrupting effects that manipulation fundamentally had on the business of the largest institution in Iceland. From there, it's easy to see how the whole economy of our country could be corrupted. For a bank, the loans it makes are its assets: it makes them expecting to get the money back plus some interest for its trouble. If the loan goes bad, the lender can seize the collateral underlying it—a car, a house, a factory—and sell it to try to recoup the principal.

Kaupþing, however, is not your typical bank. Here we have an institution knowingly and systematically creating loan upon loan with no real collateral at all, instead using its own shares as a stand-in. But at the same time, the bank was fixing the value of those same shares through daily market manipulation. Not only were the shares junk, so was the banking.[30]

---

29 No real money needed to change hands in this deal. The bank already owned the shares: it had taken possession of them already in its illegal buying on the public markets. Here they were simply moved from the bank's brokerage desk to the account of Holt Investment. The deal was booked as a trade and paid for with a new loan created out of thin air. At some point years in the future the loan would come due, meaning Holt Investment would in theory have to pay back the cash, but meantime there were no pesky interim payments of principal or interest. The Icelanders call this a 'bullet' loan. Problem solved: shares moved off the bank's books, and the bank even ends up with a shiny new loan to an 'investment company' in the British Virgin Islands.

30 What Binni did spend a lot of time investigating was how in fact the loans into these sham companies could pass muster in the bank's credit department and get through what could be several layers of internal approval. He found that these procedures were rarely

So why did the bank keep on going like this? I don't have the answer. I put down the file and look around me. I feel like sharing my thoughts with Binni, but hold myself back. I feel the bile rising inside me. With the leaked document of giant loans over the weekend I realized that the case was even bigger than I had thought. My frustration is really growing: I have been specifically hired to investigate this crisis and I didn't know about this key document before it was leaked to the press. Then I learn that it has been sitting in the cubicle across from mine for months.

Why didn't we make good use of these valuable data? Why didn't we use this exhaustive internal list of the biggest loans as a roadmap, and then systematically look at both the largest and most recent transactions? Why aren't we investigating the far bigger exposures laid out in this document? Why did we already focus so much on Holt—which, though big, is just one of dozens of shell companies?

I keep it all to myself for now. And decide to play along and do some more research on the company itself. I find the name of the owner, Skúli Þorvaldsson. His name doesn't mean anything to

---

followed, as upper management found many ways around the credit approval process when dumping shares was the goal. One of the ways the management did this was via money market loans, which are supposed to be super-short-term loans to highly reputable entities. This type of loan was repeatedly abused by the bank to finance the purchase of its own shares.

One example concerns a British client, Kevin Stanford, whose money was being managed by Kaupþing. In August 2008, an account in his name, run by Kaupþing, spent about $120m to buy shares in the bank itself. Knowing they could never get a giant loan such as this one approved by the bank's loan committees, the architects of this deal created a money market loan for $120m, due on 2 September 2008, only a few weeks away. The idea was apparently to put off figuring out a more permanent financing arrangement. Then that date came and of course they couldn't figure it out, so they just rolled it: they made a new money market loan that included the interest and principal of the old one and made that one come due on 30 September 2008. Then when the 30th came there was still no good solution for financing this huge purchase by an individual, so they extended it again with a new loan until 30 October 2008.

In the interim, Kaupþing went bust and its estate was stuck holding a $120m loan against which there was 0 valuable collateral.

Kevin Stanford referenced these transactions in a 2019 letter to the Kaupþing bosses. Further discussion of this letter can be found in Part III.

kjarninn.overcastcdn.com/documents/1.__Hreidar_and_Magnus_open_letter_.pdf

me. But I learn that his father started one of the grand old hotels in Reykjavík, Hotel Holt. Skúli inherited some of the wealth, and apparently later named his new shellco after the lovely old downtown institution.

Kaupþing owned a separately incorporated Luxembourg bank to handle business for wealthy individuals; transactions between the Icelandic and Luxembourg entities are all over the reports I reviewed during my first days at FME. It looks like the managers of Kaupþing in Iceland convinced Skúli to entrust the management of his wealth to their private bankers on the Continent. With his money under their control, they were able to create a series of entities, among them Holt Investment, used to purchase shares of Kaupþing against loans that ultimately came through from the parent bank in Iceland as well.

Skúli's story turns out to have been a common one: many of the wealthy clients of Kaupþing had 'discretionary mandates'. This meant that the private bankers in Luxembourg had freedom to manage the client's money without getting permission for each and every transaction. The bankers took advantage of this as they looked for hiding places for worthless Kaupþing shares. First they used their clients' wealth management accounts in Luxembourg to hoard these shares in massive amounts. When all the clients' money had been used up buying this junk, the dedicated team would then create shell companies in the British Virgin Islands, lend those companies money, and use them to absorb yet more Kaupþing shares.[31]

That afternoon I perform a systematic analysis. I open up the spreadsheet of Kaupþing's brokerage trades over several years and sort for the very biggest trades. It becomes very easy to see that the bank unloaded shares in huge blocks at the end of every three months: March, June, September, and December. These are the dates

---

31 In addition to its private banking clients, Kaupthing had other ways to hide the shares it was buying. One of these was to stash them in companies incorporated in Iceland, such as with a company called Mata ehf., which purchased a huge block of Kaupthing shares in March 2008, financed entirely by a short-term money market loan granted by the bank. On the offshore side, it wasn't just British Virgin Islands companies, either, as in the case of Desulo Trading Limited, a Cyprus offshore company that purchased shares in big blocks from May until September 2008.

corresponding to the end of the fiscal quarter, when the bank has to close its books and make a report. Over the years, the shares piled so high at the prop desk every three months that anyone looking at the reports couldn't help but find them. So, at the eleventh hour, brokers entered a few big trades and the shares ended up being 'owned' by a revolving list of dozens of companies with funny names. Mostly they are the same names from the PowerPoint of the largest loans the bank made.[32]

In fact, there are very few names that I recognize from my analysis of the Kaupþing broker trades. I would have expected to see some trades perhaps with well-known foreign institutions: overseas banks or mutual fund companies. But there are none to be found. I do recognize a small handful of buyers: the Icelandic pension funds. Were these the only real-world buyers of Kaupþing shares during all these years? It makes sense that regulations and investment policy would force our local pension funds to take large positions in Kaupþing. After all, the pensions are largely constrained to hold Icelandic equities and Kaupþing itself made up a third of the value of the local stock market. These retirement dreams are now zeroed out.

And it's nearly quitting time, so time to summarize what I found. And time to take the case forward, up the chain of command. Sigrún will need to see my new master list of buyers, as it should change the transactions we decide to investigate. But, for now, to the *sundlaug*, the neighborhood swimming pool. As soon as possible.

---

32 These big block trades to unload shares from Kaupþing's books aren't real trades in any sense of the word, because the risk of holding the equity position never changes hands. All that changed hands is the name of the owner of the shares, but the real owner is ultimately the bank, which would need to sell these shares to pay off the loan it made to finance the purchase. Such a trade is called a 'fictive' trade in the parlance of EU market law, and such trades are illegal in both the EU and Iceland.

This was in effect a way to just lever and lever and lever the bank, because no new equity came in via these deals and instead the bank simply added loan assets to its balance sheet as it assumed the ownership of shares that other real participants in the market had previously held. Much of the bank's loan book during this time actually reflected loans to affiliates and investment companies to hold the shares of the bank itself. It was a snake, feeding on its own tail, and somehow getting larger in the process.

11

MEDIA MEDDLING

FOR a foreign-born Icelander like me, the fact that each neighborhood in this vast and beautiful land—whether in a hamlet or the one city—comes with its own public pool doesn't stop feeling miraculous. Today I decide to go to Laugardalslaug, the big daddy of Reykjavík pools. This is just a few minutes' drive from FME, and features not one but two Olympic-size lap pools, five hot tubs covering a range of temperatures, a giant water slide, and a steam room.

Mercifully, the 50-meter outdoor pool is low on British tourists today, and thus offers smooth right-hand traffic flow in the lap lanes. I swim for a kilometer. Then I hit the 36-degree hot tub, followed by the 38-degree massaging hot tub, then the steam room, a shower and a cooling dip back in the pool, then back to the hot massaging jets at 38 degrees. It's a bit of a circuit I've developed over the years. I try to gather my thoughts on the investigation but find myself half in daydreams as I watch the thermal columns of steam rise into the evening air above.

I am also listening in on the political discussion in hot tub number two. That's something to rejoice about, five years on. My command of the Icelandic language has improved enough to be able to understand what people are saying without having to concentrate. Here in this very same hot water I had some of my early conversations, after those first few months of intensive study.

The hour soaking in geothermal waters does its job and I drive home with a clear head. I know that the master list of transactions can wait: the most pressing thing for me now is to compile all the supporting evidence and write a full formal criminal referral describing the years-long buying and hiding of shares by Kaupþing management. A lot of work awaits before that document is drafted, reviewed and cleared by our lawyers, and greenlit by my boss. And then on to the members of the board of the regulator, who will hopefully rubber-stamp it.

The next morning, back at my desk, I put together the pieces of this referral for the prosecutor. A flow diagram showing the one-way trip that Kaupþing shares took from Nasdaq OMX, the Icelandic stock exchange, through the prop desk, the brokers, and out the back door to the British Virgin Islands. The beating heart of the case. On each time period, over many years, the numbers added up: whatever the prop desk had purchased on the open market to keep the price up, it sold over the fence to the brokers, and they sold the same number out to their increasingly exotic Caribbean client base. In addition to the flow of shares through the bank, we have to compile the org charts, the emails exchanged among the participants, and the daily reports of the buying prepared by the prop desk traders for the top two men in the bank, the Executive Chairman and CEO.[33] Everything needs to be organized, described,

---

33   There is at least one cultural consideration that might have played into the ease with which the top management of Kaupthing was able to carry off this scheme for so long. Icelanders can have a very reverent attitude toward management, and perhaps this comes from centuries of domination by the Danes. The Danish ruled Iceland with an iron fist, allowing only products of inferior quality to be traded in exchange for the best fish and wool the Icelanders could produce. Icelanders resent the Danes for this brutal history, but today also exhibit a kind of Stockholm syndrome, as Denmark is often the first choice for educational opportunities, summer holidays, and living. And Danish tourists still come to Iceland and bark at others on the street in Danish, expecting to be understood and obeyed. Inside organisations, some Icelanders view management as all-powerful. They tend to view

and catalogued. I am learning from the inside why investigations like this one take so much time.

And I need help. My Icelandic may be good enough to throw politics around with the old dudes at the swimming pool, but still falls short of what's needed for a 100-page formal criminal referral. Much to his chagrin, Binni gets pulled off his cases to help me draft the document. We spend the next weeks in countless hours of conference room discussions: formatting words, sentences, and paragraphs in the old Viking tongue. This report needs to be crystal clear for a successful prosecution, and I also don't want the next set of investigators to waste time recreating discoveries we've already made. I accumulate all the data, charts, and facts, and write down bullet points in either English or Icelandic. I sit down at the end of each day with Binni and a young, driven lawyer, and together we re-draft everything formally. We go back and forth debating each section of the report: does it need to be here, can we say this? I want to make bold claims and use active voice. They push back on me, dialling every sentence back, using all the tools of Old Norse grammar and word choice to soften up responsibilities, to blur the line between cause and effect.

---

the management hierarchy as a command structure: 'If my boss tells me to do something, I have to do it.' This attitude surprised me when I moved to Iceland, after the more collaborative environments I was used to in the United States. But another strange feature of this attitude is that in general Icelanders do not view responsibility as accruing to the management, as I learned in my lunchtime conversation with the FME lawyers.

In Icelandic work culture, the fact of a manager asking a direct report to do something is often taken as enough. The more senior the manager, the more imperative it is to follow his exact instructions, even if those instructions go against the best interests of the organization.

Contrast this with Wall Street culture, which (say what you will about its overall ethics) at least is not anymore a place where senior management can command junior personnel to send cash offshore, no questions asked. I ran this scenario past a former colleague at a major Wall Street firm, when I first saw evidence of bank employees entering naked money wires in Iceland, and he confirmed for me that in his bank, the more senior the request, the more it would be considered odd and flagged for review. Legitimate money wires arise automatically out of normal daily business overseen by line employees; someone senior commanding a junior employee to move cash does not arise in the normal course of business.

Around this time I come to realize something that really helps me understand Icelanders' relationship to money: even the concept of money, as in cash money, is only about a generation old here. On a tour of the family farm where Hulda's dad spent the summers of his youth, he proudly points out the dairy barn. He says that when he was working here in the 1960s, a milk truck would come from Húsavík, about 60 kilometers away over uneven gravel roads, every three days. The truck would pick up all the milk that had been collected from the cows on that period. But that lone milk truck also served as the principal link between this farm and the entirety of the great world beyond: if the family needed something for the farm, say a strap of leather, they would affix a paper note to the milk tankard stating their request. On its next milk run three days later, the truck would return with any goods they had ordered. And the account of the farm at the dairy would ostensibly be debited by the cost of the strap.

It's a neat system, one that requires no paper scrip at all in order to function. When my father-in-law tells the story, he is clearly proud and a bit nostalgic for those times. But it also strikes me that this arrangement has a key disadvantage in that the farmers are ever at the mercy of the dairy as to the cost of the leather strap and everything else their farm requires. The good people at the dairy have no special expertise in procuring items such as these, and no incentive to look for the best price or quality. The remote farmers of Iceland—that is, the entire population of the Land for most of its existence—were for centuries at the losing end of a monopoly, first under the Danish king and later under merchants such as these. Is this why even today in Reykjavík comparison shopping for price is still so rare? Can it help to explain why Icelandic financiers made leveraged buyouts so fast they never seemed to haggle over the terms? And could the lack of cash in the historical economy of the Land explain why Icelanders during the boom seemed to go especially nuts about money?

———

One Thursday morning, Hulda and I are up earlier than usual to get out to the airport for a long weekend away. We feel very lucky that we get to take a break during this time; most of our friends with kids can't afford these luxuries. Iceland has two tiny travel companies that compete to offer charter trips in the off-season to cities and winter ski destinations all over Europe. We picked the capital of Bohemia this time.

On our little brick stoop sits the morning paper, wrapped in plastic. I stuff it in my shoulder bag on the way out to the car. It will take about an hour to traverse the windswept lava plain between here and Keflavík International and we don't want to be late.

Once we've reached the gate I remember about the newspaper. The whole top half of the front page is filled with the umpteenth photo of Iceland's latest boondoggle, a poorly built artificial harbor in the south called Landeyjarhöfn. We receive a free subscription to this newspaper, *Morgunblaðið*—literally, 'the morning paper'. The folksy name is deceptive, because it is also the mouthpiece of the most powerful political party, *Sjálfstæðisflokkurinn*. The current editor is none other than Davíð Oddsson, Godfather of this Independence Party. He was head of the central bank of Iceland during the crisis, and before that the same prime minister who oversaw the failed privatization of the state-owned banks. Now losing revenue to its competitors, *Morgunblaðið* has given us a free subscription in the hopes we will get hooked.

When I at last take the paper out of its bag and unfold it, my stomach lurches. The main headline reads: "FME Investigates Overarching Market Abuse by Banks".[34] The very short article summarizes the highly secretive work we've been conducting at the regulator, and doesn't do a bad job of it. It states that Kaupþing and the other banks were systematically trying to influence the price of their own shares, and suspected of creating false demand for them on the market. It also mentions the shell companies used to hide the shares and the loans made only against the value of the shares themselves. All of this is pretty weird for me because within the regulator we work on these cases in deep secrecy. Very few FME employees know what

34 www.mbl.is/frettir/innlent/2009/09/24/fme_rannsakar_allsherjar_
markadsmisnotkun_banka

we are looking at, apart from us investigators and the members of the board. The journalist must have been fed by someone on the inside. But who, knowing that it would be a violation of Icelandic law punishable by prison time? The article only mentions "sources of the newspaper".

Knowing the how and the why of the leak does not really matter to me in the moment. Sitting in the waiting area, I see a way to finally share a bit of my work with Hulda. For her and for Icelanders in general, it is good to see that something is actually happening almost a year after the country came apart. For some of those within the banks, a lot of this is maybe old news. Certainly the ones who faced the regulator, the compliance and internal audit people, could guess what we were looking at from our requests. And the senior executives who carried out these schemes over many years had to understand them very well. But some of the activity was so compartmentalized few line employees at the banks had the chance to realize how big the fraud was, and perhaps we at the FME were the first ones to have a God's-eye view and put the comprehensive story together. But now this journalist also has his teeth into it. And the rest of the country can for the first time get a taste of the extent to which the banks had duped them all.

"Here's something you might want to read carefully," I tell Hulda with a wink. She takes the newspaper from me, silently. She starts reading, making the face she makes when she studies something intently.

"Stop staring at me," she says.

"Okay, babe." I turn to the window to look at a plane pushing back from the gate and give her some space. The airport is not particularly busy at this time of morning—all the regular Europe flights have left—but there's enough ramp action for me to keep my focus away from Hulda. The pale bright endless sky of Icelandic autumn fills the floor-to-ceiling windows of the terminal. Hopefully, we'll get some warmer weather in Prague.

I'm both excited to share this article with Hulda and frustrated: it doesn't name any of the people involved at the banks, some of them household names in the Land. I know that my fiancée will never ask me for more detail. Ever careful not to put me in the position of disclosing anything at all about my work, Hulda's resolve amazes me. My lips burn with the secrets. It might be useful for Icelanders to know who put them in this quagmire.

"Okay, that seems like it might be pretty big," she says when she's done reading. "Don't tell me more," she adds before I can even open my mouth.

It takes a bit of time to get aboard the plane. Departure is noticeably late but nobody says anything. As we finally take our seats, Hulda opens her book to make sure I don't bring up the topic again. Until it finds its way back to us by itself in a new surprising way at the other end of the flight.

While we're waiting for our luggage in the shiny new Prague airport terminal, I spot Sigurjón, the former CEO of Landsbanki, standing across the luggage belt from us. I barely recognize him. Unshaven and wearing a white T-shirt that doesn't cover all of his midriff, he looks heavier than before and, frankly, terrible. I've never seen him not wearing an expensive suit. I do what Icelanders do when they see someone they haven't seen in a while: I avert my eyes. I grab our bags as they come around, and we wheel out of there.

Hulda and I last saw Sigurjón and his wife the year before, at the Landsbanki Investment Conference in Madrid. How much has changed since then!

"Did you see who that was?" I say under my breath.

"Yes, he was trying to catch your eye, he remembered you!" Hulda says.

"Hulda, we're gonna put that guy in the slammer," I blurt out before I can stop myself.

"I don't want to know about it," she says. We look for our hotel shuttle.

Thankfully Prague keeps us busy enough to let me forget about criminal manipulation of share prices for a few days, a break I really need. Exploring it is like walking around a living medieval castle the size of a whole city. I lived here briefly but it's the first time for Hulda, and I am really happy to show her around town. We eschew the Icelandic-speaking guide and I take her on my own tour. Some of my favorite spots are still here, nearly 15 years after my first visit. It is with a big smile that I watch my love taste her first sweet, dark Czech beer and later say, "Let's just have one last beer in this little place." A weekend of color isn't nearly long enough away from the black and white of Iceland, but we are very grateful to be out and about at all.

On Sunday night I find a link with a translation of the article into English. I send it to my parents in Boston. It feels good to share it with them too. "When are the convictions coming?" asks my dad.

12

IN GOOD HANDS

BACK at work on Monday, I immerse myself again in the case document. Writing it is like climbing a mountain with many false summits: the conclusion of the report seems ever close at hand, but the list of open issues seems to keep getting longer. I am growing more exhausted and irritable. Sigrún comes past my desk and says that we should begin thinking about how much the perpetrators of the market abuse cycle profited personally. Frustrated, I resist the extra work. But it is actually the best question to ask.

Why keep doing this? Why keep sending the bank's cash out the door, buying up shares, and then stuffing them into dodgy companies in Iceland and overseas? Why keep hastily arranging junk loans to these new firms? I realize I have had a blind spot around this question: I was so focused on understanding the machinery of share laundering, I forgot to ask who owned the laundromat!

Looking at the salaries, bonuses, and stock option grants earned by the top executives of Kaupþing, the answer crystallizes: to be a top manager in this bank meant mansions, sports cars, private jet travel, Alpine ski trips, and Mediterranean vacations beyond the dreams of any Icelander, or indeed most human beings. Until recently, Iceland was Europe's poorest country by far, a forgotten place where people lived half in the ground under sod roofs, a place that owed some of its very first roadways to the postwar Marshall Plan. As long as the Kaupþing share price stayed high, its executives could claim a healthy bank, and their lifestyle could continue at least until the next quarterly filings, three months down the road.

It suddenly seems like maybe this banking boom and inevitable bust was fabricated by a very small number of people. The top managers of the banks rewarded themselves handsomely for as long as they could keep up the facade—and left their countrymen to pick up the pieces when the house of cards came tumbling down.

Of course, nearly everyone in the bank benefited from the endless cycle of share purchases. By Icelandic standards, bank employees were taking home salaries never before seen. Some were also taking home big bundles of stock options as performance-linked payment. And those options were only valuable if the stock was valuable. This type of performance-linked payout scheme is designed to align the interests of management and employees with the best interests of the company, following the logic that a well-performing company has a higher share price and therefore the staff is rewarded for the performance.

In the case of Kaupþing, however, management made an end run around this logic, figuring if they could just do anything possible to keep the share price high they could personally profit, regardless of the quality of the bank's operations or its loan book. The game seemed to be to keep this going as long as possible so that the managers could extract as much cash compensation from the bank as they could.

To keep the party going, the bank needed to keep buying up its own shares, and to be able to afford that required constant growth. To pay those executive salaries and bonuses meant swallowing first the tiny stock market and then the whole of Iceland's economy. But the share-laundering machine and the fast growth were actually just perfect (in the short term) for the institution and its employees: for a bank, each new loan made counts as an asset it owns. That meant every time Kaupþing made a new loan to a sham company to hold its own shares, it could count another valued asset on its books and the balance sheet of the bank grew. The credit department could thus boast of new business with investment companies and its staff could claim bonuses for facilitating all of this wonderful new lending. A few floors below, the brokers could likewise book the sale of shares to the same sham company offshore as though they were trades conducted with valued clients. They could claim big commissions for these trades. After all, there was nobody real on the other end of the telephone to complain about extortionary execution fees.[35]

Apart from all the sham companies set up in Iceland and abroad during the boom years, Iceland also had a small real economic sector, focused on fishing, tourism, and energy exports. Imagine that a fishing company goes to an Icelandic bank during this time to secure financing of a new trawler or processing equipment. To the surprise of the fishing company, the bank offers not only to loan the entire amount requested, but to loan them an additional amount which would go to a new Icelandic company that the bank had created. The express purpose of that company, which would have the same owners as the fishing company, would be to hold shares in the bank itself, and the bank would lend that company all the money it needed to buy the shares. If the shares increased in value, the owners of the company would get free upside, and if they went down, the owners could walk away. Some Icelandic businesses took the bank up on these arrangements, and in this way the real economy of Iceland was also corrupted by these share-price support schemes.[36]

With the conclusion of the analysis of the benefits granted to individual managers and employees, I can finally close the big draft of the Kaupþing market manipulation case. Edited, copied, pasted,

---

35 To take the Holt Investment example, a $250m set of trades could generate $1.25m in commissions, assuming a low 0.5% rate. And who would receive these commissions? The bank itself, plus the individual brokers who booked the trades, straight into their annual bonuses.

36 It's not clear how much these clients understood their role in the share-parking schemes; we did not have time or resources to pull the threads on the dozens of such deals.

reviewed, spell checked. Written in proper legal Icelandic, and all relevant laws cited, chapter and paragraph. A central focus of the document is a who's who: a section introducing the prosecutor to the main players inside Kaupþing who were involved in the manipulation of the share price and the hiding of shares offshore, based on the evidence we painstakingly collected from contracts, trades, and emails. We send an advance copy of the case document to the members of the Board of FME, for approval at their next meeting.

I am invited to sit in at this event, where I give a presentation of the highlights of this historic case, perhaps the biggest of its kind anywhere in the world. A culmination of many months of hard work by me and the team, I expect it to sail through, to get big smiles of approval from the board for a job well done. For getting to the core of a giant criminal case that had helped to bring the country down. Here are the culprits, in black and white!

But I can tell right away there's a problem. There are murmurings and grumblings around the table, and a couple of questions about some of the individuals named in the document. This board of somnolescent old lawyers never signed up for approving criminal case referrals against some of the country's wealthiest and most powerful people. They thank me gruffly for my presentation and I step out of the meeting. Sigrún stays behind in the makeshift boardroom.

She comes back upstairs to our offices and confirms what I had suspected: the board doesn't like to name names, and they don't want to approve a big criminal referral document that lists any actual human beings as perpetrators. Their collective view seems to be that we can list the bank itself as the perpetrator. Let the special prosecutor name individuals if he likes.

So in the eleventh hour we change the final document, removing all the individual perpetrators. The who's who is out. Now it's just a surgical operation: a faceless bank buying its own shares and shipping them off to funny Caribbean companies. The board is happy. Approved.

Hey, not so fast! The special prosecutor gets an advance electronic copy of the neutered referral. He calls Sigrún. "Banks don't commit crimes. People commit crimes," he says. A referral for criminal prosecution from the FME needs to contain the names of the people the regulator reasonably believes were involved, based on the evidence the agency collected in its investigation.

We crack open the Word documents again, turn on track changes. And at the very top, the very first paragraphs, we list the names, addresses, and ID numbers of the fourteen key participants in the scheme, based on our investigation. To me it feels right, having these people listed. But it again erupts into an extended discussion at the next board meeting. "Are you sure the prosecutor wants it that way?" We have to reiterate his request. And in the end they finally assent.

So, at long last, the case has the grudging approval of the board and is ready to go out the door! The report itself is close to 100 pages. On top of that, there are hundreds of pages of emails and internal bank documents. As well as our detailed trade-by-trade analysis, formatted carefully in locked Excel spreadsheets. On this, the first day of October 2009, a courier picks up the bulky envelope at FME and drives it a short way to the new offices of the prosecutor.

Iceland's special prosecutor, Ólafur Þór Hauksson, is almost as fresh as me at his position but we've met already. His curiosity and positive attitude have kept me going through the long slog of the past months. He has a broad mandate: prosecution of any crimes committed leading up to the financial crisis of 2008.

Appointed to the role early this year, Ólafur Þór didn't have to face fierce competition to get the job. Rather the opposite: the only candidate, kindly pushed into heading what would turn out to be the biggest investigations of their kind, anywhere, the 44-year-old former *sýslumaður* (literally, 'man of the county', something akin to county magistrate) has no previous experience in the financial world or financial crime. He has headed two offices in more remote parts of the Land, dealing with issues like child custody and settlement of divorces and estates. On the one hand, it looks to many like Iceland's powers-that-be are merely trying to make a show of investigating the crisis, but in reality rendering these investigations toothless by putting a novice in charge. On the other hand, Ólafur, one of the few senior legal professionals in the Land who has no links to the financial and political elite, is thus not at all conflicted. On top of that, he is brilliant.

Our first encounter was in May 2009, five months before we finally send the referral. The Kaupþing market manipulation case had grown so large after the first weeks of my investigation that Sigrún and I thought we should give him and his staff a preview. We went down to his original tiny office on Borgartún, a stone's throw from Kaupþing. That day we sat with him and his handful of staff around a giant white conference table he had procured for free from a remaindered government furniture warehouse at the edges of Reykjavík.

I told him I had something big to show him. As I booted up my laptop and tried to get it working with the projector, he asked me, "Is this as big as the Al-Thani case?" This was in itself a giant case, and had already kept him and his team busy.

"Al-Thani is just a small part of this one," I replied carefully. "I think you'll see this case is like the umbrella around Al-Thani." He raised his eyebrows and chuckled. It seemed he didn't shy from big cases.

The Al-Thani case is named after the Sheikh who bears the same name: Mohammed Bin Khalifa Bin Hamad Al Thani of Qatar. This member of the Qatari ruling family had become Kaupþing's third largest shareholder by investing $285m to buy a little more than 37 million shares, or 5%, of Iceland's biggest bank. At the time of this transaction, in September 2008, Kaupþing was in serious trouble and Lehman Brothers had just declared bankruptcy. A spokesperson for the bank told Forbes: "Kaupþing had most of the shares, as the bank had been buying [its] own shares in recent weeks. The rest was bought in the market. There was no discount."[37]

The transaction had two goals: to prove the strength of the bank, since a wealthy foreign investor had enough confidence in the institution to be willing to take such a stake, and to make the bank known in the Middle East.

37 www.forbes.com/2008/09/22/sheikh-kaupthing-iceland-markets-face-cx_ll_0922autofacescan02.html#26b70f0973e5

Except that Kaupþing then collapsed about two weeks afterwards. A big loss for the poor Sheikh, right? Actually, no. Despite the headlines, he never put up any of his own money. What he did was to agree to have his name associated with yet another Kaupþing fraud: the executives created a new company in the British Virgin Islands to which they extended a loan worth hundreds of millions. With this cash, the sham company was able to sop up shares that Kaupþing's prop desk had already purchased on the open market, the latest iteration in the same scam they had perpetrated for years. This time, they did it publicly and appear to have paid Al-Thani $50m for the use of his name on the deal. Sigrún, my boss, had concluded this investigation before my time at FME, and sent it on to the special prosecutor. By the time of our May meeting, he was still in the early stages of planning the prosecution of what would now become merely a bite-size piece of the biggest market manipulation ever.[38]

I showed Ólafur Þór how Al-Thani was only the most visible and recent of a years-long conveyor belt of criminal on-market share purchases and Enron-style off-the-books concealment. I showed the flow from the stock market through the bank's trading desks and out the back door. Once finished with my handful of slides, I could feel how engaged he and his small team had become. I had a good feeling about Ólafur Þór Hauksson from the get-go. An outsider to finance, certainly, but he appeared genuinely interested in what we were showing him. He asked good questions. He wasn't afraid to say when he didn't understand something, and then he picked up the thread very fast. I could feel that we were on the same wavelength, each of us eager to uncover what had really taken place in Iceland during the boom. I left his office inspired, feeling on the right track—and, above everything else, convinced I had finally found a strong ally.

---

38 What was in it for the Sheikh or any of the other buyers who put their names to these deals? From the perspective of the individual, he was offered a no-lose bet by Kaupþing management. If the shares went up, his newly created company would keep 100% of the gains risk free. If the shares went down, he could walk away from the shell company and the bank would be stuck with a loan which had no good collateral behind it.

Since our May meeting, Ólafur Þór has moved with his team to a larger office space but it still has a very temporary feel. A white sheet of copier paper with *Sérstakur saksóknari* ("Special Prosecutor") in inkjet letters is taped to the entrance door. He shares his modest offices with a handful of staff. The main feature remains the giant round white conference table with a projector and nest of cables on top. No decoration adorns the walls. Still, the place somehow feels more welcoming and open than my home at the FME.

Close to two meters tall, and big too, the special prosecutor is a giant of a man, filling entire door frames as he passes through them. He offers a warm handshake and his hand is the size of a pie plate, his head the size of a lion's. He laughs easily and often, and his laugh can be heard echoing down the corridors of his offices.

I have organized the salient points of the big Kaupþing criminal referral of October 2009 into a slide deck. Ólafur and his top lieutenants take their seats around the Arthurian table, and I walk them through the flow of shares, the offshore companies, the org charts, the best of the emails, and the personal gains of the executives. The whole scheme is now completely clear. They pepper me with questions, then break off into discussion. The fact that we named 14 individuals in the referral poses a logistical challenge: one wise old attorney on staff points out that no courtroom in the Land can hold that many defendants at once! In under an hour, we have covered the whole sorry story of Kaupþing's systematic market abuse and explained a big part of the economic implosion of Iceland.

This second sit-down confirms the first impression I had back in May: Ólafur Þór is a consummate professional. He runs the show with an effortless grace, letting everyone speak and share, and then brings everything to a clean conclusion. Inside his offices, his smarts and clear perception are obvious, but in TV interviews he seems to play the role of a country bumpkin. That, too, is smart. He just might catch the masters of the universe of Icelandic banking and their big-city defense attorneys off guard.

With the big case now in good hands, we can move on.

13

THE INVESTIGATION MACHINE

I N a way, sending that first big Kaupþing stock market manipulation case off to the special prosecutor at the beginning of October 2009 feels anticlimactic. We have so much more to do, so many more angles on Kaupþing alone: years of bad loans, secret trading portfolios full of unknown assets, the bank's dealings with its affiliates abroad, sham customer accounts, and on and on. Add to all of this two other gigantic failed banks, Landsbanki and Glitnir. Next come the array of Icelandic investment companies, investment funds, failed investment banks, failed savings banks, and the stock exchange itself. And those are just the institutions. What about individuals? The insider trading cases, the deals done offshore... the list seems never to end. Around this time, a friend asks me how my job is going and I have to shake my head. "I wish just for once I could open a report on one of these firms and have it be clean," I tell him. "It's dirt as far as we can see."

We don't throw a party or indeed do anything at all to celebrate the big Kaupþing milestone. But that doesn't mean we aren't happy about it. I can speak for myself and some of my colleagues too: I feel so good, proud of the work we have done. We have proven to ourselves that we can investigate and send off a case of this magnitude.

And if there were to be a celebration party, who would pick up the tab? I don't have that kind of money, nor do my colleagues, and certainly the FME doesn't have a budget for such niceties. Times are tough in the Land: the deep darkness of the crisis has become our new normal. I am just grateful to have this job after so many months of no income combined with our mercilessly rising mortgage payment. Many of my countrymen and women have no job at all. At home, we behave carefully with our money. For Hulda's birthday this week I will pick up a card and a small gift; the trip to Prague was already a big splash. The days of going out for a great meal or buying her a beautiful present are well behind us. If I'm meticulous, I can end up with an extra $50 or so in my bank account at the end of the month. So, no party.

I often can't help but see a parallel with a scene in my favorite movie, *Heat*, released in 1995. Al Pacino's character, a detective, waits up all night in a laundry truck to catch De Niro the master criminal on a precious metals heist. As the score is unfolding, a careless SWAT team guy sits down, the butt of his rifle clanging against the floor of the van. Hearing the noise, the disciplined criminals simply walk away from their heist, and Pacino lets them. Emerging from the cramped truck to the brightening sky of a new day dawning, the detective tosses his radio to his lieutenant and proclaims gruffly: "Back to work."

In this job I end up dropping a lot of quotes from *Heat*. To my surprise, some colleagues have never seen this classic. A few of us talk about our favorite moments at lunch and the others get curious. One of the lawyers suggests a movie night at his place and invites us over. Maybe this can count as a party for the big case after all.

Back to work, then. In the movie and at the FME, too. I've never had such an important job, a job that could make such a difference for my struggling country. So this is not a time to feel tired and empty and go home early. Knowing this fuels me. I am a junkyard bulldozer ready to face the next towering pile of financial crime. We have finished a case, yes, even a big one, but we need to keep going.

The same day we sent the big Kaupþing case to the prosecutor turned out to be important for another reason: I had a new colleague start. For the first time, I have help on the investigation work. Unlike Binni running around on his own, the new guy Högni joins my now-respectable team of two full time. He looks and acts humble and quiet, and in fact doesn't seem to mind that I'm unable to show him around the office or give him a proper orientation that first morning. I am busy with the logistics of getting the big Kaupþing case file packed and sent with the courier.

I print out a copy of the thick referral document and give it to Högni, telling him to read it over for starters. From my perspective, it's the most explosive document on the Icelandic financial crisis to date. And nobody outside of a tiny circle of us has seen it. No one in the public knows these details. But on the inside, it can be a great teaching tool for a new staff member. It clearly shows both the scope of the crimes we are dealing with and the level of professionalism we expect from our finished product.

It hasn't been so hard to convince Sigrún that we needed reinforcement. She saw how the big Kaupþing case swallowed all of my time and ended up taking a couple months of Binni's and a lawyer's too. And it is pretty clear by now that the other two big banks were involved in a similar kind of malpractice with their shares. Thinking I would have to do the same trading analysis and endless digging in management emails for the next two banks as I did for Kaupþing is overwhelming. Sigrún agreed to get us some temporary support for the number-crunching component of these huge share manipulation cases. And finding someone has been the easiest thing to do. Over the last months the FME has received dozens of applications from unemployed people trying their luck the same way I did a year ago. We have our pick of whomever looks most promising.

Högni looked way above average on paper. He gave me a really good impression the minute I met him too: smart but understated. Balding, though still quite young and with a red beard, Högni could have been the inspiration for the phrase 'salt of the earth'.

Högni gets really fired up reading about Kaupþing's market malfeasance, so I think he can dig right in and work on the next name on our list: Landsbanki, the second biggest of the failed banks, and the oldest bank in Iceland. For a time, Landsbanki even served as the nation's central bank. The bank recently celebrated its 120th anniversary in style, right on the eve of it going out of business. Despite its past glory, or maybe because of it, the institution seemed to demonstrate a similar pattern of buying up its own shares as its new-kid-on-the-block rival Kaupþing. At least this appeared to be the case in the trade extracts we received from the stock exchange back in the spring. At that time we requested data for all three big Icelandic banks trading in their own shares. We focused on Kaupþing first simply because it was the biggest actor, the standard-bearer, and because of the connection to the already-sent Al-Thani case. But the original letter from the exchange had made clear that all three banks had engaged in some form of this behavior, so now, six months later, it is time to move to the next name on the list.

Högni starts crunching the data on Landsbanki right away. And he's much faster than I was. After only a day he tells me he has his first results. We go to a conference room on the fourth floor and spread out the pages. We can see basically the same scheme going on at Landsbanki as we had at Kaupþing. The old, once prestigious bank had also been buying up huge volumes on the public market. We can see it even more clearly this time because this bank's shares were only traded in Iceland, while Kaupþing was listed both here and in Stockholm.[39] The Landsbanki story does, however, bring a new twist. The number two bank had also been hiding lots of illegally bought shares offshore, but under a different cover story. Whereas Kaupþing had made it look like rich people were buying the shares into their offshore firms, Landsbanki had found a different and crazier way to muddy the waters.

Iceland's oldest bank had also set up a series of companies with funny names in the British Virgin Islands and elsewhere, which had

39 Kaupþing had two prop traders assigned to cover its daily market manipulation: one covered Iceland and the other Sweden.

bought the bank's own 'LAIS' shares directly, usually at quarter's end. But this series of companies seems to be linked to the bank itself: indeed each of them has as its listed representative in Iceland a bowtie-wearing tax attorney who was himself an employee of the bank. It beggars belief: buying up hundreds of millions in your own shares on the open market, stashing them offshore, all in the clear light of day.

Ultimately around a fifth of the bank's share capital ended up in this small handful of offshore companies, themselves controlled by the bank, voted at the bank's annual meetings by the bank's own tax guy. It was nuts. I summarize the information into a few charts and bullet points and take it down the hall to Sigrún's office. My late-afternoon meetings with her have become something of an institution.

I knock. She waves me in with a tight smile.

"You are not going to believe this latest craziness!" I start in. She arches her eyebrow. We both enjoy the discovery aspect of these investigations the most. I lay out the charts for her.

"Oh, but that one's OK!" she says and her smile turns cold.

"What? How is it OK?"

"The bank came in here and explained all this to us a few years back. Don't worry about it. That was approved long ago. I was in those meetings."

"How did they explain hiding all these shares offshore for so many years?" I press.

"Well, they were warehousing these shares for the employee stock option program. So they'd have them ready in a few years when the options vested. Here, I think I have the papers here somewhere," she says. She fishes around in the tidy file drawers by her desk and pulls out a stack of A4 paper in a plastic sheath.

"But that's not how employee options work," I say. "When the employee options come due, the company just creates new shares to fulfill them. Everyone else gets diluted."

She looks puzzled. I continue:

"In fact, accounting for this dilution was a big Silicon Valley topic a few years ago. Why would Landsbanki spend all this effort and expense warehousing shares offshore for years, when the bank can create new ones from thin air any time it wants to? It doesn't make sense to me."

"But, like I said, they informed us about it. It's OK."

She hands me the file and I take it back to my desk. Landsbanki had indeed come to the FME a few years before, seeking approval for this mad scheme. They stated clearly that they needed a series of warehouses offshore where they could keep their own shares for many years, off their balance sheet. They needed to have them ready for the years-off exercise of employee options. They would finance these companies themselves. And, check! The FME approved it. Sigrún's signature was at the bottom of some of the pages.

The bank coming clean with this nonsensical scheme had in a way made it okay by itself. In those halcyon days of the Icelandic economic boom, a bank visiting the FME at all to seek counsel or approval was such a rare event that it really helped the regulator feel important. Seen this way, of course they had approved! Whether the stated rationale for the scheme made economic or legal sense didn't seem to have been a factor.

Given the way of business during the boom, and Sigrún's personal involvement in this little saga, I understand that I will have to back off. Admitting that the FME didn't understand what it was approving, while I myself now work for the same regulator, is tricky indeed. It's the first time the conflict inherent in my role has become so obvious.[40]

It's also increasingly clear to me that my idea of what market regulators do, versus how this one has historically functioned, are vastly different. Back in my Wall Street days, I discovered at one point that I had easy access to all the trading information for a number of the bank's hedge fund clients. I showed my boss, who sat over the cubicle wall from me. "Ah, but acting on that would be insider trading. And the SEC always gets their man," he'd warned. He feared the crime-fighting power of the SEC, a fear I inherited, as well as a view of the market regulator as an elite crime-fighting force. But

40 FME did send the case of these offshore companies holding Landsbanki shares to the special prosecutor on 2 December 2010.

here at the FME, regulation of the securities market is policies and checked boxes. Whenever the boxes are all checked we can go home for the day. And whoever checks the boxes best gets a promotion.

It will be hard for me to let go of Landsbanki's sleazy offshore shares dumps, all the same. But I'll need to choose my battles carefully. I won't be able to fight all of them.

14

THE OLDEST MANIPULATION
IN THE LAND

HÖGNI looks up as I walk around his desk on the way to my own cubicle.

"Jared, do you have a minute?"

"Sure, what's up?"

"I've been looking at these Landsbanki trades. Something just doesn't make sense."

I look over his shoulder at his two monitors, covered width-wise in an elegant spreadsheet. Clearly he's taken ownership of the data analysis from his Excel-hobbled boss.

He puts his finger on the very left of a graph. It shows all the shares that Landsbanki bought from the market with the bank's own money, month by month.

"See this?" he says. "Even back in 2003, Landsbanki was buying a big piece of the market—*before* the other two banks started this crap."

"So when did they start? And are we sure these are the prop-desk trades?"

"I only have back to 2003," Högni frowns. "But yeah, I'm sure it's the prop traders."

"Let's see if we can go back further," I say. "When did Landsbanki start trading anyway?" The next day we have our answer. Högni is that fast. Landsbanki shares started trading in 1998, when part of the bank was still owned by the Icelandic people. And Högni already has all the trade data from Nasdaq OMX.

"You're not gonna believe this, Jared." Högni's face wears a familiar puzzled scowl. I can't wait to see what he's found. It turns out to be even more bizarre than we could have imagined. Landsbanki, the storied old bank of the Land, the institution that just celebrated its 120-year anniversary to great fanfare, the former central bank of the country, and my old employer: *that* Landsbanki was engaged in the same trading pattern all the way back to 1998! And *í stórum stíl* (in grand style) as Icelanders would say: there are many months during the boom and bust years of 2000–01 when Landsbanki's buying of its own shares exceeded even that of 2007–08.

In a decade trading on the market, Iceland's oldest bank—the bank named after the Land itself—was engaged in systematic manipulation of its own share price in each and every month. There was never a time when the market for these shares actually reflected a fair price.[41]

We are flabbergasted. Controlling its own share price seems baked into the DNA of this bank, and thereby the stock market of Iceland itself. So we do some more careful analysis and then package up all the information and visit Sigrún's office together. She casts her pale eyes over the printouts of Högni's beautiful graphs while I walk her through the uncomfortable truth.

Sigrún grimaces. "This is going to be a problem," she says. There's a statute of limitations that rules out some of this period from consideration.[42] Nevertheless, I think it's important to give the full

41 Given this analysis, perhaps unsurprisingly Landsbanki had already set up LB Holding in the year 2000. This was an offshore Guernsey company that it used to hold its own shares, among other things.

42 There's another problem, too. A new law entered into force in 2003: law 33/2003, on

picture to the prosecutor so he can make use of it as he builds his criminal case. She reluctantly agrees.

But there is an even bigger problem that comes to light as we write up the findings. As with Kaupþing, I want to see who was in charge of these prop traders at Landsbanki back in the early 2000s. Who was authorizing them to spend the bank's cash on devious market manipulations?

We get the old org charts back from Landsbanki. At least their compliance officer seems eager to help us—or recognizes our authority anyway.

It's ambiguous to whom these bank traders report directly, if anyone, but in the levels above them in the org chart is: Gunnar Andersen! Now this is a name we do know. In fact, his office is on the floor just below ours. He is Sigrún's boss and the new head of the whole FME, and he has recently asked me to write some speeches for him in English.

Brought in as a 'clean' face to replace the disgraced former director

---

Securities Transactions. This law is the first time "market making" is mentioned in the Icelandic legal code, according to the legal review article *Þróun löggjafar um verðbréfaviðskipti* by Aðalsteinn Egill Jónasson.

This 2003 law states that a market maker must not be influenced by the issuer of the security in which he makes a market. Could the banks claim they'd been "making a market" in their own shares legally before this point, as crazy as this idea sounds?

www.althingi.is/lagas/128b/2003033.html

[Normally, a market maker is someone who's willing to both buy and sell a given security in a market, and makes a profit on the difference in the price. The best example here might be a guy standing outside Fenway Park in Boston calling out, "Anybody need tickets? Got tickets?" He's a classic market maker, buying extra tickets from fans for one price and reselling them higher to the next people coming down the sidewalk. Generally, he wants to be holding no tickets by the start of the second inning, having sold all the tickets he had bought.

Icelandic banks, however, were almost always net buyers of their own shares, rarely selling them back. This would be like a scalper who buys up all the unused tickets from fans and then walks home with them in his pocket; it's behavior that doesn't make any sense without a different motive behind it.]

In its 2016 decision on the Landsbanki market manipulation case, the supreme court states that this 2003 law, combined with a subsequent law in 2005 (31/2005) made market making by an entity in its own shares impermissible.

Hæstiréttur Íslands, case number 842/2014.

general, he maybe doesn't look as clean to us now. The oldest bank in the Land spent its own cash to keep up the false appearance of a healthy share price starting more than a decade ago, ultimately bringing ruin to the whole country. And this behavior began ostensibly somewhere in the shop of the man who's now our boss, the head of the regulator tasked with cleaning up after the crisis?

Any case referral including this behavior is going to have to cross his desk. Or at least be presented to the FME board with him in the room. How will we handle this? Nobody knows. We decide to discuss it informally with the special prosecutor at our next meeting, like so much else of our work in progress.

I suggest that we send a formal criminal referral covering the Landsbanki manipulation of 2004–08 and provide a separate informational memo detailing the 1998–2003 share buying that seems to have happened partially under Gunnar's watch. The prosecutor can then do as he wishes—but, as he points out, under Icelandic law he is only allowed to investigate market transgressions that come as formal referrals from the FME. Anything in the informational memo will be out of bounds. We are in a jam.

In the end, we place both the trading analysis and the informational memo onto a shared drive belonging to FME that the prosecutor can access. And nothing happens with the pre-2004 trading activity.

The Icelandic public does not get to learn how they were deceived for more than a decade by their oldest financial institution, even while they themselves owned it.[43]

---

43 They actually do get to find out—later. But by that time maybe nobody was paying attention: the news of the 1990s-era share buying comes out in the small print of the supreme court documents for the big Landsbanki case, where it looks like both 'we were making a market in our own shares' and 'everyone knew and it was always happening' were exactly the defenses employed by senior Landsbanki personnel. It appears, according to court testimony, that Icelandic banks buying up their own shares is deeply rooted in the DNA of these institutions, even when they were under state control, stretching back to at least 1998.

CEO Sigurjón Árnason stated that Landsbanki Íslands hf. had been conducting "market making in its own shares" before he took up his position as CEO in 2003, when he moved over from Búnaðarbanki (the Agriculture Bank that soon formed the bulk of Kaupþing). He said that Búnaðarbanki had also been engaged in similar activity while he worked there,

As for Gunnar, maybe he knew and maybe he didn't. Referring to the big market manipulation cases, he tells me himself, unprompted: "You know, they tried to pull that shit at Landsbanki when I was there too." Did he try to stop them and think he had?

---

that his lead prop trader and "his men" had taken care of share-buying for Búnaðarbanki before he moved over to Landsbanki with Sigurjón. The activity was by then also already happening at Landsbanki, and the lead trader had merely assumed control of the share-buying when he took over prop trading.

For his part, the lead trader also stated that Landsbanki's trading in its own shares had begun long before he joined Landsbanki. The fact that the bank traded in its own shares had been known to "everyone", both other market participants and the authorities, including both the stock exchange and the FME. These were normal business practices that had always been above board, according to this man. The regulators had not objected or commented on the trades.

One of "his men", a trader on the desk, backed up this view, stating that the employees of the Landsbanki prop desk had acted in the same way ever since the bank was listed on the market in 1998. "Everyone" had been informed of this arrangement.

Hæstiréttur Íslands, case number 842/2014.

15

'BARA BANKING'

I HAVE been asking for additional manpower for months and months and although Högni is working out stupendously, I really could use a lot more help. I make this known and Gunnar Andersen, the director general himself, calls me into his office one autumn day.

"I hear you are looking for more support," he says.

"I'll take whatever help I can get. We have so much more to go on these cases."

"Well, fine," he says, "there's a new woman who's starting this week and they can't use her in the credit division yet. Would you like a temporary team member for about three weeks?"

"Sure!" I say. "I can let her work with us on the next big bank case."

The next day, a woman with bobbed blonde hair and big glasses is sitting in one of the empty cubicles in my area, sipping a coffee and flipping through the welcome booklet for new employees. I go and introduce myself. I tell her I will really appreciate having her as an analyst for the next few weeks.

"Anything I can do to help out!" she blurts, almost too enthusiastically. She goes on to tell me in an I've-seen-it-all-already tone that she worked for years in one of the big banks and really knows this stuff inside and out.

I explain that we have opened such giant criminal investigations so far that she might be shocked to learn about them. I hand her the formal referral document for the Kaupþing market abuse case. I explain that this material is top-secret, that only a handful of people know about this one. Her eyes go a bit wide.

"Why don't you read over this material and I'll come back in an hour after my meeting and we can talk about it?" I say, handing her the 100-plus-page file. As with Högni, Sigrún and I have agreed that this is the best way to bring a new team member up to speed on the scope and nature of our investigations. The completed case is a very comprehensive look into both the big crimes and the type of work that we need to do.

I return after my meeting, excited to hear the feedback from the new woman about the massive crimes committed by the top execs at Kaupþing over so many years.

I can see over her shoulder that she's about a third of the way into the report, the page open to a graph showing just how many shares in itself the bank was buying each month.

"So, what do you think?" I ask.

She looks up at me with a blank expression.

"Þetta er bara 'banking'," she says: "This is just banking."

16

CREDIT-LINKED NIGHTMARE

ONE of the things that puzzled us as we reviewed Kaupþing emails and meeting minutes in the preparation of that big market manipulation case are some references to an internal trading book called YFST or *Yfirstjórn*. This previously unknown and secretive portfolio took significant positions in the bank's own shares in the last days before the collapse. Not only that, it turns out to be our first key to an even more dramatic story of market abuse by the biggest Icelandic bank.

The word *Yfirstjórn* rings both arrogant and humorous. It translates literally as over-steering, or in this sense, the management-above-the-management. As in, most companies just have a management, but this bank is so important that it has a management *of* the management. The word appears to refer to the most senior executives of the bank, in this case the CEO and executive chairman. But what doesn't make sense to me at all is that it's also the name of a trading portfolio. Why would these top executives require their own trading book? Didn't they have other things to do at work? How did they have time to think about trades at all? Didn't they trust their proprietary trading desk to take care of this? After all, those are the guys they paid to take risks with the bank's money.

After the usual delaying and dissembling, Kaupþing agrees to send us the trading books of the YFST, which, sure enough, is stuffed with shares of Kaupþing itself. These, like the others, were bought to keep the price high, this time in the name of the CEO of the bank.

I go through each item in the YFST portfolio on different month-end snapshots. Besides the shares, I find a series of other investments with funny names: they each start with CS, for Credit Suisse. They jump out because they are also large positions. They look like they might be Credit Suisse bonds. Their names have interest coupons and maturity dates specified.

Down the rabbit hole I go: in later months, the CS rows disappear but others pop up in their place named KAUP, for Kaupþing, and with the same coupons and maturities. This makes me even more curious about these 'bonds'. How could a CS bond suddenly become a Kaupþing bond?

It turns out these were the same investments after all. Someone at Kaupþing had likely renamed them, probably in the Zodiac static data system for tracking information on investment products.

So these are some kind of investment that look like a bond, but aren't regular Kaupþing bonds. After some more prodding, Kaupþing sends me the documentation they have. These are custom credit instruments issued by Credit Suisse and referencing Kaupþing. Each one has several pages of documents attached, describing the investment in thick legalese.

It turns out they are something very esoteric-sounding indeed: credit-linked notes, or CLNs. I have to study these to figure out what they are. I dig a little deeper on these mysterious investments. But it doesn't take long to uncover this little trickery.

To understand what these CLNs are and why Kaupþing senior management wanted to buy them, it is helpful to first understand the credit default swap (CDS) market. The CDS market sprang up on Wall Street in the 1990s to meet the demands of investors for insurance on their bonds, and over the next decade or so it became among the most important and tracked financial measures in the world. None the more so than for the Icelandic banks. Here is how I explain CDS to my colleagues at the FME.

CDS is an insurance policy on the debt of a particular borrower. Because anyone can see the price of this insurance (it's publicly quoted), the CDS spread is also a good measure of the financial health of a borrower, like a company or a country. It is a simple indicator of the market view on the chance of a particular borrower not paying its debts, and is therefore extremely useful.[44]

So the higher the CDS insurance premium (or spread), the more risky the borrower, and the less valuable are outstanding or future loans made to that borrower. Unlike the loans or bonds themselves, which once made are often kept in a drawer until their due date, CDS is quoted every day. So the CDS spread becomes a proxy for the credit risk of a borrower. Seen from this perspective, CDS is a useful financial innovation. Every big borrower now has a publicly and globally viewable credit score, and it's also now possible to buy insurance on their debt.

Starting in 2007, the CDS on Kaupthing showed clearly that the bank was in trouble, much more clearly than had its share price, which as we now know was being illegally bid up on two markets each day. The price of insuring bonds issued by Kaupþing was very high. The Yfirstjórn (top bosses) of Kaupthing presumably did not like this state of affairs, because the CDS market, one they couldn't easily control, was correctly reflecting the global market perception: the biggest Icelandic bank had a high and growing chance of going bust. The issuers and traders of this CDS protection had presumably taken a good look at the shambolic financials of the bank and bid the price up to levels not seen elsewhere in the world for a financial institution that was a going concern.

Given this state of affairs, and their modus operandi with their own shares, perhaps there wasn't much to do but try to manipulate the very large CDS market, too. In this case, however, the Kaupþing bosses couldn't rely on the home-grown market manipulation

---

44 Essentially, the CDS is priced as an additional yield over a 'safe' debt, like a German government bond. But you can still think of it as an insurance policy. The more speeding tickets you get, the more risky you are, the higher your insurance premium. Nothing so esoteric there.

techniques they had perfected for their own shares, but had to enlist the help of unscrupulous London bankers. Fortunately, these were not in short supply.

From my investigation, it looks like Kaupþing gave Credit Suisse around $70m in total (in early 2008, on a few different occasions) and in exchange got back a credit linked note (CLN), a piece of paper that pays back periodic interest. The amount of that interest was dictated by the CDS spread, the measure of riskiness of Kaupþing.

If Kaupþing was still an operational firm in five years, the holder of this note would receive back his initial investment. In this case, the bank itself held the note. So the bank was betting it would be around to get its own $70m back. Why hand over your valuables on a bet you'll be around to receive them back? This is a bit like someone giving away the keys to his house and saying, "Give me these keys back if I'm still alive in ten years. Otherwise, keep the house!"

There was clearly no reason to do this deal other than to try to manipulate down the CDS spread of Kaupþing. The Icelandic bank was putting up its creditors' money in an attempt to sell insurance on itself: this could not look good. And Credit Suisse apparently agreed: as a condition of issuing these notes, they demanded that Kaupþing publicly announce the transaction at the next quarterly meeting, in April 2008. Kaupþing never did. CS stopped selling them notes at this point.

I compile all this information into a summary document and take it down the hall to Sigrún. She says, "Oh! But they also bought these kinds of 'notes' from Deutsche Bank in the Chesterfield and Partridge story. And those were much bigger deals, over €500m in total."

"What?" I say. "That would amount to a massive attempt to manipulate their own bond prices. This is another giant manipulation case!"

"No, we didn't see it that way," she says. "That case is already gone. Binni sent it over a couple months back. It was just a big fraudulent loan, is all."

But it was much more than a fraudulent loan. The core issue was the manipulative intent of Kaupþing, and the willingness of first Credit Suisse and later Deutsche Bank to go along with that, at a key time, early 2008, when the CDS market was correctly telling the news: the bank was on its last legs. Deutsche Bank seemed to have even fewer scruples than Credit Suisse, as the Germans continued working on these types of deals all the way until the collapse of Kaupþing in October 2008, and on a far grander scale than the Swiss bank.

But perhaps this intense interest isn't surprising, given the major-player role of Deutsche and other German banks in the obscene growth of the Icelandic banks: the Germans had real skin in the game all along in this process. Between 1998 and 2003, the three Icelandic banks nearly quadrupled in size, and that growth was almost entirely on the back of bonds they issued in the European debt markets. These tiny savings banks for fishermen and farmers carried more than €2bn debt in 1998, and then borrowed more each year after that, with total debts of more than €10bn in 2003. By that point the banks already owed around €35,000 for every man, woman, and child in Iceland. But that paled in comparison to what came next: from 2004 to 2007 the banks grew by another 700%! In 2005 alone, Landsbanki issued more than €3.5bn worth of bonds in Europe, Glitnir around €4bn, and Kaupþing €4.5bn.[45] These are staggering numbers for a country with the population of a Manhattan neighborhood.

A key player in the issuance of all this new Icelandic debt was Deutsche Bank, and buying up much of that debt were the German regional banks. It was a match made in Heaven: the Icelanders never met loan papers they wouldn't sign, and the Germans could not seem to pass up the chance to make a bad loan. So maybe a little credit default swap market manipulation in the end times was just what the *Hausarzt* ordered.

I go back to my printed out (and already well-worn) copy of the Icelandic securities law 108/2007.[46] The way the law is written, right there in section 117, it clearly applies to these giant CLN deals as well. I try to get anyone around me to listen. The CDS market is far more

---

45 Source for borrowing numbers: *Aðdragandi og orsakir falls íslensku bankanna 2008 og tengdir atburðir, Rannsoknarnefnd Alþingis, bindi 2.*
46 www.althingi.is/lagas/nuna/2007108.html

important than the tiny Icelandic and Swedish stock markets. That's why Kaupþing had to try to manipulate it! I show the various legal staff of FME... look: here's the grandest manipulation of all.

But nobody seems very interested. It's too abstract for them. Since the manipulation happened offshore on an unregulated derivatives market that they don't really understand, to these lawyers it's like it never happened at all. Never mind that the CDS market was at the time arguably the most important market on earth, and that what happened there had direct price consequences on all the (regulated) debt markets of the world.

So my second big Kaupþing manipulation case is dead in the water. I eventually settle for writing up the YFST portfolio contents and sending it off to the special prosecutor as an informational memo.[47]

47 Years later, a pair of sharp London liquidators came to the same conclusion, namely that these trades were made for purposes of illegal market manipulation. In a section titled 'Unlawful Nature of the Chesterfield CLN, the Partridge CLN and the Partridge CDS' (paragraphs 142–5) of their claim, they make a clear case for how the trades violated market abuse laws in the UK, Luxembourg, and Iceland, explicitly citing the very same section 117. kjarninn.overcastcdn.com/documents/1._Particulars_of_Claim_-_28.11.2014.pdf

17

GOOD INTENTIONS

WE'RE obviously not real cops. But it might not hurt to learn from them. This is, anyway, what our human resources director has proposed—and I have jumped at the chance. So, one morning, in the middle of the dark month of November, I'm heading to an all-day interrogation class with the police. Not quite the very darkest time of the year, but about as bad as it gets. Sunrise won't happen until around 11:00, but we won't see any sun anyway through the low iron-grey clouds that blanket the city.

We will meet at the Icelandic police academy, located in the very last neighborhood of Reykjavík, right before the main artery splits west or south. Taking a city bus this far out would be a ludicrous adventure, so I've got no other options but to take my car, trying to see patches of black ice on the worn roads of the capital in the pitch dark. The wind blows so hard that sometimes the car shakes on its springs at stoplights. Fortunately, the city usually salts the important roads and I can get there on time. Not that punctuality always counts for so much in Iceland, but the cops do intimidate me a bit.

Flanked by Iceland's largest state-run liquor-store-cum-warehouse and a car wash, the police academy stands right in the middle of one of the sad industrial areas that dot the forgotten hinterlands of the city. After parking at the edge of nowhere, I have to practice a type of walking at which native-born Icelanders are old pros, sliding my feet along the icy sidewalk to keep from falling hard. This technique gets me from my vehicle to the doorway without incident. The city rarely bothers to remove ice or snow from pedestrian paths and each winter I suffer a bruising fall at least once. Hey, they don't call it Iceland for nothing.

Inside, the friendly desk sergeant asks if I'd like coffee without bothering to find out who I am. Then he waves me into a small break room off to the side. The floors are made from the same standard-issue linoleum found in most of the schools, medical offices, government buildings, and companies all over the Land. Sitting on a hot plate in the corner is a glass carafe, half-opaque from years of use, and about half full with a black liquid.

The bitter smell makes clear that this is coffee well past its prime. I pop one of the ubiquitous white disposable thermoform plastic cups into a holder and decant some. It's both tongue-burningly hot and also the worst coffee I have ever tasted. This includes diner coffee served by New England waitresses who ask, "Want me to warm that up for you, hon?" as they dish out bottomless refills. This patrolman's special, months or even years ago roasted (the Icelandic police academy seems not to be a daily-use facility), and ground and kept in a foil Merrill bag that's never been resealed, has probably been sitting on this burner for well over an hour already. I am at least savvy enough not to ask these Icelandic cops if they have any cream to add. "You still breastfeeding?" I'd been asked by a Zodiac co-worker within weeks of my arrival, when he saw me sullying my drink by adding milk. I can only imagine what the cops might say. I check in the refrigerator anyway. Of course, it's completely bare. Black it is. *Svart og sykurlaust.*

About half of the attendees for this interrogation class come from the police. There's a small group of us from the financial regulator. Many others from FME were also invited but never bothered to register. Binni had told me that it was a waste of time.

The police instructor takes us through the theory and practice of interviewing: the euphemistic Icelandic word being *skýrslutaka*, or report-taking. We watch some example report-takings in videos. The last part of the day will be a mock interrogation using students from the class. The case study is designed for street cops, not investigators of multinational billion-dollar financial crime, so it's focused on petty larceny. But actually isn't this in effect what we are also investigating? Grand, grand larceny. I can learn a lot here.

I sit at one of the classroom desks, observing the role play at the front of the room. I have made big strides in Icelandic for sure, but not to the extent that I feel confident enough to participate in the exercise. I'm actually dying to be in the ring with them, but the questions and answers are too fast for me. One of my colleagues, a lawyer, is playing the guilty criminal. She stonewalls the ones playing the police. It's very amusing to watch the back-and-forth. And it makes me realize something that is true for any interrogation: how much preparation is required for success. Everything must be set up tightly to minimize the opportunity for a stonewall. First and foremost, all the supporting material has to be in order and easy to access. Then the order of the questions is all-important: the slow and strategic reveal of information is key. There are ways to keep the interviewee off balance and guessing. My colleague sticks hard to her cover story but the rookie interrogators chip away at it.

The biggest takeaway for me is that I am grateful I don't have to do much of this type of work. We have agreed with the special prosecutor that his team will handle the interviews for the largest cases. I realize that he has his work cut out for him. His team is currently preparing to interrogate dozens of Kaupþing participants in the largest market abuse scandal in the world.

18

MARPLE AND LINDSOR

A T work there's one project I can't let go. I keep it for my spare time, and I will have a little now. I come into the quiet office over the dark Christmas holidays, days when most of the country is still comatose on leftover *hamborgahryggur* and *hangikjöt*. I'm also looking for a chance to prove to myself that I still have it, that I can still bring in a big case. With Högni at the helm of the big Landsbanki case, my days are now getting eaten up more by meetings with little time for the hunt.

This case has been burbling along in the background for a while, and now as the Dude might say, "new shit has come to light": after some delays the authorities in Luxembourg have sent us responses to our spring and summer information requests. I finally make space to dive once more into the depths of this ever-crazier unfolding story.

At first blush, the Marple case involves trades done back and forth between a BVI shell company named Marple and Kaupthing Bank Luxembourg S.A. The latter was the separately incorporated Luxembourg private bank owned and controlled by its Reykjavík parent Kaupþing and nicknamed KauLux. On a number of days in spring and summer 2008, Marple did trades back and forth with KauLux, mostly in bonds issued by Kaupþing in Iceland. These up-

and-down trades were often executed at vastly different prices. But the debt instruments traded normally change price only incrementally, and over long periods. Here, Marple would buy a bond from the KauLux trading desk for 60 cents and sell it back for 90 cents, days later or even the same day. The net effect of these trades was that KauLux was giving cash to Marple: 'the little shellco that could' always ended up with no bonds and net gifts of cash. In addition Marple had done all the transactions on credit: it had taken loans from KauLux to pay for the bonds in the first place.

To delve deeper into Marple, we needed to see the cash and trading accounts of the company in Luxembourg. And now I have these, and others, in front of me on my desk.

It turns out that Marple is owned by Skúli, the one who inherited the Hotel Holt fortune. His little company profited mightily in these trades. Every time it bought bonds it sold them back for more, and more and more cash accumulated in the company. The bank itself was always the loser in these trades. By the collapse of Kaupþing in October 2008, the total profits left behind in Marple were in the millions of euros.

A mystery here: what was in it for the bank? Why would KauLux do so many losing trades with the same customer? I can't answer this.

But it was not only Skúli and Marple who benefited from such generous trades with the bank. In our back-and-forth with Kaupþing in Iceland and Luxembourg over the past 18 months, we learned that there were also four employees of KauLux itself who traded in a similar manner. These are the other accounts I have on my desk now, printouts of scanned PDFs in tiny typewriter font. I need to use a straight-edge and highlighter to follow the money as it moves through these account statements.

The four were each given a loan by their employer, KauLux, to do trades on the market, so they put in no money of their own. And all four of them used that credit to do the same thing: buy Kaupþing debt from the bank's own trading desk, in July and August of 2008. They bought these bond issues at a substantial discount to the face value, like a 40% or 50% off sale, because the Icelandic parent bank was already in trouble and its bonds were trading cheap. Why did the employees do this? What did they know that would make them gamble on these junk bonds?

Clearly they didn't know much. Within a handful of weeks, Kaupþing in Iceland went bust. These employees at KauLux were screwed. They had purchased bonds issued by the Icelandic bank and these bonds were now worthless. Moreover, they had bought these bonds on credit and now had huge loan balances, money they owed to their own employer. These amounts ran to the hundreds of thousands of euros for each employee.

But then, magic happened! On the same day that Kaupþing in Iceland was falling on its head (to use the Icelandic expression for 'going bust'), KauLux bought all the worthless bonds[48] back from its employees, and Marple, too, of course! And not only did it pay them back what they'd bought them for, it paid them full face value. One hundred cents on the dollar! The executives turned out to be geniuses after all. Windfall profits of hundreds of thousands each were credited to their trading accounts. Mysteriously, some of them promptly wired these profits to another cash account at KauLux, one belonging to the motor yacht M/Y Mariu, a vessel commissioned by Giorgio Armani and named after his mom, and now used by Kaupþing's top brass as a party boat. Were they all going to go on a cruise? Or was the yacht's bank account a good hiding place for ill-gotten gains?

Then at last came a final piece of this nutty case: Lindsor. Yet another blank-slate company created in July 2008 in the British Virgin Islands. No sooner had the KauLux trading desk bought back all the bonds from Skúli and the four executives at such wonderful prices than it turned around and schlepped them off to Lindsor Holdings Corporation. So, no trading losses for the KauLux traders either. Poor Lindsor paid full freight, though, and it was a huge sum: €171m cash. Where did a newly created BVI company like Lindsor come into such a fortune? The whole amount came from Kaupþing

---

48 These were 'subordinated' bonds, so they paid back 0 even after Kaupþing bankruptcy proceedings.

in Iceland in a giant wire. Where did Kaupþing in Iceland get such a large amount in such dark days? That one is easy: it sent Lindsor this huge amount on the same day it received €500m from the central bank of the Land, 6 October 2008. So the Icelandic people paid Kaupþing to pay a British Virgin Islands shell company to buy some bonds that were now worth 0, bailing out a wealthy investor, four bankers, and a trading desk in a faraway country.

All of this is right there, plain as day in the tiny hard-copy account statements. But what's more, no legal contracts or other documents substantiate or explain this deal. It seems to have been done on the fly, and it has taken us a long time to piece it together, using information from Kaupþing in Iceland combined with what we can get from our CSSF colleagues in Luxembourg. At first, there do appear to be documents dated in September 2008, setting out the Lindsor deal before it happened. These were signed by the CEO of Kaupþing himself, Hreiðar Már. But they are oddly worded; something is strange about them. And the numbers don't add up: the round-sum €171m wire had to be justified after the fact, by bank employees in Iceland and Luxembourg. And they just can't seem to make the bond prices match the amount.

It comes to pass that the September documents were themselves faked, months later, after Kaupþing had fallen. The former CFO of the bank, miraculously still at that time on the inside, emailed the disgraced CEO to get him to sign backdated papers explaining both the money transfer and the purchase of the bonds. The €171m wire transfer itself was justified on the basis of a demand guarantee issued by Kaupþing to KauLux, part of billions in such guarantees we discovered, which ensured the Icelandic bank would be gutted like a fish if it ever fell on hard times.

One thing that has quietly astounded me in all the thousands of emails I've read and hundreds of internal bank documents I've seen so far is that no employee has stood up for the integrity of his role. Nobody has said, "wait a second, this isn't right" or "it isn't my job to do this" or "these actions contradict our own policies". But with Lindsor, I finally find her. A smile spreads across my face as I read her words. She is such a breath of fresh air. Her message is so stark, her words so black and white they jump off the page. Hallelujah!

This woman's boss is the treasurer of Kaupþing, the same one who presided over the prop desk traders. He emails telling her to execute the €171m wire transfer to Lux, as the Icelandic financial sector crumbles all around them. She's the boots on the ground: the one who actually needs to enter these wire instructions into the money transfer system. And she doesn't want to do it. She emails back her boss saying this. She points out that according to the agreement with KauLux, the foreign bank has to request such a transfer in writing and provide seven days' notice. They have done neither, and there are no legal documents on which she can base this massive movement of funds. She wants to hold off. She is, after all, acting to protect the assets of her employer.

Her boss will have none of it. "Do it," he emails back. She gives in. The money moves. And their bank, Kaupþing, goes bust within hours.

19

DISAPPOINTMENT IN
THE DUCHY

INVESTIGATING these massive cases of fraud has brought me a love of my work that is completely new. I have never enjoyed a job like this one. And I've never been so all-in, either. It takes all of my brainpower to stay on top of the myriad details in the ever-growing tree of open cases, and to keep the cases moving forward. But I also need to maintain a clear big-picture vision: the truth that comes out with these cases might help restore sanity and credibility to the corrupt financial system that has taken down the country I love so dearly. Increasingly, I also need to bring others with me on this journey.

It is the first Sunday of 2010 and as I think ahead to the work week, I find myself eager to get back to my desk and open the case files. I haven't felt Sunday sadness for many months. Quite the opposite: I thrive in there.

Research continues with the help of Högni, who is turning out just as well as my first impression had led me to believe. I also spend more and more time on the phone with other regulators.

The FME generally relies on formal requests for assistance to obtain information from its counterparts abroad. These are formatted as signed letters addressed to another regulator, usually in mainland Europe.

Because of the uncertainties inherent in letters sent between regulators in the native tongue of neither, and the long time lag inherent in these formal requests, I prefer a more direct approach. I have started a friendly exchange with a fellow investigator at our Luxembourg counterpart, the CSSF. Her name was on one of their responses, so I picked up the phone and cold-called the switchboard, asking for her. We got along well on that first call and now we chat openly on the phone about our work.

She and her employer, the Lux regulator, have been very cooperative since the early days of the crisis, feeding us trading and account data and information on many open cases. As some of these investigations touch their jurisdiction, I have even considered going there in person to present the facts in depth. I brought up this idea with my counterpart previously but now we agree on dates for late January. She will set up the meetings. I just need to convince Sigrún that the travel is worthwhile.

To my surprise, my boss not only agrees to the trip but wants to come along as well. I had been expecting to have to do a lot of persuasion. I don't know if it's the prospect of travel abroad at FME expense that energizes her: these trips 'out' are rare events often seen internally more as a bonus than a work assignment. Or maybe it's just the genuine curiosity she shows for the investigation.

We have few days to prepare. I need to pull together a presentation of the big Kaupþing market manipulation case. We want to show Lux the scope of our work, and the extent to which financial crime took down our small country. We also want to brag a little, to try to overcome the inevitable inferiority Icelanders feel when on the mainland.

More importantly, we would like to use the trip to send one investigation back to CSSF and this means drafting a formal referral. Every investigator has a file he can't let go of. The Marple and Lindsor case has become mine. Sigrún has an attachment to this one, as well. It has mystified both of us since I started. It's got a lot of moving pieces: trading of subordinated (read: junk) Kaupþing bonds back and forth between Kaupþing Luxembourg and some clients and bank employees, sometimes on the same day at vastly different prices, and mysterious large cash wires too. Marple became a side project for me, for my evenings or when I needed a little office relaxation, a little bit of spice for when the big market abuse cases felt stale.

We would go as far as we could on Marple, and then inevitably hit a dead end where we needed more information from abroad. So we'd dash off a new request to Lux and wait a while for the next pieces of information to come back. And each time that fat envelope from CSSF hit my desk it felt like Christmas morning. But the twists and turns seemingly never ended.

The Luxembourg regulator has been especially helpful in getting us all the information we requested. But it turns out that a big part of this case actually involves banks of, employees from, and trades conducted in the Grand Duchy. So we think it proper to refer this part of the investigation to these colleagues at CSSF. There is a lot to set out in our formal referral, and many unanswered questions. Another few days of writing and preparation and we are boarding a plane for two whole nights in the heart of old Europe.

We do not expect warmer weather in Luxembourg than in Iceland, at least not at this time of year, but we can count on at least doubling our hours of daylight and cutting the wind speed by two thirds, so it's already halfway to the tropics for us. Despite this promise, we land on a cold grey and wet January afternoon. After an 04:30 wake up it has taken us all day to get here from Iceland via Copenhagen, and the light is already fading. We travel from the airport along a new commercial strip where the big banks have their main offices. Kaupþing Luxembourg, now rechristened Banque Havilland, sits prominently among them. Looking out of the taxi window, I marvel a bit at the new cars, models of BMW and Mercedes I have never seen. I feel a bit like a country kid come to town for the first time: in Iceland no cars have been imported in nearly two years.

Our hotel is near the old town. Across the small city is where the Commission de Surveillance du Secteur Financier has its headquarters. We will head there tomorrow morning first thing.

My CSSF contact meets us at the door. It is very good to meet her in person at last. She has set up a day of meetings with her boss and their small team of regulators. The stately conference room is panelled in dark hardwood, a far cry from the haphazard facilities back at FME. I start as planned with my presentation of the big market manipulation case. Under EU and Icelandic law, we are allowed to share information for the purposes of good supervision, so I can freely explain this top-secret case to show just how unusual were the daily business practices of the largest Icelandic bank. But our counterparts don't really look impressed and sit watching us with stone faces. They do seem to listen, but hardly ask a single question, leaving us a bit uncertain. My sentences start to trail off as I speak into the silent room and look around the big table for any reaction. They are not dismissive of us, but neither do they show much interest. Considering the effort we have put in and the consequences the market manipulation had for the Icelandic economy and its people, this is an unexpected reaction from another small nation. It is also surprising considering the local Luxembourg subsidiary of Kaupþing played a big role in the story.

It does not get any better when we show them the Lindsor case referral[49] after a formal lunch at a nearby restaurant. The atmosphere remains quiet, their faces impassive. We are extremely grateful for the work they have done and the information they have gone to great lengths to collect and share with us, and we state this clearly. But now, that spirit of cooperation seems to be lost in some financial, regulatory, or diplomatic limbo. The reaction is at best muted, especially when we point out the facets of the case that we are transferring back to them. We leave their offices with a persistent feeling of unfinished business.

At the hotel, I wonder what happened exactly, what we got wrong back there. Perhaps presenting in English and not in French didn't help, but neither of us speaks French. We thought we were doing the Luxembourg regulator a favor by handing over a very interesting

---

49 The January 2010 referral letter from FME to CSSF regarding these employee trades and the Lindsor cash is available here: kjarninn.overcastcdn.com/documents/10.__FME_letter_22_jan_2010_.pdf

case with a lot of good work already behind it. We thought their eyes would go wide at what we showed them, and they would say, "Wow, thank you! This is great! We will jump on this!"

We were probably naïve. They were maybe embarrassed that some hillbillies flew in from the land of *Immigrant Song* and plopped themselves down in their Old World conference room to give them a talk on things that had been happening right there under their noses. Maybe no regulator would like that.

I am feeling a bit down, and I think Sigrún is too. Now we do not know what will happen with a case that we both care a lot about. Was it wrong to come down here? Probably not; it's always good to make personal contact with our counterparts. But the experience is a reality check. It is an opportunity to be reminded that, in Luxembourg or elsewhere, not everyone is concerned with doing the right thing. Not everyone experienced the 2008 crisis as viscerally as we did in the Land. These people have other priorities, or lack the courage, willingness, or ability to act. More often than not around the globe, those are the forces in control. We need to make sure these forces don't also win in Reykjavík. One economic implosion was enough.

We fly back to Iceland somewhat dejected, as if the blockbuster we had envisioned has turned out to be a flop. I feel unsure whether to invest more time and energy in working so closely with other regulators. But international cooperation has many facets, and in the weeks that follow I am able to forge a new agreement with the British Virgin Islands on information sharing. Now we can find out (very slightly) more information about the many BVI shell companies connected to our investigations. And that accomplishment gives me motivation again to push forward on our IOSCO application, one that had been languishing since the crisis started. We are the only European country still not a part of this important international regulatory association, and we get accepted just in time to be named alongside Syria, Saudi Arabia, and the Maldives in the global press release.

20

WE MADE IT!

WINTER temperatures in Reykavík don't hit as hard as people who live outside the Land generally imagine. It snows sometimes, yes, but it rains too, hovering just around freezing. The bone-chilling Boston winter cold of my childhood wins out for sheer brutality. And as dark as it gets by Christmas, the daylight starts increasing by seven minutes per day from late January and we overtake the southern countries in a matter of weeks. The change of seasons in Iceland is tied very closely to drastic shifts in the amount of light. By the end of March, the days are very long.

The rapid return of sunlight lifts everyone's spirits. I have something else to be cheerful about as well. Alongside work, the prospect of our wedding this coming August keeps me busy. Hulda has planned everything long ago. Even her plans have plans. Every few days I get a reminder of an important upcoming appointment: meeting with the priest to go over the ceremony, then with the photographer, then sitting around beers in *Íslenski barinn* with two of the baddest-ass musicians in the Land, trying to convince them that, yes, they really do want to play a wedding for the first time.

At work, business as usual has a new twist: the annual competition for the best beard at the office, meant to raise awareness of men's cancer. We start from clean-shaven faces on the first of March. It seems like every guy in every office in the city takes part in this thing, with individual and team pages up on a communal *Móttumars* website. We can grow whatever facial hair we like. I have an idea how ridiculous I am going to look, but I'm also going for the win this year—committed to sprouting a 'full trucker' honky-tonk moustache.

The endless series of work competitions and events does serve to keep things lighthearted, but sometimes the office environment is less serious than I would like, outside of our little investigation team. We are doing real work. It matters a lot to me that the Icelandic people understand how much the malfeasance at the banks cost us. Icelanders are used to thinking of their country as so small as to be insignificant in the world. News pieces never convey the fact that these bank failures were huge not just by Icelandic standards but by global standards. So, between investigation work, coordination meetings, updates with the prosecutor, wedding preparations, and studying each night for the Level III CFA exam, I try to squeeze in some time for a little PR. Sigrún encourages me to draft a newspaper piece that will give a bit more insight on the sheer size of the Icelandic banks and their place in the history of corporate collapse.

Morgunblaðið publishes my piece on 11 March 2010.[50] It compares the collapse of each of the three Icelandic lenders to the biggest American bankruptcies. In order to ease comparison, I have converted the sizes of each bank's balance sheet into U.S. dollars. Put together, the three entities were worth $182bn the day before they went bust. My stomach shrinks at this number, as it had back at the beginning of the investigations. These were huge institutions. At least 11 times the size of Iceland's economy.[51]

When I superimpose these three Icelandic failures onto those

---

50   www.mbl.is/greinasafn/grein/1325468
51   By comparison: the balance sheets of the banks in the U.S. taken all together were less than the size of the U.S. GDP (93%) at the end of 2008. Iceland's financial sector at collapse was thus proportionally 15 times bigger than that of the Americans. Source: U.S. Federal Reserve Consolidated Balance Sheet Depository Institutions, 2008.

from America, I end up with an odd-sounding collection indeed: famous American names like Texaco and Chrysler interspersed with old Viking words. Landsbanki, Kaupþing, and Glitnir slot themselves easily among the top ten U.S. bankruptcies of all time. Yet the U.S. economy is the world's biggest: 1,000 times that of Iceland.

The analysis puts numbers around the devastation that Hulda and I felt in autumn 2008. American friends and family had said "things are bad everywhere". Perhaps, but the U.S. would have needed to experience not just one but 300 simultaneous Lehman Brothers collapses to get to an event of similar magnitude as Iceland.[52] Nobody in either country could believe how giant this failure had been.

The beard competition comes to an end. I've gotten used to the new look and don't shave the thing off as fast as possible. In fact, I still wear the full trucker for the next item on the endless FME events calendar, the annual Friday-night karaoke competition. At the end of the evening, I am crowned for my Elvis and Coldplay stylings. In the world of FME employee competitions, I am, for a brief time, the King.

---

52 Or the Northern Rock bankruptcy in the UK happening 140 times over.

21

A REAL PAGE-TURNER

"LOOK at this, my AmEx card just doubled my credit line!" Hulda says, beaming.

"Did you ask them to do that?"

"No, they did it on their own. I just got this letter today. They say it's thanks for being an 'A-list' customer." She hands me the letter. Her credit line has been bumped up to 400,000 ISK (about $3,500). They thank her for always paying her monthly bill on time.

We have come home together from work and are standing in our entryway opening the day's mail.

Hey, wait a sec! I am also a good customer of the local American Express, a credit card that lets us accumulate frequent flyer points on Icelandair. And my credit line is merely 150,000 ISK ($1,300) but I take home around double what my fiancée does. I had no idea until now that she has so much credit; sometimes my own low limit has been a problem, like during months when I am traveling.

Honestly, this news makes me a little jealous of Hulda. From the very beginning in Iceland, getting a credit card at all has been a challenge: for my very first one in 2004 my company itself had to co-sign for me, complete with a lecture from the former-cop HR guy on how spending too much wasn't a good idea. Hulda herself, at the time my preferred customer service rep at the bank, had also made an Icelandic credit card seem like an unattainable dream. I felt like I was back in fourth grade.

I express my frustration and Hulda suggests that I request a bump up to 500,000 ISK per month ($4,350), just to see what happens. She thinks they'll probably give it to me. Kreditkort, the company that issues AmEx cards in Iceland, has an office right up the hill from FME, so I stop by there at lunch the following day. Like many Icelandic offices, it has a friendly vibe with soft pastel decor, parquet floors, and a machine dispensing free coffee. There's a row of desks for customer service staff, and I take a seat in front of the one woman working.

"I'd like to request a higher credit limit for my AmEx card," I begin, after we exchange the requisite pleasantries. She asks how much I would like. "500,000," I tell her.

She looks at me oddly and with a matronly note of suspicion in her voice asks why I need access to so much money each month. I tell her that I am a good customer: I pay off my balance every month in full and on time, but that a couple of times the limit was so low as to cause me problems on travel abroad.

"I can't make this decision on my own," she says. She will need to take it to the head of credit. I ask her if she needs any supporting documentation, like bank balance statements or recent payslips. She says it won't be necessary. I am surprised; what will they use to make a determination about me?

Meantime Hulda writes Kreditkort online and asks for another bump, up to 500,000 ISK per month. Just to see what will happen. Within an hour, she gets an SMS back: request granted!

I am not so lucky. My SMS, a few hours later, comes back negative. They say they can give me 300,000 ISK ($2,600) only, which is at least something. But they offer no explanation for refusing my original request.

So I return the next day at lunch to speak to the same lady. She says she is very sorry, but that they won't be able to offer me any more credit. I ask why, and she can't provide a reason. (I think I know the real reason: my name and accent both mark me as a foreigner. It's like a flashing red light here in the Land: second-class citizen! But nobody official will say this explicitly.)

I return to my desk and type a courteous email to Kreditkort, and I get Hulda to proofread it. It asks for written reasons for why the request was denied.[53]

I have an ulterior motive here. One of the main criticisms made by the International Monetary Fund after the crisis was that Iceland had no clear process to measure creditworthiness for individual borrowers. There's no credit score—or, if there is, it's the number of seconds spittle takes to dry from a moistened finger stuck in the air. Here it is nearly three years after the historic collapse, and I am surprised to discover evidence of the same apparent sloppiness that helped crash the country in the first place. A couple living under the same roof has different credit limits, with the one making half as much getting nearly double, and nobody can tell us why.

So I also draft a formal letter to FME, my own agency. This will get routed to Guðfinnur, the head of credit supervision. I lay out the situation and say that it looks like solid evidence that this major Icelandic credit card firm has no clear process by which to score credit risks or allocate personal lines of credit. Always stirring up the pot, me. But I figure we are friendly colleagues and this could make a clean-cut test case for his team. A real chance to do some good.

"That's a very, very sophisticated type of case you have there," says Guðfinnur, after calling me into a meeting room. He has my formal letter printed out in front of him. He's smiling his inscrutable smile. He says that this behavior clearly shows that there is something fishy going on inside Kreditkort, and that he thinks the team should get to the bottom of it. He says one of the lawyers on his team will contact me to get all the facts.

When I get the email from the guy later, my heart sinks. I know this lawyer a bit. I've seen him around the FME and he doesn't give

<hr/>

53 They do respond after a few weeks' delay, and tell me it's because I don't own any real estate, but by this point, neither does Hulda. They also say I've been a customer for less time than she has.

me a good feeling. Always dressed impeccably in skinny suits, he seems prematurely jaded at probably 24 years of age. He invites me to stop by his desk and go over the case.

His desk is hidden in the back corner of the second floor, above a storage room for the Asian grocery store. The window shades are down and it is dim and sickly back here. He doesn't offer me a seat. He stays standing and so do I. He tells me he doesn't think the FME has jurisdiction over consumer credit.

"Then who would have jurisdiction?" I ask, surprised.

"Probably *Neytendastofa*," he says, indicating the consumer affairs bureau of the Land.

"But this is an issue of credit scoring and rating, highlighted by the IMF as a key problem for Iceland," I point out. "And our agency has the responsibility to regulate the credit markets of Iceland."

He stares sideways at me, his jaw clenched: "I don't think so."

I remind him of the name on the side of our building. It means: *The* Financial Regulator. I ask him what Jón Jónsson out on the street thinks we do in here all day. I ask if there's another financial regulator in the Land who takes care of these types of matters.

His jaw pulses once or twice as he flips silently through the Icelandic legal codes. He's got a binder of them open on his desk and stands over it while I watch, flipping the pages at an achingly slow rate of perhaps one every ten seconds. This guy has all the time in the world to figure out why he doesn't need to spend time on something. Long minutes pass this way.

"Here it is," he says at last. If he were Texan, he would be drawling. He stubs his index finger onto the page in muted triumph. "Right here: it says FME doesn't need to do this."

By this point in my new career as an investigator I have read enough legal codes to know that there's almost always a way to justify either action or inaction. These second-floor credit boys seem to default to the latter. In the time this jaded paralegal spent flipping through pages, he could have a formal letter out the door to Kreditkort, asking them to describe for FME the high-level view of their credit-scoring process. A letter that would have potentially caused them to realize their process was nearly nonexistent, and that maybe they needed to develop one. Something that would leave both the firm and its customers better off.

But instead, this. Dead-eyed flipping and disinterest so intense it's aggressive.

And that's about enough of that. After all, we have bigger *þorskur* to fry. I head back through the cafeteria and up to the fifth floor to the bright light.

22

THE COMMISSION REPORTS

THE oldest parliament in the world, the Icelandic *Alþingi*, set up an investigation commission, co-chaired by a respected judge and a Yale economist, in the wake of the financial crisis. This body was mandated to describe the causes of the Icelandic collapse, and in fact even visited us at the FME around a month after I started. I presented my early findings on the banks' unannounced purchases of their own shares. Their final report is due in early April 2010. We wait eagerly for it, curious to hear their conclusions but also worried that the commission will uncover something big that we've missed.

I watch the press conference unveiling the report[54] on TV in the cafeteria, joined by around half the FME. High drama unfolds before us; we can feel the nation all tuned in simultaneously, waiting with baited breath. But the commissioners lay out talking points from jetstream altitude, stating mainly that the banks simply grew too fast. As ever, I want to dig into the details.

That night on the way home from work, Hulda and I stop off at the venerable Mál og Menning bookstore on Laugavegur. They have given the Special Investigation Commission reports pride of place,

54 www.rna.is/eldri-nefndir/addragandi-og-orsakir-falls-islensku-bankanna-2008/
skyrsla-nefndarinnar/english

right inside the entrance to the store. A wooden pallet is stacked high. I pick myself up a copy, or should I say a brick: nine soft-bound volumes wrapped with plastic and sporting an integrated carrying handle. A few other customers stand in line at the register buying their copies. Everyone coming into the store is looking over the giant reports. Hulda says she feels proud of me for running right out to buy this voluminous set, but for me it's a must-have. My curiosity for the details, the real juice of the story of this financial collapse, is boundless. Today really marks a turning point.

The amount of careful work that went into the final product is obvious; it was clearly meant as a document for the ages. Color graphs pop off the beautifully typeset pages. The authors delve deeply into each aspect of the saga of the Icelandic banks. They start with detailed chapters on the economic and political environment, and then go in depth into the privatization of the three banks in the late 1990s and early 2000s. Next they get into how the banks financed their growth through borrowing from foreign lenders, and how they grew their loan books by lending (very often to 'related parties', friends and family members of the banks' own managers). The report spends whole chapters on the ownership structure of each bank, the compensation structure of the managers, the internal and external auditors, the domestic equity market, the market for the Icelandic *króna*, and the role of investment funds. Each of these massive chapters contains detailed analysis, anecdotes, quotes from managers, shareholders, and politicians. It is a bit overwhelming, and this is only the first four volumes!

Legal and supervisory issues come next, starting with a careful analysis of the European legal landscape, but then a lot of focus on the failures of my very own FME to supervise the banks during their rapid growth. Next up: the undercapitalized Icelandic deposit insurance system, especially as it related to the savings accounts these entities opened abroad after their troubles borrowing from foreign lenders in 2006. The report rounds out with a careful blow-by-blow of the events of the hellish week during which the three giant lenders went bust. Glitnir was the weakest of the three and the first to fail, but then much transpired both within the banks and the government through the collapse of Kaupþing three days later.

The Special Investigation Commission does not shy away from naming names. In its final chapter, the report lists 12 individuals who through "mistakes or neglect" allowed the crisis to unfold as it did. Among them are Geir Haarde, former prime minister, and Davíð Oddsson, another former prime minister, the architect of the banks' privatization, the head of the central bank in 2008, current editor of *Morgunblaðið*, and the puppet-master of Icelandic political life.

But up front, in a long-ish executive summary section, the report states that the problems for the Icelandic banks lie first and foremost in their too-rapid growth, the easy access to foreign capital they enjoyed in the middle of the decade, and the fact that their owners took advantage of their position to force the banks to make the biggest loans to themselves. The authors go on to conclude failures with supervision by both the central bank and FME, as well as by the Icelandic government.

One analyst makes a very crucial point, in an English-language addendum to the report: "It is important to note that the analysts' concerns and the 2006 funding mini-crisis completely predated the U.S. subprime crisis, which developed into a worldwide financial panic. The market was reacting to bank characteristics that would complicate funding for any bank, anywhere in the world, even under normal financial market conditions." In other words, the Icelandic banks were in trouble starting in at least 2006, and absent corrections (which he says elsewhere that they did not make), they would have run into serious problems even in a beautiful blue-sky world. The U.S. subprime crisis and the collapse of Lehman serve merely as convenient scapegoats for the Icelandic cheerleaders of the sector. Yet these sycophants continue to cite these causes over and over, unwilling to look deeper to the rotten core of the institutions.

After 2006, the way the Iceland Three continued to survive was classic Ponzi economics: keep taking in new money and growing to try to outrun the bad decisions of the last financial quarter. They needed more and more new capital in a continuous stream to keep the scheme going. One method to collect more money and thus stave off collapse was by using the so-called EU passport scheme to open retail savings accounts in other European countries. These new accounts were nevertheless not always regulated in those countries, by EU design. Both Kaupþing and Landsbanki did this, via the online sites Kaupthing Edge and Icesave, respectively. They used these to take in the money of private savers and keep their banks growing, even though the financial markets had realized they were in trouble. Icelandic culture has long celebrated the crafty Viking, the guy who bends or breaks the rules and comes out ahead, and the EU passport scheme must have seemed custom-crafted for this kind of abuse.

However, the parliamentary report dances around the original sin: the illegal purchase of the banks' own shares on the market to maintain an illusion of financial health and the use of their own loan books to hide those very shares. The Commission describes both of these things, but uses weasel words: "weak equity" (an expression invented to mean the banks held way more than the legal limit of their own shares) and "loans to holding companies" come up a lot. It also points out the "big time" (*í stórum stíl*) buying of their own shares on the Icelandic stock exchange, especially when prices were falling, to create artificial demand. But the report does not overtly connect the share purchases on the open market with the lending to shell companies to make the same equity disappear offshore. And although the commission hints at it, it also does not come out and say that potentially serious financial crime undergirds the growth of the banks.

But for those of us on the investigations these nine volumes nonetheless become a valuable resource: a go-to guide, like a *Yellow Pages* for shady shell companies and impenetrable deals. Whenever we open a new case file, the first thing we do is look at what the Special Investigation Commission has already described.

"Eldgos í Eyjafjallajökli!!!" reads the email from Hulda. This one-line, subject-only message tells me all I need to know: there's a volcano erupting under Eyjafjallajökull, the 'glacier of the island mountains'. The date is 14 April 2010.

A smaller eruption, merely the size of Manhattan, already happened near this site a few weeks before. Along with many childless and/or bourgeois Icelanders we decided to go see this once-in-a-lifetime event for ourselves. So we splurged on a helicopter flight over the hot lakes of lava. When the chopper turned on its side briefly, a few hundred meters over the eruption, I could feel the heat ready to sear me through the sheet metal hull of the aircraft. We landed not far away and were left there in the swirling wind and snow as new land was created high in the mountains a couple of football fields away.

Just like with the crisis of March 2006, we'd thought the mini eruption the big deal. But what Hulda refers to in her email is that the volcano under the glacier itself is now in action. When this happens, the roof of ice melts, causing massive flooding and ash ejections. The big one is here.

The giant eruption of Eyjfjallajökull continues for weeks and becomes world news as it shuts down European air traffic for a few days. Locally, the lightning-filled ash plume builds into a tower that can be seen 100 kilometers away. The farms in the shadow of the glacier are forced to slaughter all of their livestock, and the national highway along the south coast is quickly cut in two by work crews to keep the inevitable *jökulhlaup* (glacier flood) from causing even more widespread damage. The ash itself is silica—basically sand—but with the consistency of flour, so light it can hang in the air. When the wind changes, it blows toward Reykjavík. I come out to my car to find it coated with a fine powder, and when I turn on the wipers to get rid of it, they scratch the windshield. Of course, it is even worse to breathe. I come to my office after a weekend, and with a window cracked the whole place is covered in a layer of fine ash. The investigations will have to wait until I can get the black stuff sponged up somehow. Months later, glass like flour still lurks in the crevices of my keyboard and desk phone.

The volcano becomes everything. The careful discussion of the many fascinating findings and conclusions of the parliamentary report that had begun in the Icelandic media are consumed by a lightning-pierced ash cloud that towers into the stratosphere.

23

BRIGHT DAYS

EACH month, one of my FME colleagues organizes a wine lottery. A tall and somewhat awkward guy who rarely says much, his lottery reminder emails nonetheless land in my inbox with Swiss-watch regularity. This *léttvínsleikur* (literally 'light wine game') costs participating employees a thousand *krónur* (around $15 pre-crisis and $8 post-crisis) per month. Co-workers crowd around in the sparse office of my colleague as he draws the winner's name out of a hat. Behind him stands the expensive bottle he has purchased that month, solitary on an otherwise empty wooden bookshelf behind his desk. High drama.

Despite my success at karaoke, I have never won the wine lottery and my interest in it is waning. I have stopped going to watch the name be drawn and instead I usually just wait for the email announcing the results. So many things pull one away from work in this agency.

I am having a hard time finding enthusiasm for Icelandic employee games more generally. Signing a work contract can bring with it many hidden obligations to join multiple competing sets of lotteries, competitions, contests, raffles, and events. The underlying idea of the light wine game is sadly symptomatic of a common trope in the Land: gambling one's way to prosperity. The allure of truly expensive booze for less than half the price of the very cheapest bottle strikes many as a good bargain.

I joined the wine lottery in an early attempt to fit in at the FME. Working as the rare professional foreigner in Iceland, I felt a lot of pressure to conform. Especially in the early days, in 2004, each time someone came by my desk with a new contest or game, I eagerly signed up. It was all very exotic, and I didn't want to appear even more foreign than I was. But from the beginning I found that the level of peer pressure in daily life could be brutal.

Most companies have a separately managed *starfsmannafélag* (employee association) for which a not-insignificant dues payment is automatically deducted from each month's salary. Separate from the labor union (although most people are in those, too, and they can have real power), this is rather a slush fund for 'fun' activities. The most loudmouthed and influential in each office deploy the fund on parties and events they themselves plan (sometimes at their own houses) and then guilt the others into attending. Withdrawal from this little club is, of course, possible; Icelanders aren't communists. But that action could send a very provocative message to the heavy-hitters in charge of the association. Some colleagues and I pondered dropping out of my first association at Zodiac (there was one lonely martyr in that office of 25 who did not participate) but backed off at the extreme level of offense taken by the co-workers in charge. The not-so-subtle threat of retribution in the form of isolation at work and exclusion from all manner of activities hung over us free-thinkers like a sword of Damocles.

But here at FME I am beginning to feel my status as a leading investigator of the same crisis that cut the buying power of all those employee association bank balances by half or more. So maybe it's OK to skip the wine lottery. And the next foosball tournament too.

Along with the ongoing eruption of Eyjafjallajökull on the south coast, a media earthquake begins to shake the Land. Even though I've been working at the regulator for a bit more than a year now, and have intimate knowledge of some of these cases, the first headlines come as a shock to me. No rumors in the news, no whispers in the back alleys of the FME, no heads-up from my counterparts at the prosecutor's office. But on 6 May 2010, it hits the news: Hreiðar Már Sigurdsson, former CEO of Kaupþing and one of the golden boys of the Icelandic boom years, has been arrested and taken into custody by the special prosecutor.

I call Hulda at her office and tell her to check the front pages online. I end up spending most of the day glued to the web, guiltily hitting the refresh button and swapping between Icelandic news sites, relentlessly chasing every bit of new detail. I have lots of work on my desk, but this story is hard for me to let go. And not only are the Icelandic media having a field day; some big international outlets are covering it, too.

Incredulous, I study the news photos and video of Hreiðar Már being escorted by a plainclothes police officer, late on a bright May night. A short stretch of concrete sidewalk leads from the office of the prosecutor to a waiting police vehicle. The suspect doesn't wear handcuffs, yet there is no doubt what is going on. The self-styled banking genius is now flanked by beefy Icelandic cops, his path back to the auto and the detention cell delineated by the law. The images shock even me. Hreiðar Már is suddenly no longer in control, the one being led along. The same man who received the Order of the Falcon award from our president for his contributions to Icelandic society, the high-status power broker, has had a terrible fall from grace. Seen by many as a top mind, a shining star, an incredible story of success—even as the one who single-handedly brought Iceland the staggering good fortune of the boom years—Hreiðar is spending his nights in a holding cell and his days in an interrogation room.

On top of my shock that this is really happening comes a nascent sense of relief that some of our hard and secretive work is beginning to bear public fruit. Even though I am relying entirely on news reports to guess at what's going on inside the prosecutor's office, I know our labors helped in getting things to this point. I feel vindicated too. The past year and a half has brought countless discussions among

Icelanders eager to know the truth about the banks and the actions of top bankers during the boom years. More liberal-minded Icelanders see the top bank management as "of course" responsible for the dizzying collapse of the country in so very few days. ("How could they not have known?" say some friends and family.) However, this arrest also serves as a response to that other thread of thought, more likely to be espoused by those on the political right (and the banks' top management themselves): that the crisis was solely the result of troubles outside Iceland.

To those with this apologist viewpoint, the gathering steam of public outrage and then the massive report from the parliamentary commission, sometimes led to a reluctant admission that "OK, maybe something was afoot in our banks". Maybe they weren't as shiny as everyone believed in 2007. But still, anything untoward that happened inside them had to be confined to a few "bad apples", a few "rogue traders": low and middling bank employees too crooked or incompetent to do their jobs.

But with the arrest of CEO Hreiðar Már it has to be obvious to all but the most shameless: the Kaupþing fish had rotted from the head. Innocent until proven guilty, yes, but for a judge to issue a warrant at all for such a high-profile executive is in and of itself big news. For me, this outward confirmation that a very top executive had some demonstrable knowledge of dirty business represents a new horizon for the society.

Apart from Hreiðar Már, who voluntarily flew back to Iceland from his new home base in Luxembourg never expecting an arrest, his friend and colleague Magnús Guðmundsson, the former head of Kaupþing Luxembourg, also returned to be placed unwittingly in custody. Each is housed in solitary confinement and only given access to his lawyer.

A judge granted the prosecutor these arrest and custody warrants on the back of big accusations: forgery, theft, and violations of securities laws, including market abuse. Both men could be eligible for up to eight years in prison according to the press but I'm not sure to which cases these warrants pertain: the same two individuals are named in many investigations. The media only refers to the Al-Thani matter and states that referrals and data from the FME formed some of the basis. An even more senior executive, Sigurður Einarsson, the former executive chairman of Kaupþing, is also under warrant. He resides in a mansion the bank bought him, choosing his expensive bottles of red from a cellar the bank stocked, in the posh Mayfair neighborhood of London. No wine lottery for him! He shows no intention of returning and seems safe for now as no extradition treaty binds Iceland and the UK.

I get up early the next day to pore over the accounts in both *Morgunblaðið* and *Fréttablaðið*. Then on the weekend, the tabloid *DV* is filled with even more photos of the arrests. It feels like we are suddenly in a big country. In Iceland, changes to the fishing quotas and single-car accidents routinely make the front page of both mainstream and gossip publications. Now we are in the big time!

Hreiðar Már plays the lead role in this weekend's account because he was truly a superstar of the golden age. Few Icelanders could boast of his extravagant salary, duly reported down to the *króna* by the press each August,[55] and few in Iceland embodied the financial success of the country during the boom years as well as he. His youthful looks caused many to perceive him as a boy wonder of financial markets. One friend ruefully told me after the crash, "We weren't really sure how these guys were doing what they were, making so much money out of nothing. We thought they were geniuses."

The tabloid does not focus only on Hreiðar Már. The reporters also shine a bit of a spotlight on the special prosecutor, Ólafur Þór Hauksson, whom they call the most important man in Iceland. The editorial board of *DV* writes that the country should thank him for not being in the same category of leader as those in charge in the past. Big praise.

---

55 Incomes in Iceland are a matter of public record, at least for three weeks each August when the tax office lets anyone come in and view a paper printout of the summary tax information of each resident. Icelandic reporters look up individuals of interest and publish a glossy magazine called *Tekjublaðið* (the salary paper) that lists the monthly income of anyone deemed a public figure.

Despite this adulation in the media, the small team at the prosecutor's office does not have much time to read the papers. They are working double and triple shifts to conduct more than 40 interviews with Kaupþing staffers, making use of every minute of custody they've been granted. One of them later explains to me their "decapitation" strategy, favored by Icelandic law enforcement in drug-trafficking cases: place the kingpins incommunicado for a few days and talk to everyone lower down in the meantime. Without the big guns to give orders, the smaller fish will flail. And some of them will talk.

The spotlight remains on the investigations a while longer. In a profile a couple of weeks later, *DV* publishes a front-page special on the prosecutor. They praise Ólafur Þór for being a role model, for his sense of humor. The newspaper describes him as a great cook and a family man, calls him well-read, and says he has an answer to all questions. He can apparently quote the law verbatim and discuss court precedent off-the-cuff while he tromps around the countryside in waders, looking for the best place to drop a hand-tied lure into a bubbling Icelandic brook.

I couldn't agree more with this praise. I have developed a deep respect for the man who's been nicknamed Heavy Special by some of the disgraced bankers, a name he laughs off boomingly. His good humor and brilliance have been a whiff of hope all along for me. I know it will take more time for the bankers to be convicted—if they eventually are—but what a huge step forward his team has made over the past weeks.

In this environment of adulation, I am deeply honored when Ólafur Þór invites me to travel with him and his top team to The Hague. We have a meeting at Europol headquarters with law enforcement from several countries: the Serious Fraud Office from the UK, as well as cops from the Continent. Some wider interest is arising in the big criminal cases developing in Iceland, and the modest vine-covered brownstone tucked away on a leafy street is the right forum for sharing them. My voice shakes as I describe our big investigations to the stone-faced police gathered around the U-shaped table of a bland Europol conference room. But at the break, a former mafia prosecutor from Italy shakes my hand and says, "What you showed us today is organized crime!"

Literally a head taller than other men, our special prosecutor really sticks out in a crowd. As we enter the Amsterdam airport to catch the plane home, I notice again how his lieutenants try their best to secrete him away from the public eye. One of them says under his breath that these trips are like traveling with Big Bird. They have a difficult task in helping him travel incognito. Ólafur suggests a restaurant near the gate and his men steer our little group to the very furthest back alcove they can find. But it doesn't matter. Some drunken Icelanders on holiday spot us from far down the concourse. "Er það sérstakur? Sérstakur saksóknari!"—*Is that 'the special'? Special prosecutor!* They begin yelling proudly at us, across all of the airport, as only Icelanders abroad can do. "Áfram!" they yell... "Forward!" Go get 'em! A tiny bit embarrassing, but it is also hard not to feel like heroes right now. *Erum við loksins á uppleið?* Are we finally on the path back from 2008?

We board the Icelandair 757 and struggle our way back to a block of seats somewhere around row 23. The last one of our group down the aisle, I watch Ólafur humbly try to squeeze his frame into an economy-class chair. I am just finding my seat and stowing my carry-on in the row behind him when I hear a flurry of activity to the fore of the plane. The purser has burst down the aisle. "Aren't you the special prosecutor?" she asks Ólafur in Icelandic. "Come with me," she says. "*Strákar!*" she adds, and motions to us, indicating that all his 'boys' should also come along to the Saga Class section at the front of the plane. Again the last one there, I find the only empty business-class seat is next to the man himself. We fly back home together, flipping through the day's newspapers from Iceland and chatting. Opposite a thoughtful editorial page, a bright yellow Bónus supermarket advertisement with blown-up cuts of raw meat jumps out of the page at me. Running out of conversation topics, I try to convey to the big guy how jarring I find these photos of food bargains in the midst of serious content. But I don't think he sees anything odd with it.

Hulda picks me up at Keflavík airport in the late afternoon in her dad's big Land Cruiser. We've planned to drive directly to Ísafjarðardjúp—the Deep of Ice Fjord!—to spend the long weekend with friends. Hulda wants to get ahead of the weather but warns me it might be rough going. A May snowstorm is predicted to hit the west of the country and the weather office can't predict yet how bad it will be. I'm feeling so tired with the trip to the Netherlands that I drive only the first three hours or so and then gladly hand the wheel to Hulda. She pilots us through an increasingly thick blizzard, the only car on a desolate narrow and winding track through the West Fjords, with visibility just past the hood ornament, the road surface broken and patched. The snow really slows us down and we make maybe only 40 km/h for what seems like an eternity. The wheels keep slipping on the snow and the big vehicle drifts from side to side on the sloped and rutted road.

Finally we reach the town of Hólmavík[56] after 10 at night. We have already heard on the radio that we can travel no further. The big pass over the high heath—*Steingrímsfjarðarheiði*—that connects to the main set of fjords that lie to our north and west is closed under a couple of meters of new snow. So the last stop for all of the holiday traffic is this 70-person outpost. We have reached the very end of civilization.

The two modest hotels were long ago full by the time we turn in past the town service station. Even the floor of the gym at the local school can't take any more visitors. We pull the car off the road on one of a tiny handful of residential streets and decide to try the guesthouses, knowing it's in vain, but hoping they can suggest something for us anyway. Iceland's 1,100-year tradition of taking care of wanderers in snowstorms keeps us hopeful. I admire Hulda's polite Icelandic on the phone as I sit worried in the passenger seat. Heavy snow tumbles down outside and starts freezing on the windshield.

---

56 The same settlement where young law school graduate Ólafur Þór first made his mark as *sýslumaður*.

But about then the magic of the Land begins to manifest: a man comes out of his house, curious about why we are parked in front of it. He apologizes right away that his extra bedroom is being used by his son's family (also up for the long weekend) but is on his way down to ring his neighbor's doorbell and enlist that guy on our behalf when the second guesthouse owner tells Hulda by phone that she'll put us up in her own house. She says she knows the layout of the miniature town can be confusing for new people and so even comes to get us in her car, so we can follow her back home, a street and a half away.

We enter the modest house through the front door and straight into the kitchen. With a gesture of seamless fluidity, our hostess hits the power button on a 12-cup drip machine and the bitter black smell of Icelandic coffee hits us like home. It doesn't matter the time of day or night: in Iceland, *kaffi* equals hospitality. We sit at her light-blue painted kitchen table and drink half-full black cups from plain white porcelain. The heat from the bottoms of years of hot mugs seems to have rippled the paint on the table surface and it has peeled off in places, revealing a darker coat beneath. The powerful smell of livestock creeps in at us from another entrance on the left. The woman and Hulda compare notes and try to figure out whom they know in common: Icelanders' second national pastime.

The woman's teenage daughter bursts into the room, thrilled about the turn of events. "I've got the new *Séð og heyrt!*" she proudly exclaims to Hulda. "Want to see it?" The glossy weekly *Seen and Heard* gossip magazine is apparently a thing of great value this far west. How could Hulda refuse? And the girl bounces with glee for another reason too. She'd been grounded for the evening after an argument with her father. But now the parents need her bedroom to put up these strangers from Reykjavík, and she eagerly applies makeup in preparation for a sleepover at her best friend's place.

I go out to the car and fetch one of my duty-free bottles of Italian red wine from the Holland trip. The mother and daughter accept this gift reluctantly, exchanging quizzical expressions like we've handed them an exotic bird. The girl shows us to her room, where she powers on a couple of lava lamps. The ceiling is covered with glow-in-the-dark stars and after she leaves we snuggle together on the single teenage bed and feel just a little bit lucky.

The next morning shines bright and hopeful. The mom offers us breakfast—toasted bread and thin-sliced *fjölskylduostur*—'family cheese' that melts a bit on top of the runny butter. She won't hear of taking any payment for our room. The mountain pass is being reopened—we overtake snowblower trucks clawing through snow drifts taller than houses—and we can drive the rest of the way to the Deep and meet our friends. It's beautiful country, seen by very few, so we are grateful that the Land has decided to allow us humans to once more traverse and experience it.

24

TASK FORCE IN THE (212)

OUR shiny new membership in IOSCO, the International Organization of Securities Commissions, at last lets us legally share information with other "competent authorities" (that's legalese for regulators) the world over: anyone who's a member. And that includes the Americans. I am really interested in the possibilities here because of how the U.S. markets were used by the Icelandic banks.

After the mini-crisis began in early 2006, the European debt markets closed to the Icelandic banks, and they were forced to go further afield to raise the cash they badly needed to survive. For Kaupþing, the next logical place was New York. Subsequently, in 2006, they issued €3.7bn worth of bonds in the U.S. markets, underwritten by some of the biggest banks around: J.P. Morgan, Morgan Stanley, and other titans of Wall Street.

I found the prospectus for this U.S. Medium Term Note program in the sheaves of documents we had from Kaupþing and it looked scandalous. Right there in the early pages was a graph of the share price development of the biggest Icelandic bank and discussion in the text of how the strong performance of the bank's shares were indicative of its great financial health. But we knew already from the big Kaupþing case that the share price of the bank was a fiction dating all the way back to 2004. I thought the U.S. Securities and Exchange Commission might be interested to know that American investors had been defrauded to the tune of billions when they bought these bonds. With our communication channels now open, I can share the still-secret details of the biggest shares market manipulation in history with my counterparts from the world's biggest market.

I met one of the lead investigators from the Enron Task Force at an SEC event in Washington the previous November and he had been friendly. By the time we gain membership in IOSCO, he's working in international relations for the agency. I call him up and he seems genuinely happy to hear from me.

We chit-chat and then I tell him: "I can finally fill you in on our confidential investigation of Kaupþing Bank." We arrange a more formal call, and I prepare some slides to send over a secure channel, showing the magnitude of the market abuse perpetrated by the bank.

On our second call, we go through the presentation in detail. He seems interested. He tells me the right people to investigate this will be a team at the New York office of the SEC, and he will get us in touch. I am overjoyed: this thing is starting to move!

The day comes and the meeting is set. I call into the (212) number from my desk, looking out across at grey Esja while I speak to a conference room full of SEC lawyers in Manhattan. I take them through my few slides, showing first the background of the share-price manipulation, and then how the manipulated shares were used to sell a much vaster amount in debt to American investors (many of them pension funds, entrusted with Americans' retirement[57]) by the biggest blue-chip names on Wall Street. I tell them we are thin on resources but would be happy to help them with what they might need from our side to take this case forward on their end.

---

57 Some of the largest creditors to Kaupþing, according to a 2010 list from that bank, are American pension funds: Oregon PERS, Iowa PERS, Florida State Board Administration, Maryland State Retirement Agency, Minnesota State Board of Investments, Utah Retirement Systems, and California State Teachers Retirement System, to name just those on page 507: wla.1-s.es/kaupthing-claims.pdf.

Their responses are muted. And from their questions, I sense they can't seem to connect the dots. When I mention the likely manipulation of the credit default swap (CDS) market, arguably the most important market in the world pre-2008, they don't seem to know what this is. After 20 minutes or so, they thank me for the presentation and it's "don't call us, we'll call you".

The FME has granted me a study week and I am spending the long days in Bókhlaðan—literally, 'the pile of books'—the combined National and University Library of the Land. My third and final CFA exam looms on Saturday, and outside the window of the library the skies of the capital are hazy brown with airborne ash. I will be glad when this week is behind me.

"The funding is approved and we have to start to advertise immediately for the new team additions," the email from my boss leads off.[58] Sitting in a study cubicle, I look out towards Öskjuhlíð, one of the little hills of Reykjavík, through an atmosphere that is nearly opaque. My desk sprawls with notecards and formulas to memorize. "We need to discuss what skills we need," Sigrún continues, insisting that I go into the office during this high-pressure time to discuss the structure of the new team with her and Binni.

Distracted as I am with the exam prep, I am happy with the idea of an expanded investigation team. I have been pushing for more staff for the better part of my first year. The two-hour meeting ends up being a respite from hastily written investment policy statements and sheets of formulas to memorize. After all, she didn't call me back from a sun-drenched cabana on the azure sea of Calabria.

More than a month later, in mid-July, the three of us are still trying to come to a final decision on how to enhance the team. We rehash every detail in an interminable string of meetings. Eschewing the normal practices of a securities regulator, we plan to hire from

58 In a classic Catch-22, as the funding for the FME was still provided by the banks themselves, we had to wait for the decrepit shells of the fallen institutions to approve the expansion of the very teams investigating the malfeasance that led to their downfall.

a wide variety of relevant backgrounds. This means not just lawyers and paralegals, but also those who have worked as traders and asset managers. However, the legal staff we *do* plan to hire cause a point of friction. The question is: should they be slotted directly into the new investigation teams headed by Binni and me? I think so, but Sigrún disagrees. She says she can't imagine legal professionals performing this type of work. I point out that at the SEC, for example, all of the investigators are lawyers. Once we find and document market abuse or sham loans, for example, we will need to report those findings in a way that is in harmony with the law. Sigrún finally opts for an in-between solution: she creates a pool of legal resources that reports to her. Binni and I will have to come to agreement between ourselves, or do battle, to make the best use of these new staff.

In the middle of this horse trading, Guðfinnur, the head of credit regulation, invites me to join a meeting with the CEO of one of the many B-list financial institutions in Iceland. Besides the 'big three' failed banks, a frightening number of other financial institutions still dot the landscape of this country of just over 300,000 people. This sad self-styled investment bank of a couple dozen employees has asked the FME to approve their new organizational chart. But the diagram has the same manager directly overseeing both the bank's proprietary traders and the brokerage desk, indicating such an obvious conflict of interest that even in the pre-crisis go-go years the bigger banks at least created the appearance of a 'Chinese wall' between these operations. My colleague doesn't seem to have the temperament to have a throwdown with a bank CEO over this issue, but the new structure apparently also bothers him. He comes by my desk to discuss their request.

"What do you think of this?" he asks me.

My hackles are up. "Everything we have been working on in these criminal cases shows us how important it is to separate these functions," I tell him. "Sure, it's a small bank, but you could have the prop traders report to the head of Treasury, and keep the brokers in the Markets area." I give him concrete examples for why the two desks have to be separated in order to avoid a conflict between the bank and its clients: if the proprietary traders know a big brokerage order is coming in, for example, they can front-run the customer on the bank's behalf. But here in Iceland we have all just lived through a much bigger example: the giant market abuse cases now at the prosecutor's or in the pipeline. Here the collusion between prop desks and brokers has arguably taken down the whole country. This is the maybe first time my colleague has wrapped his head around the corrupt trading inside each bank that underpins our still-secret investigations. He seems to get it, nods his agreement and we go downstairs to the meeting together.

Already at their places in a windowless second-floor room, two men, one in his late forties and the other in his late twenties, fidget in their government-issue chairs. Having seen the offices in many of the banks, I know the shabbiness of our facilities at the FME can be almost offensive to these types. Buttoned up in bespoke suits, with their perfectly deployed full- and half-Windsor knots respectively befitting the age and social status of each man, they appear imprisoned behind a couple of chipped formica desks, pushed together to form a conference table. The table pushes its way out a little too closely to the walls on either side, meaning the backs of the chairs can barely swivel. Wires run from a speakerphone along one table to the floor. This space was furnished in less than 15 minutes. There is no art. Just off-white walls, not very recently painted.

Guðfinnur opens the meeting, and soon the senior executive is sliding a piece of paper across the table at us, with the motion of a *fait accompli*. This discussion for him is obviously just a formality. Make nice with the regulators.

"Here's our new organizational chart," he says. "Our board has approved this already and we are content with it too." He evinces a done-deal Icelandic male-banker arrogance that guys on Wall Street and in the City of London would do well to come and study.

"My colleague Jared has some comments on this," the head of credit states, throwing me immediately to the wolves. After all, he sits on top of the division that regulates this bank, so he should be the one making the comments. These executives don't report to me and have never met me; I was brought in as a consultant, or so I had thought. But, OK, bad cop it is.

"My question here is: how can you have the proprietary traders and the brokers all reporting directly to the same guy," I jump in. "In our investigations of the failed banks, this kind of conflict is exactly what brought them down."

"Well that 'guy' is right here next to me, and I can vouch for the fact that he is a good man," counters the CEO. "He will be able to manage the conflicts. Plus our board has already approved this structure." Icelanders love structures. They maybe love the word "structure" even more. The race between creating structures and saying the word "structure" among this class of Icelandic businessman would come down to a photo finish.

"Sure, he might be a good guy, but with all due respect, what if he leaves your firm in 6 months and the next guy is not as good?" Both men stiffen at this implication, throats swelling a little above the Windsors. The "good guy" looks hurt I would suggest such a thing. "And anyway, I am sure your board can just as easily approve a better structure."

We go back and forth a bit. My colleague Guðfinnur, the one ultimately responsible, and the one who brought me into this fruitless meeting, remains on mute. We do not find any common ground. Walking back upstairs, I am not sure why I was even invited. What was the point? I tell Sigrún I am not interested in any more distractions like this.

Later, I learn that the FME ultimately told the B-list bank to do whatever it wanted. I feel deeply frustrated—but less and less surprised. I am beginning to see that despite such a national catastrophe less than two years ago, not much will really change in the corrupt world of Icelandic business. In a country of so few people, nearly everyone is afraid to make waves at work for fear that the splashback might hit that very same evening in the local grocery store. It is the land of no consequences.

I decide to devote no more energy to these side issues and keep my focus locked on the big criminal investigations. Maybe when some of these stories come out, the country can begin to look itself in the mirror. For now we are in a race to get the facts down on paper and sent over to the prosecutor.

Meanwhile our wedding day edges closer and closer. The pace of the reminders showing up on our shared calendar is accelerating. Hulda finds the only hall in Reykjavík that can hold a hundred people without making us buy their food, a function room attached to a football field. We get Waingro's older brother, a professional chef, to put together a catering plan for us. ("Are you OK with Minke whale carpaccio, if I can get a good cut?" he asks. "Sure, the Americans will think it's beef," I tell him.) An old colleague of Hulda's mom and mine is a classy older dude who may well be the finest *maitre d'* in the Land. He tells us to leave everything to him: he'll come with tablecloths and waitstaff and dress up the old locker room into something magical. We put together our event piece by piece on personal acquaintance, truly Iceland-style. A friend of Hulda's uncle has some old cars and says he'll polish one up and drive us around in it. The photographer worked on the wedding of Waingro and Ella. Our priest has been with Hulda's family forever, with the added benefit that he's formally allocated to the district church of Þingvellir, the oldest church in the Land. Our nuptials will be registered on sacred Viking ground.

By the beginning of August, the guests start to arrive. One particular Icelandair redeye from Boston is especially jammed with family and friends, and Hulda's people take them all in with style and grace. We do a big rehearsal in the church, and try to brief the English speakers on all the beautiful traditions of Icelandic weddings. And then the big day arrives. We are married on 7 August 2010, smiling brightly at each other across the altar.

25

CAVALRY

WHILE I'm off getting married and taking our foreign guests around, developments inside the FME unfold with uncharacteristic speed. We took time to hash out every detail, but once everything was decided our new staff arrived quickly. Four of them join Högni in our group, and we will share a new administrative assistant with Binni's team of four. Three new legal staff will serve in a pool reporting to Sigrún. Binni and I went back and forth to pick our team members. I play a bit of poker: make a big deal about wanting certain people, but then relent and let Binni have them. In this way I manage to get exactly the new staff I most want to spend my days with.

We had to find a way to narrow down the hundreds of applications FME received for these investigative positions. I created a case study from part of the Marple investigation, but changed around all the dates, amounts, and names. The applicants got a timeline of events and details, and within this narrative at least seven items might cause an experienced or inquisitive person to raise his eyebrows. Each candidate had 90 minutes to read over the case, describe the biggest red flags, and generate an investigation plan for the next steps. The disparity of answers we received back from my test scenario genuinely surprised me. Some of those with the most beautiful résumés nonetheless returned hasty and ill-considered answers, one only a few incomplete sentences long. But then, one person who had no work experience at all and came straight out of university answered very thoughtfully, including making a convincing investigation plan. We used these test case results to create our interviewee list. This quantitative process sometimes meant hiring people with less or more varied experience.

Like us at the FME, the Office of the Special Prosecutor started out with only a handful of staff. The special prosecutor was able to expand that office, partially by taking over the entire open casebook of the economic crimes unit of the national police, and grew his team to over 100 people. It was his success in requesting additional resources that at last guilted Sigrún and FME management into taking action to expand our tiny investigation team of three. More than a hundred is a lot for a small country, but not compared to the number of employees still working at the collapsed banks, and certainly not a lot compared to the number needed to investigate all of the complex financial crimes we have uncovered.[59]

We end up with an investigation team of 16, which is still nowhere near enough. By comparison, the Enron Task Force numbered in the hundreds, with seasoned investigators allocated from multiple branches of the United States government including the IRS, the Justice Department, and the SEC. And that was to investigate only one firm. We have three collapsed firms of that size, as well as dozens of smaller savings banks and investment companies, and only 16 people. And the authorization to make even those hires has been a struggle.

Our new staff arrive at the beginning of September. Some of them are, like me, former employees of the failed banks, including the

---

59 It would however have been very difficult to bring in outside resources to investigate these banks, at least on the government side. The country was in dire economic circumstances after the crisis, and with a very weak currency was not very able to afford the services of investigative firms from outside Iceland. The winding-up boards of each bank did have enough assets in some cases to hire outside investigators to look into some of the open matters within those institutions.

one who will become my deputy. Sharp, iron-willed, and a diligent worker about my age, her knowledge and insight are honestly a bit intimidating. I make sure my new team has their desks, give them tons to read, outline some small cases they can begin, and leave them under the care of the now senior and experienced Högni. He'll know how to keep them more than busy and help them find their bearings while I'm off for two weeks. Finally our honeymoon has arrived: first an Italian beach and then what turns out to be a very intensive paragliding course in Verbier in the Swiss Alps.

Upon my return, I present the big Kaupþing market manipulation case to all of our new investigators: both my new team and Binni's as well. Many of them have had the chance to read it over during my weeks of sand and mountains. This case on its own can actually come across quite dry, just day upon day of trading data. But when I lead the team through the whole narrative—the stock exchange, the colluding trading desks, the backdoor companies with silly names— ears perk up. Sure, their eyes might have flicked across the headlines that FME was looking at some big cases—but having the nuts and bolts of the scam laid bare is another matter entirely.

Show the timeline—how this had been going on for years and years, in fact throughout all of the golden years of the Icelandic miracle—and their eyes begin to get wide. Then I build the story to the final months and weeks when the prop desk was buying virtually all of the shares that came across the market, making tremendous cash outlays known to the senior-most executives in the bank, themselves household names in the Land. By this point anyone with any financial market background is sitting in shock. Our new teams prove no exception: first stunned, and then angry. I hope to light a fire under all the important investigations yet to come. The big market abuse cases form just the outermost layer of the onion.

The shape of my weeks is changing now that I have a team. More meetings, less digging and investigating on my own. One thing holds, though: the ancillary work entertainment and events that the FME employees seem to love are still coming at us in full force. This autumn each floor of the agency must hold a Friday party with a theme. Our investigation teams all sit on the fifth floor, and our crew organizes a pink party, with pink outfits mandatory on the day. Mid-afternoon all the investigations shut down so we can get prepared. An especially brilliant young investigator files away his sheaf of case papers and makes a run to Ríkið, the state-run booze store, for crates of Breezers and beers. Another investigator decks the walls and desks with pink streamers and balloons, and by 16:00 people are starting to trickle up from the lower floors. We fight hard to ensure that the fifth floor receives the most points in the inter-floor rivalry. The third floor had done their own theme party two weeks before, and we think these pink balloons are really gonna seal the deal for us.

FME is, after all, a very typically Icelandic workplace. Despite the attempts most staff make to execute their duties professionally, the Icelandic blending of work with personal life often overrides. One of the office admins shouts across the floor at me one Friday lunchtime preceding an FME party, "Jared minn! Eigum við ekki bara að detta í það í kvöld?" Or, "My Jared! Shouldn't we just fall into it tonight?" Getting rip-roaring drunk together is the cornerstone of many a friendship in the Land.

26

THE THIRD THIEF

AFTER Kaupþing and then Landsbanki, the time has come to look at the third biggest institution, Glitnir. We have been dreading looking into this bank. Even by the flimsy standards of the other two, it was a ramshackle operation. For example, they seem to have restructured their entire senior management plus division structure every six to eight weeks during 2007 and 2008, so it takes one member of our team nearly a month of full-time work to piece together a series of org charts just to know the very basics: who reported to whom and when. And even with her new charts, a lot of questions remain.

Add to this a new dimension in complexity: immediately following the collapse, each bank was split into two, a new and an old bank. Foreign journalists interpret this as good bank and bad bank, which might be a reasonable assumption. By this they assume that good loans and other good assets would be placed in one stable entity for the future, while non-performing loans and shady securities would be placed in a different, bad entity.

Icelanders, however, have their own ideas of what constitutes good and bad. A first-pass, default assumption in Iceland would be that everything of the Land itself is good. Everything 'across the stones', *í útlöndum* (in the out-lands), over the seas from the country is bad. This applies to individuals just as much as it applies to financial instruments. In the heat of the crisis, when they needed to partition the banks, Icelanders placed all the domestic assets and liabilities in the new bank and the foreign stuff in the old one. This method was in keeping with Icelandic psychology, although not so much with the numbers; many of the foreign assets (like investments in real-economy companies and real estate abroad) had significant value whereas many of the domestic assets (loans to bankrupt sham Icelandic investment companies, for example) were worth zero.

As an example of this partition, we now have old Glitnir and new Glitnir, the second one having been created out of thin air and given a gift of all domestic loans, deposits, employees, and the brand and logo and allowed to keep running its local banking business within days of the meltdown. The old Glitnir was left with foreign loans, foreign obligations, and a massive IOU against the new Glitnir for all the domestic pieces of the bank.

Guðfinnur, the same FME apparatchik who handles bank regulation (and who dragged me to the fruitless meeting with the B-list suits), is responsible for the monitoring of this new arrangement, but the partition of the banks also severely hampers our investigations. Strictly speaking, the legal entities under investigation are the old banks. They were the ones in business before the crisis, the ones that illegally bought up their own shares, the ones that broke so many other laws. But today, post-crisis, these 'old' institutions have been reduced to tiny offices staffed with lawyers winding things down, paying off creditors and getting ready to close the doors. Most of the information we need and all of the loyal employees are sitting in the new banks, the real banks, which have been up and running the whole time like nothing ever happened. The division between old and new amounts to an extra layer of misdirection for an investigator.

Our preliminary work shows us that with Glitnir, as with Kaupþing and Landsbanki, some internal traders were buying up the bank's own shares on the market each day to keep the public deceived that this junk had real value. We need to confirm then that these traders were on the prop desk, spending the bank's own money to do the buying. For this we simply need the list of names of prop desk traders and their boss. However, who worked the prop desk of Glitnir during these years is murky indeed: the bank organization charts are as fickle as the chattering class of professional Eurovision pundits in the Land (yes, this is a real thing).

We need this in writing, so send a letter to the old Glitnir asking for clarification. It's a pretty straightforward request: who was working prop desk on these periods of heavy share buying? Please let us know in the next two weeks. But nothing comes back at all, not even an acknowledgment of receipt of the request: no phone call, no email, no snail mail. Ignoring the FME's requests, even after such a massive regulatory failure as the Great Icelandic Crisis of 2008, is still very much par for the course. Iceland is a culture where finding ways to skirt laws and regulations is a celebrated pastime dating back to settlement times.

Indeed, stacked up against the actions of a celebrated outlaw like *Eiríkur rauði* (Erik the Red), the man who named Greenland in a brazen Viking marketing attempt and subsequently lured hundreds of Icelanders away to his frozen colonies there, what's ignoring another annoying letter from the FME? The lackadaisical attitude pervades: to be serious about enforcement in Iceland requires some persistence and pushiness, maybe a bit like that displayed by old Eiríkur himself. Högni, who had sent the original request and is getting worried at this callous lack of response, calls the old Glitnir for an update. They don't even bother to return his call and he comes to me, worried. "What should we do?"

"Grab your coat," I say, "let's take a drive."

We go outside to my trusty 14-year-old silver RAV4 and drive down to the offices of the old Glitnir. They have rented a floor or two in a dingy building on a side street behind Borgartún, the ugly commercial strip that's styled itself the Wall Street of Iceland. I could see the resemblance—that is, if the Street was a collection of car washes and protein shake stores. You'd never guess the legal address of one of history's largest bankruptcies was there.

The main door is locked so we ring the bell and wait. The

receptionist is a crafty woman in her late 40s. She cracks open the door and peers around it.

"Do you have an appointment? Anyone expecting you?" she asks.

"No, we are from the FME. We are here to see your general counsel," I say.

"Oh, *strákar*," she says. Her tone and choice of words is meant to indicate that we are naughty boys. She opens the door and whisks us into a conference room just off the reception area.

The GC comes in not long after, affable and accommodating. "We got your letter," he says, "but the new bank has all this data and they still haven't come back to us. Let's get them on the phone and figure this out."

He punches some numbers on the speakerphone, and right away it's clear who owns the voice at the other end. The head of compliance of the new bank is the same guy who was in charge of compliance at the old bank before the collapse. This type of baked-in conflict of interest and conflict of role appears so common as to be unquestioned in the post-crisis financial landscape. This guy has an interesting nickname too. Although I insist on calling him by his given name, he likes to be called *Reddari*: the Fixer.

"Ho ho ho!" the Fixer says. "Yes we got your request and we are working on that!" Full of confidence, his jolly voice booms down the line.

I glance at my colleague Högni, a nice guy, a bit shy. He's mostly been impassive since the beginning of this trip down information lane, but his nostrils flare at the sound of the Fixer's false good humor.

"OK," says the General Counsel, turning to us, "so you can follow up directly with the Fixer." No need to come back here, he doesn't need to add.

Now we have what we need: the green light to bypass the old bank and go directly to the source. We have followed the right channels, proceeded up the chain of command. "See you soon," I say, bending close to the speakerphone. We shake hands with the GC in a quick goodbye. The receptionist wags her finger at us. Hey, isn't this the job?

Now the chase is on. We are both fired up as we dash across partially frozen puddles to my old car. On the move again, rolling out to the real Glitnir HQ at Kirkjusandur, the Church Sands. I'm feeling nervous, too, though I attempt to hide it. Going on these spontaneous visits always wracks my nerves. But having Högni along helps keep it under control. He knows the case inside out, he is ten times the analyst I am, and he has dug really deep on these trades. He's a native-born Icelander and that too is a comfort. No issue with the content, no issue with language, and less issue with the ever-present prejudice against those born abroad.

We haven't reached the parking lot of Glitnir Bank a handful of minutes later when my personal mobile phone lights up. It's a number I don't know.

"Hallo?" On the other end is the Fixer. He's not supposed to call on a personal cell, he should have called the switchboard at the regulator first. He must have scrambled online in these few minutes and looked up my personal mobile in the Icelandic phone directory. This smacks of desperation. And now this guy is *really* getting on our nerves.

"We don't think you should come today," he continues. "The person responsible for this work is home with a sick child." He's deploying the oldest excuse in the Icelandic professional playbook, the dog-ate-my-homework of the Icelandic business world. I've been here nearly seven years now and am far too seasoned not to see through this charade.

"It's merely an IT issue," he adds, now tying in the business world's number one global excuse, "this guy is the only one who can access these systems."

"Can't this man be reached at home?" I ask. "Doesn't he have a phone there?" Then: "We will talk about it in person soon anyway. We're just arriving. See you in a minute." We are in the parking lot of the bank, pulling into a visitor space at the main entrance.

As we come through the revolving door, ducking quickly into the warmth, we hear someone running down the stairs into the lobby. Then we make out the portly silhouette of the Fixer rounding the final flight. We don't even bother to announce ourselves to the receptionist.

"Welcome, please, come in, come in!" he says, all smiles and good humor again, pumping our hands in enthusiasm. We follow him into the elevator and up to the third floor. We sit down in a conference room at a table piled high with papers. Högni's letter is there in the middle of one pile, in a plastic sleeve.

"See, I have the request right here," the Fixer waves the folio proudly, to show how good he is at cooperation. "I used to work at the FME, you know," he says. "It was before your time, but I worked very closely with…" and thus begins his attempt at name-dropping and rank-pulling.

Högni and I remain unmoved. "So, let's see what we have here!" he continues. And now it becomes clear that this is the first time he has even really read the request letter, nearly a month old. I can also tell that nobody has ever dealt with him like this. Despite the chaotic collapse of the bank for which he supervised compliance, and for which he somehow still miraculously works, he's never experienced even the mild pressure of a couple of mid-level regulatory employees on an unannounced visit.

He soon gets the famed "IT guy" on the speakerphone from his home. But it turns out to be just another smokescreen. The IT guy says, no, I've told you before, that information resides with the SAP lady. "Well, we'll just have to talk to her and get back to you," the Fixer says to us, ready to end the meeting.

"Why don't we go speak to the SAP lady now?" Högni tells him. My reserved teammate is beginning to bristle at the audacity of these Icelandic compliance types; for me it's not the first time I've tried to make them dance.

The Fixer gets on the phone, and sure enough, the SAP lady is not suffering from a sick child. In fact, she works just down the hall on the same floor. He leads us reluctantly down the hall to her office and she suggests another conference room. She is somewhere between 50 and 60 years old and not happy about missing her afternoon coffee break. It becomes obvious that this is the first she has even heard of this request.

"What's your question for her?" the Fixer asks, trying to make it seem like we are the ones getting put on the spot.

"You've had the letter for more than three weeks. You even read it?" My patience is by now wafer-thin.

Högni steps in to smooth things over, his voice nonetheless shaking with exasperation. He explains what we need: employee records for who worked on the Glitnir prop desk and when. She pulls up the information on the conference room screen in less than 30 seconds. Högni suppresses a huge smile of relief, and seeing the first of the names, starts digging in with specific questions. Jumping up to point at the screen on the wall: "This guy, was he fired or transferred internally?"

The woman states that she needs a few hours to cross-check the results and give us a proper written answer. "We'll send it to you tomorrow by ten o'clock," the Fixer intervenes. We thank the hapless SAP lady and head downstairs with the Fixer. He shakes hands with us at the bottom of the stairs.

"Always nice to see you guys, but Jared, please make an appointment next time," he says with a nervous smile.

"You know we never need an appointment," I smile back, fingering the FME badge. "We'll hear from you tomorrow."

The sense of unease I felt all through these interactions doesn't vanish in the evening, nor when I wake up the next day and get ready for work. The Fixer himself makes me uneasy: he likes to buddy-buddy with us but does not take the formal legal requests of his regulator at all seriously, despite the fact that this agency is now clearly investigating the actions of the bank for which he handled compliance. During the time he held this important role, his employer likely committed the third-largest market abuse of all time, worldwide, as it sought to keep pace with its domestic peers in the number one and number two slots.

From these three disgraced banks we see no humility at all; we have to push hard for every scrap. Gathering even the most basic information involves a sort of a crusade against red tape, bad faith, incompetence, and organizational jigsaw.

I try to concentrate on one of my many open cases that morning, but at ten sharp Högni leans around the side of my cubicle, looking worried. Exactly what has been bugging me ever since we left Glitnir the day before: they (of course) haven't done as they promised, again.

"Let's wait another hour," I tell Högni, knowing pretty well nothing will happen in the next 60 minutes. At 11, we ring the Fixer. "Where are the names?" I ask. "We haven't received anything. We'll see you again after lunch if we don't get them by then." I hang up before he can come up with more excuses.

This finally proves enough. The Fixer collects the names—all five of them: three on the prop desk and two garden-variety brokers—and has them set out in a formal letter by the time Högni goes down to Kirkjusandur to collect it. In the end, we had to go through all this drama to take delivery of a single sheet of paper listing the names of five people and their departments. Granted, the bank HR system may not be 100% accurate—perhaps they needed to confirm some information internally, or their SAP and Excel records do not always sync. But still, what an endeavor to come home with the most basic facts! We investigators end up becoming experts in the banks' internal systems and management information. This phenomenon parallels the big share-buying schemes themselves: virtually nobody on the inside of the banks had the same broad view of the fraud as we are able to piece together. But too late.

On his return from the Church Sands, I see Högni laughing triumphantly with the team, recounting our adventure at Glitnir. ("And then he said: 'You know we don't need an appointment!'") It feels like we won this week and now this investigation can move forward after months of stagnation. Comic relief like this inspires the team, and, frankly, me too. Making a case like this requires so many intricate tactics, so much patience and energy, and I am suddenly exhausted from it all. I decide not to think about how many more expeditions of this sort we will have to launch to build the big Glitnir case, and join in the laughter and storytelling in the bright light of our little circle on the top floor of the FME.

27

INSIDE JOB

WITH these robust teams of investigators, we can now at last begin to really dig into the failed banks. Because my team has one more member than Binni's, we have also stepped up to take on all the potential cases of insider trading. To date, we have amassed a list of dozens of individuals and trades, meaning potentially years of work ahead. We now need to decide which cases to tackle first. Sigrún, Binni, and I maintain a shared mind map showing all the open potential issues by institution, but these insider deals have until now been an afterthought. Now we have the luxury of including them in our master investigation plan.

One big insider case has already left for the prosecutor. The events took place just days before the collapse, in mid-September 2008. The head of the finance ministry learned about the poor state of the finances of Landsbanki in the course of a confidential high-level meeting with that bank's CEO. A large shareholder himself, the official realized that the institution was in real trouble. The day after the meeting, he rang up his broker and told him "sell!" He owned around $2.3m of shares in Landsbanki, which he simply unloaded, then left the proceeds sitting in his savings account. This cash on deposit was soon after that insured at 100% thanks to the emergency law passed by the Icelandic parliament, while the bank's shares dropped in value to 0.

But this really obvious case only scratches the surface. Such insider dealing pops up everywhere we look, in and around each big bank. The clusters of smaller thrifts and investment companies seem to be even dirtier. Not all the potential cases look to be as spectacular as a high-ranking government official using privileged information to preserve his own financial well-being. But the pervasiveness of this type of activity is stunning. Every stone we turn over is squirming underneath.

A particular pattern jumps out at us right away. It looks like an open-and-shut case. One of my new colleagues gets hooked. The behavior of this insider seems particularly egregious: every once in a while my teammate will laugh out loud as he reads a new email or makes a new connection, and the rest of us jump up to crowd around him and see what he has found. From moments like these we find the motivation to press forward on what is most of the time very tedious work.

Friðfinnur Ragnar was the deputy treasurer of Glitnir. In this role he served as the head of inter-bank borrowing, meaning he secured the credit from larger financial institutions abroad that could keep the Icelandic entity afloat. His was a supremely important role in the bank, as the very existence and ability of the institution to operate day-to-day was contingent on a steady supply of these large loans and credit lines.

Commensurate with his high status, Friðfinnur received a grant of over 2m shares of Glitnir, his own employer, at the beginning of 2008. (One of the ways Glitnir dumped the excess equity it had illegally bought on the open market was giving it out to its top employees for free.) But right away he began selling what he had received, a little at a time, until he was rid of it all. He sold Glitnir shares in January, February, March, April, May, and September of 2008. Right after that, his bank collapsed.

To his credit, Friðfinnur did ask his head of compliance for permission to sell the shares, at least before completing his first trade. He wrote an email directly to the Fixer, asking if it was OK. The Fixer wrote back, "Are you sure you're not an insider?" To which Friðfinnur replied that he wasn't an insider.[60] Approved. Game on.

Despite his claim to the contrary, it seems to us that Friðfinnur was actually the consummate insider, one of the few executives who knew the real-time story of the failing bank. For the whole period he unloaded his shares, Friðfinnur was the point man on the deteriorating cash status of Glitnir. The emails he wrote and the meetings he attended bore this out. By the beginning of March 2008, things were looking especially tough for the bank. Friðfinnur sent an email on 4 March to the other senior executives, warning them of the imminent danger and referring to the bank's credit lines with a maritime metaphor: "We have used our rescue boats a few times now and the beautiful new rescue boat [an expected credit line from Citibank] is half finished in the dry dock."

Four days later, Friðfinnur attended a treasury meeting where the discussion centered on the fact that the bank was burning through its cash reserves, and was down €400m since the beginning of the year. Then, on 10 March, he sent yet another urgent email imploring the executive team to "draw down the Deutsche Bank credit line sooner rather than later" because they would have to wait 20 days to receive the cash from the big German lender.

Two days later, on 12 March 2008, he sold 250,000 shares and pocketed $63,000 for himself.

The pattern continued like this. The same day as this trade, 12

60 Quotations paraphrased.

Iceland is a member of the European Economic Area, and as such is bound by treaty to incorporate all of the securities law of the EU into its national legislation. The relevant provision covering insider trading in this case was the EU Market Abuse Directive of 2003, set down in Icelandic law 108/2007. Under this statute, inside information is defined as non-public information that if disclosed would have a significant effect on the price of a security. Insiders are defined *inter alia* as those who have access to such information in the course of their duties as managers.

March, he emailed his colleagues to say that the bank would need to borrow an additional €1.6bn, with the cash on hand now down €515m.

Two days later Friðfinnur and other top executives received an infamous email from the head of Glitnir's leveraged finance division, urging them to seek immediate cash assistance from the central bank of Iceland. On this day the London branch of Glitnir had lost a credit line worth £76bn, and the mother bank in Iceland owed 90bn Icelandic *krónur* over the next 30 days and could not pay. So came the famous line: "*Að öðrum kosti verða hlutabréf bankans svo gott sem verðlaus um páskana.*" This lovely Icelandic prose has the rhythm of grizzled Vikings rowing an open boat across a rain-spattered fjord, and it translates as: without an emergency loan, the shares in the bank will be as good as worthless come Easter.

On 15 March, it turned out that the "beautiful new rescue boat" from the 4 March email would remain indefinitely in dry dock; Citibank pulled access to the €435m credit line. Next came a treasury meeting on 26 March where Friðfinnur reiterated that the bank could not cover its obligations with the cash on hand. Two days after that, Friðfinnur sent an email with the subject line "it gets worse": trust in Glitnir was by then so low that Svenska Handelsbank would not even agree to a spot FX deal, a same-day cash trade, with the Icelandic bank.

By the last day of March 2008, deposits at the London branch of Glitnir had dropped by £440m since January, and management expected a further outflow of £380m. Also, the Bank of England was no longer accepting most of the bank's collateral. Meaning, they wouldn't lend to Glitnir. The Icelandic bank was failing.[61]

So Friðfinnur did some more selling. On 3 April and 9 April 2008, he dumped 500,000 more shares in his own bank and pocketed over $120,000 from those two trades. In May he dumped 300,000 more shares and took home nearly $64,000. Things slowed down over the summer and then in a final two trades in September, he converted all

---

61 Glitnir managed to stay alive for a few more months by selling off some of its assets to raise cash. In this way, it was the only Icelandic bank to begin to wind itself down before the October 2008 crisis.

his remaining shares into cash. Less than three weeks after his last sale, Glitnir shares were no longer trading at all, with a listed value of 0.

In all, in 2008 Friðfinnur sold more than 2m shares in his own bank, all the while attending meetings and sending emails to indicate that the institution was on its last legs. His total proceeds were nearly 35m ISK, or more than $468,000.[62] Reading over his emails and the minutes of the meetings he attended, we have to grudgingly appreciate his shameless bravado.

With this case at last written up and ready to send to the prosecutor, we turn back to our spreadsheet of insider cases. There are already dozens more to go, and the list grows with each new file we open.[63]

62 *Hæstiréttur Íslands*, case number 193/2013.
63 One of the next files we open is a long-lasting insider trading scam being run by a prop trader at a small bank. He sits across the trading desk from brokers who are taking large orders from the Icelandic pension funds. When he hears a big order come through on the phone, he quickly books a trade to front run the bigger price-moving order, not in his own name but in the name of one of his childhood friends. In this way his friend profits by a few thousand dollars at a time, at the expense of the legitimate client, and the men share instant messages to celebrate their windfall profits and then go back and forth about which hunting gear they should buy with the proceeds.

The identity of the prop trader? He's the same "good man" from the fruitless meeting in chapter 24.

28

THE DAWN RAID

O N a dark November morning in 2010 I get out of bed extra
early. I have to report to the office of the special prosecutor at
06:30 and not a minute later. I park across the street at the same hotel
where our wedding guests stayed and walk to the seaside building
in a stinging rain. Friendly faces greet me. Someone holds the door
open. The small cafeteria is warm and cozy, but also full of nervous
energy, already jammed with uniformed and plainclothes police, and
seemingly the entire 100-person staff of the prosecutor. Someone
has brought some pastries but they're mostly going uneaten. Coffee
is, however, being copiously slurped. I grab a cup myself and sit at
a cafeteria table, flipping idly through *Morgunblaðið*, waiting for the
organizers to send us off.

They've told us this will be the largest search and seizure in
Icelandic history, and it has been meticulously planned. Teams will
search around 20 first targets, homes and offices, simultaneously at
08:00 in Reykjavík, Akureyri, and even tiny Hvolsvöllur, a village a
few hours' drive to the east. Following that, there will be a second
and even third wave of sites.

The teams are five or six strong. I have brought a few FME
investigators along for the experience, but those of us from the

199

regulator are thankfully allocated to different crews, each headed by a seasoned officer. The head of my search squad is a lanky chain-smoking police detective, a tough-guy loner with whom I have only ever exchanged grudging nods—and always secretly feared.

Then the door frame fills, and we get a gentle pep talk from Heavy Special himself. The cafeteria empties rapidly, men and women streaming down the stairs. Outside I look for our team leader, who ushers us toward a silver Toyota Land Cruiser. The raid is so big that the police needed to requisition extra vehicles to get everyone around. The big truck, normally rented by well-heeled foreign tourists, has thankfully been running and is warm and dry inside.

Our team has been assigned to search the Reykjavík offices of Saga Capital, high in the city's only skyscraper. It's a short quiet ride in the dark. I try to look calm, but inside I am shaking. I can feel the same nervous energy in the others around me. The darkness is like a sixth person in the car with us. It's nearly 08:00 now. It won't begin to get light for another two and a half hours.

The cop driving pulls us up on the sidewalk in front of the glass high-rise. The building is still partially completed and we ride a cardboard-lined elevator in silence to the 17th floor. Arriving in the foyer, we see the glass doors frosted with the Saga Capital logo. But our entrance proves to be anticlimactic; apparently nobody works here at this early hour. The reception area is vacant.

We hear the noises of a drip coffee machine being put into service and then the receptionist appears from around the corner. She's visibly on edge.

The slim detective breaks the silence. "We are here to speak with the head of this office."

"Was he expecting you?" she asks, her voice trembling a little.

"No, this is a police raid," he says, letting his badge holder drop open. I have never seen an Icelandic police badge before. It is much bigger than I would have guessed. Carried in a black leather folio shaped like a sandwich board, it seems to be about the size of a license plate. The poor woman's face turns white.

She drops into the chair behind her desk and he shows her the search warrant. She tells us the head of the office is on his way in to work now. The detective says we will take over the boardroom while we wait for him to arrive. The receptionist seems to relax a little. I feel sorry for her.

Inside the boardroom, our leader passes out copies of the search warrant, stating the names of several shell companies on which we are seeking documents and info. It is not a case with which I am very familiar, having been run out of Binni's team at FME, and with more work done since by the prosecutor's people. I read over the list of inscrutable names, trying to memorize as much as possible. Then I notice the man named as the head of this office on the warrant. In my excitement over the raid, I have completely forgotten who the local office head of Saga Capital is: the old head of asset management at Landsbanki, the one who wouldn't let me go until the cakes came.

And here he comes into the conference room now. Smooth and calm, with a long black cashmere overcoat hiding his pot belly, the office chief is a model executive. Unlike his receptionist, he doesn't seem at all nervous. He notices me right away and nods without surprise. The detective lays out the parameters of the raid. One policeman, an IT specialist, will go to the server room and start an immediate extraction of the emails of several employees. The rest of the team will search the desks of staff, looking for material on the companies listed in the warrant.

The executive says he will need to go and call the CEO of the firm, his high school friend in Akureyri, to let him know of the raid.

"Trust me, he knows," says our detective.

The guy keeps inventing reasons to go to his office and make a phone call.

"You can make any call you need to from here," says our lead cop.

All at once the raid is moving fast: the detective has to take a call on his cell, the cops are all in the server room and suddenly I am there alone in the boardroom with my old boss. "How do you like it at FME?" he asks. The attempt at chit-chat surprises me and I don't know how to answer. I keep my replies monosyllabic.

Luckily, our leader appears again, framed by the conference room door, staring directly at the office head. "We will go into the main offices now, so maybe it's a good idea to get your people out of there." Turning to me, "OK, Jared, you know what you are looking for, go get it."

The exec leads us down to the other end of the building, where most of the desks are located. The open-plan office is walled on three sides by floor-to-ceiling glass. Beyond, it's pitch-black. The endless rainy night of winter Iceland.

Since our arrival, a few employees have trickled in, unaware they've walked into a raid. Their boss goes ahead of us, turning the corner into a partitioned area. I can't hear what he says, but three vacating workers come past us with puzzled looks on their faces.

I recognise the third one. He's my old direct supervisor from Landsbanki. Skinny-tie man! The one who threw me under the bus over the mysterious cash wires. The one I quit rather than be fired by. Recognizing me walking past him, still clad in my black raincoat, flattened cardboard boxes and packing tape in hand, it's like his face is suddenly made of rubber. I have of course heard of someone's jaw dropping, but this is the only time I have ever seen the thing really happen. Then I am past him and into the large four-person office space.

Inside, it's just another office in an Icelandic financial firm: an outward sense of sparse organization that belies the dusty, chaotic jumble of binders and loose papers tucked out of sight. I start with the bookcase behind one desk, while my colleagues seize and tag a laptop. I go through each binder, looking for any of the names on the search warrant. It's stressful work, as it needs to be done with perfect accuracy yet with thousands of pages of documents in this messy collection of binders. I can also feel the edginess in the cops working nearby.

I find one binder that appears to refer to a different kind of financial crime, and one that was popular post-crisis: using falsified invoices to cheat the Icelandic central bank out of its meager supplies of foreign currency, in effect stealing again from an already-gutted Icelandic society.[64] This blatant fraud became a popular money-making scheme among many ex-bankers in the Land, some of whom even set up consulting companies to exploit it. I call our leader over and ask if we can take this evidence as well. "Do you want it, Jared?" he asks. "Yes," I say. "Then take it."[65]

After about an hour, we have gone through everything. We leave most of it behind. The majority of the contents consisted of junk like slideshow decks for investment 'opportunities' run by other dodgy firms. We do, however, find three or four binders referring to companies listed in the warrant. These we log on inventory sheets and place inside a cardboard box that we seal onsite. By this time Þorvaldur Luðvík, the CEO of Saga Capital, has arrived. He wasn't in Akureyri after all. He strides into the room as we are wrapping up, his face bright red. I am standing at the front with my hand on top of the sealed evidence boxes, waiting for the all-clear to carry them outside. 'Lulli' stands across the boxes from me, veins in his forehead bulging. He looks like he might punch me in the face and grab the evidence.

But then we roll out. Our leader asks the CEO to come with him separately. He arrests him in the elevator as they descend.

Back at the prosecutor's place it's just beginning to get light. As we pull up to a parking space across from the main doors, I see the cameras. I am going to have to carry one of these evidence boxes inside, right across the path of a TV crew and some news photographers. I put on my best face, avoid eye contact, and walk with determination into the building and straight to the giant evidence room.

Back upstairs in the cafeteria, the mood is jubilant. Many of the

---

64 One of the principal efforts at stabilization of the economy after the crisis was the imposition of capital controls. This meant that from inside the country, one could only exchange ISK for hard currency, like USD, GBP, or EUR, by presenting an invoice for goods or services from abroad. But by dummying up a fraudulent invoice, a scammer could get hard currency wired from Iceland into a foreign bank account at the central bank's favorable rate. Then he could use the hard currency to buy unwanted ISK from overseas at a much cheaper rate, printing profits at the expense of his countrymen.

65 Upon subsequent examination back in the evidence room, there is not enough to build a case, and we return the binders.

search teams have returned. Released from the stress of the raids, and with the protective walls of the prosecutor's office around us, we are free to share stories. Now the pastries are being gobbled down, and coffee consumption continues to be high even by Icelandic standards. So much has happened across the Land in the last few hours. But we are only in the eye of the storm; in a few minutes we will have to head out again, to hit the second round of search sites. What a gruelling day.

That night, the clip of me walking with a brown cardboard box rolls over and over on the evening news.

29

IT WON'T HAPPEN AGAIN

I TAKE a week off to do some paragliding in Nice in early December. And return to find that Hulda performed one of her magic tricks. She's found a new place for us! She takes me straight from the airport to look it over and sign the lease. Finally, we are back in Vesturbær, the west end of Reykjavík, the 101, with a big bay window looking out to the sea. Most importantly, we're able to get rid of that albatross around our necks, the old apartment in Kópavogur. Our mortgage balance is still about 10% more than the sale price, the bank having already written off an even larger overhang. But we find a young couple who agree to take both the apartment and the loan as-is, and by the end of the year we are ready to move. We end up paying the realtor a million *krónur* for finding us these 'buyers'.

The next year, 2011, turns out to be a good one for our newly formed investigation teams. We close the big Glitnir market manipulation case in March and send it to the special prosecutor. And the team becomes a machine. We standardize our investigative processes and our referrals are getting better and better. A crack young lawyer helps us create standard templates for each kind of criminal case and makes sure all our dozens of cases pass legal muster before going out the door. Things click, we are in the groove. We have even moved offices and no longer have to walk past a noodle shop on the way to work; now we are high up in one of Iceland's two skyscrapers (the same building we raided the previous year!) with a big room for our team where we can finally all sit and work together.

It feels to me like the roles on the team have coalesced. Each person has found his or her niche. The value we are collectively creating is gigantic. My time is becoming freer to get back to my own small collection of open cases. There is just so much to do: uncounted numbers of insider trading cases stand open. The big banks' loan book cases have only been haphazardly tackled, and nobody has yet taken a systematic look at the potential culpability of the Big Four firms (KPMG, PwC, EY, and Deloitte) in Iceland that audited the financial institutions. Then comes Iceland's Housing Finance Fund, which made the strange decision to invest public money in dicey Kaupþing derivatives, the same CLNs as in the Deutsche Bank case actually, just months before the collapse. And the central bank of Iceland, which gave away all of the country's foreign currency reserves, €500m, to Kaupþing just hours before it collapsed. Then add to all this the B-list of collapsed Icelandic financial institutions— savings banks and investment companies—that were up to dirt we haven't even scratched.

This is to list just the events that happened before the crisis, but FME is principally an agency focused on current matters. And there is a lot to suggest that the biggest crimes, like the stealing of money out of the central bank via fraudulent invoices as well as new kinds of insider trades involving Icelandic government bonds, might actually be going on under our noses, three years after the trouble of 2008. In March 2011, my deputy and I kick off a project to try to make sense of all that we are learning, both from the pre- and post-crisis crime wave. What lessons can we at the FME, and Iceland more broadly, learn from this crisis and its aftermath? We don't want to let this opportunity go to waste.

Then in October, just when our little world is starting to feel good and stable, Binni drops a bombshell. He and I meet privately every few weeks to coordinate work and issues on the investigations, but mostly to fight over access to our small pool of shared lawyers. At the end of this meeting he tells me: "I am leaving the FME." He plans to return to the private sector and become managing partner in a corporate advisory firm. And now that he has announced his decision, the true measure of his dislike for this work becomes apparent. I have been savoring the chance to dive deeply into our home-grown equivalent of three simultaneous Madoff scandals,[66] and feel like the fraud behind these giant bank collapses makes for career cases. Binni, on the other hand, tells me he was always eager to get back to the world of corporate finance.

Then, a second bombshell. All of the managers of FME leave for an offsite at Flúðir, a tiny hamlet near the south coast that leads Iceland in the production of mushrooms. On the agenda is a possible restructuring of the agency. In the middle of the morning session, my cell phone lights up. It's Högni. He sounds ten times more distressed than the day Glitnir Bank wouldn't give him his data.

"Jared, I'm really very sorry." His voice is almost a whisper.

"What's going on?" I ask.

He plows ahead: "They wouldn't give me a permanent contract at FME, so I'm gonna have to leave. I got a nice job at the bank. I've got my kids to think about, and my wife is studying abroad soon for a year."

It hits me like a ton of bricks. My heart sinks, my stomach with it. Högni is a key man, the master of all of the trading data for all the investigations, and indeed all the hard-core number crunching we need for cases across both investigation teams. He is also by now one of our most seasoned investigators, with an encyclopedic knowledge of our past and future cases.

Unbeknownst to me, and because he was originally hired as 'temporary' help before all the others on the teams joined, Högni was never given a permanent contract. I always assumed that his employment was permanent; he always assumed I knew it wasn't. Sigrún knew the situation all along but kept me in the dark. Now

---

66   Or 26 simultaneous Allen Stanford Ponzi schemes!

he's walking out the door. Without Högni, we will need to spend months getting a new resource up to speed on all the data analysis we need. It is a hollowing loss.

The approaching departure of Binni, and now also of Högni, raises the question of the future of the two investigation teams. Specifically, should we maintain two separate groups going forward? In my opinion, there isn't any longer a need. The cases we open, even across financial institutions, are intertwined. I have thought about making a push to merge the groups under my leadership, but am already so busy that I am not sure if I even want it. So I wait and see what Sigrún has to say about her thoughts for the future.

Soon after, she invites me to her new office. She clearly means to talk about the future of the investigations, but I wait for her to raise the topic. And, as it turns out, she also thinks that forming one big new team makes sense. We discuss the various options but at the end of a three-hour discussion we agree that the way is clear. She asks me whom I'd like to choose as a deputy for the new, merged team, suggesting it should be someone from Binni's team. She closes the meeting by saying she'll let HR know about the plan and we will begin to take it forward the next day.

I go home quite confident about the future—with me as head of a unified team, we will be able to deliver even more comprehensive and useful cases—and tell Hulda about it. I am also quite apprehensive about the new workload, but looking forward to the challenge. I'm thinking that it is going to take a bit more time for the HR and FME senior management to agree on this course of action so I go back to work the next day as if nothing has happened.

I'm taken aback the next morning when Sigrún barges into our team's workroom and tells us she has an announcement to make. We get to our feet uncomfortably; Sigrún is not one to put people at ease. Something doesn't feel right. We stand by our desks in a circle. I feel a growing mistrust.

Sigrún starts by announcing that Binni is leaving for a new challenge. There is a collective gasp. I have known the news for weeks but some on my team look shocked and upset. Then, a little hesitantly, she moves to us and our organization. "We will of course need a new team leader for Binni's team," she says. Wait, what? So, no unified team after all. As if that isn't infuriating enough, she winks at my current deputy at the same time. Then she turns heel and walks out.

I sit at my desk and put the puzzle pieces together. I am fuming at both the deception and the decimation of my team. Högni is going soon, and I don't know how we'll replace him. Another of my team is going back to her studies. A third is leaving for extended paternity leave. And now this: not only does Sigrún announce exactly the opposite of what we agreed yesterday but she seems to want to take my deputy away from me. She will move to run Binni's team of five, while I'm left with only two. I try to calm down—without much success. After a while I can't hold myself back and walk down to her office.

"What about what we agreed during our conversation yesterday?" I ask.

"Oh that? We were just tossing ideas around," she says.

"Tossing ideas around?" I'm startled. "And you're taking my deputy away too? What message should I take from this?"

"I don't see why you should take a message."

"The message I am taking is that you are unhappy with my work and want me gone. You leave me as leader of a team of two."

Then Sigrún plays the classic card. I never thought she would stoop so low. "Perhaps next time we should have the discussion in English so you understand better."

That's enough for me. I tremble with shock—but try to put on a brave face and head back up to the open plan office, where my whole team will see me. We have a lot of candid discussions over the next few days. I realize that of course Sigrún couldn't merge the teams, even though that would have been the right thing to do. She would have put herself out of a job: that of coordinating two separate groups of investigators.

It still doesn't make me feel good about my situation and the way I've been manipulated. Nor does it bode well for the future of investigations at FME, one of the only regulators in Europe not to possess a dedicated enforcement division that handles civil and criminal proceedings.

I take a final shot to save the investigation teams and expertise. I speak to Sigrún's boss, Gunnar Andersen, and explain the situation.

"I don't trust Sigrún anymore, based on her actions. I would like to report directly to you pending the reorganization of FME," I tell him. "Otherwise I don't have a choice but to see that I am being moved out."

"Don't take it like that. I'll think of something to improve your situation. But I can't promise anything."

"Why don't you think about it over this weekend?" I say. "If you can't come back to me with a temporary solution for my role, I will resign."

I wait as promised. A full five days and nothing happens. No word at all from the director general. On the appointed day I walk to his office with my resignation letter and he is out for the day. It seems my days at the agency are soon to be over, the job I loved most of all ending with a whimper. I tender my resignation on a dark day of the first week of November 2011, two and a half years after I joined, in April 2009. I have a three-month notice period and file-cabinet drawers full of open cases. It will take me the full 90 days to wrap those up and try to send as many on for prosecution as possible. But most of all, I want to spend the time I have left working on the lessons learned document, trying to help the Land I love to avoid a crisis like this ever happening again.

I don't get the chance. Sigrún tells me she wants me out by the Friday of that week. And so those open cases and projects remain open forever.

One encounter around this time should have enlightened me about the general attitude toward our investigation work. At the offsite strategy meeting in the mushroom capital of Flúðir, I made the case that going forward the agency needed some enforcement capacity, some team to look at alleged violations at financial companies. But our general counsel told me: "We don't need you or this kind of team anymore. Don't be naïve, the financial crime that happened here, that was all back in 2008. It won't ever happen again." What can I possibly reply to that head-in-the-sand view of the world, after world-class financial crime tore this country to its very core? I am stunned and silent.

Soon after that, she became the head of the FME.

PART III—THE OUTCOME

30

THE GREAT DISMANTLING

WITH my team being taken apart and reassigned from under me, and no clear sign from management that there would be any mandate to continue the investigations, I left the FME in November 2011. In my file drawer were dozens of unresolved cases and open issues. The project to document all the lessons we had already learned in the investigations in order that we might build a more resilient financial sector and a better regulator in the future was another casualty.

Everything was up in the air as the troubled agency was at the start of a restructuring into three new divisions: onsite, offsite, and oversight. There were many ways this new organizational chart made little sense, not least that within this new scheme there was no clearly delineated enforcement division or team. That meant no group within the agency would have the mandate to do investigations of past or future wrongdoing in the Icelandic financial sector.

The chaos at FME continued. As part of the transformation, my former boss Sigrún was relieved of her title and position just days after my departure. She learned that she would be able to re-apply to be a manager in one of the units, along with many other applicants. She departed the agency. The investigation team members themselves were reassigned to new roles and new managers within the new structure. Only a handful of the cases remained open.

I traveled to Switzerland for one week in December 2011, as Hulda and I had been contemplating a move there. The high salaries, higher Alps, and cosmopolitan vibe beckoned. I met with the Swiss regulator FINMA as well as some of the auditing firms, which were building up their own investigation teams.

The director general of FME, Gunnar Andersen, was forced out early in 2012. He had used a contact at Landsbanki, his former employer, plus his status as top dog at FME to try to gain access to bank records linked to a member of parliament. The Landsbanki staffer whom Gunnar had asked for help took the documents to a third person, who delivered them to the tabloid *DV* at Gunnar's request. Gunnar fought against the FME board in the Icelandic press before finally stepping down.[67] With this departure, the chain of command under which I had worked had completely evaporated, mere months later.

There was no enforcement division at the FME when I arrived there. Today there still isn't one. Throughout all the years of the Icelandic banking boom, the regulator had no way to look at trading data in a systematic way, nor was there expertise for email and document searches. The dedicated investigative teams built up a substantial amount of infrastructure, including world-class document search. But, more importantly, during these investigations the FME developed a team of seasoned professionals who dove into some of the largest and highest profile financial crimes in the world. That team was long ago scattered to the four winds.

In March of 2012, I joined my former counterparts at the Office of the Special Prosecutor, where Heavy Special greeted me warmly. By this time the agency had grown to around 120 people. But the job turned out to be disappointing after the big role at the FME. Because a significant percentage of the cases at the prosecutor (around 40

---

67 Gunnar was later convicted in this case and sentenced to 12 months in prison, suspended, by the Supreme Court of Iceland.

Hæstiréttur Íslands, case number 326/2013.

in all) had come from either my team or me, I was forbidden from working on them. A defense attorney could after all point to my repeated involvement as a conflict of interest. I was left with smaller cases, matters that had originated elsewhere in the FME or directly from the old banks. Binni, whose dream job in the private sector quickly turned to dust, came over to join me at the agency and also felt demotivated. As neither of us was a lawyer, we felt marginalized. I participated in one interrogation. During the break, the witness—a former top bank executive who had decamped to Luxembourg and came back for the interview at the request of the prosecutor—let it be known that he knew all about me and my career, seemingly in a bid to throw me off balance. It worked.

During this time, some former colleagues lobbied me to apply for the top role at the FME, director general, convincing me that there would be nobody better suited for this position. I did apply, and made it as far as an interview with the hiring panel. One of the panelists, an economics professor from the University of Iceland, dinged me for not having any formal training in economics or finance. "That's not true," I replied. "I am a CFA charterholder." "Yes, I saw that here, could you explain to us what that is?" replied the professor.

I packed my car with some interview suits and drove to the east of Iceland in early September 2012, to catch the last ferry to Denmark before the winter snows began. After close to four days at sea, I drove off the massive ship and onto the mainland. I made my way down Germany to Switzerland, to pursue a better life for Hulda and myself in Zürich.

At the beginning of 2020, the FME was merged into Seðlabanki Íslands, the central bank of Iceland.

31

WHY DID FME DROP THE BALL?

AFTER the dramatic collapse of the three banks, the build up of investigative capacity at the FME happened at a snail's pace. It took the agency six months to hire its first dedicated investigators—Binni and me—and then another 18 months to get a team approved and hired to help us to conduct the investigations. The FME sent around 80 criminal cases to the prosecutor in all. Yet another 12 months later things were already winding down.

I still do not know exactly what chain of events caused the investigations at the FME to be dropped so rapidly. But I believe both the 2011 restructuring and the subsequent chaos at the top of the agency made good excuses for the incoming management to scuttle the open cases and close things down early. When I left the agency in 2011, although we had successfully investigated the three largest cases of market manipulation in global history, we had only scratched the surface of the potential criminal cases within the big three banks. Most of the ancillary activity that supported this massive share buying we never touched, including never really taking a systematic look at the use of bank loans to prop up the share price over a period of many years. (We did manage to look at some of the larger and more recent loans, but these cases were developed willy-nilly. We never thoroughly cross-checked the biggest sales by the banks' brokerage desks to simultaneous loans by their credit teams. We left some of the largest and most mysterious deals unexamined.)

The massive buying of their own shares over so many years inevitably corrupted every relevant department in each bank, directly contradicting their original purpose: the prop desk traders were supposed to be making profitable trades for their bank's own books, but instead made losing trades in the bank's own shares. The brokerage desk was supposed to be making commissions by executing trades for real customers, but instead they were entering fake trades with bogus customers. The credit department was supposed to be making high-performing loans to good firms that would benefit the bank's future profitability, but instead they were making massive junk loans to offshore firms with no collateral other than the bank's own shares. The risk managers were supposed to be identifying ways the bank could potentially get in trouble down the road, but instead sometimes became patsies for the prop traders, generating on-demand reports on how many shares the bank had bought in itself. The compliance staff were supposed to be ensuring that the bank followed relevant rules and regulations, but in some cases instead were taking it upon themselves to clean up the messes made in the other departments, in order to *become* compliant. This activity also involved the general counsel, the internal auditors, and of course the most senior executives. Some of these departments and employees escaped our scrutiny.

Nor did we get into what was very likely accounting fraud at the big banks. Were their Big Four auditors at all culpable in covering up misleading filings? Broadly speaking, we don't know. (We do know that in one case where the actions of these professionals were examined closely, two auditors from KPMG were found guilty of gross negligence and each sentenced to nine months in prison, although the sentences were suspended. They were also banned from practicing as auditors for a term of six months.[68] They submitted a

---

68 *Hæstiréttur Íslands*, case number 74/2015.

claim to the European Court of Human Rights, which announced in March 2021 that it had "struck the applications out of its list of cases after receiving friendly settlement declarations". In these, "the Icelandic state acknowledged violations of the applicants' right to a fair trial and undertook to pay them €12,000 each".[69]) We also know that many insiders and connected parties to each of the three banks sold shares and profited with impunity.

Leaving aside the big three banks, we also never looked into the role of Nasdaq OMX, the Iceland stock exchange. We know that they made use of the industry-standard market surveillance system and also that the pattern of a single buyer hoarding shares every day in each bank using iceberg orders is almost impossible to miss. Did they know something about the criminal trading patterns that the banks' prop traders engaged in for many years?

Moving outside of the inner circle of Icelandic finance, there was a surprisingly large number of B-list banks and brokerage firms, as well as the regional savings banks. Many of these had collapsed, and we had open files on them, with early signs of staggering malfeasance in several. And even more broadly, the Icelandic industrial sector was certainly tainted by the years of corruption at the banks, with their shares likely stuffed into fishing companies and related shell companies.

Finally, the criminal activity did not stop in 2008. It took on new forms and continued in 2009. We saw some glimmers of this in a 2009 insider trading investigation involving Icelandic government bonds, especially in the massive effort to defraud the central bank of Iceland of its precious remaining foreign currency, which did warrant a small task force. But, generally, nobody was looking at the present day.

Of the potential criminal cases for crisis-related activity that FME could have originated under its governing law and mandate, I estimate that we only conducted serious investigations on under

69 According to the declarations seen by the ECHR, "the applicants are free to apply for the reopening of their cases" hudoc.echr.coe.int/eng-press#{%22item id%22:[%22003-6954127-9356139%22]}

10% of the total. To do the rest would have required a team of 30–40 and an additional five years, a time scale entirely normal in cases of white-collar fraud. To investigate a big case successfully takes deep analysis, and access to documents and materials that the entities and people under investigation often stall in providing. Perhaps asking for this level of resources in such a small economy was too much. But I think we could have done it.

Having said all this, I am proud of the approach we took. We started with the biggest institutions in the economy, and went for the easiest cases we could make that implicated the very top management of each. A spreadsheet[70] from the Icelandic outpost of Transparency International summarizes the good work of FME and especially the staff at the special prosecutor during these frenetic years: 24 criminal cases concluded by the end of 2017, with 71 individual charges (often the same person shows up in a few cases) and a 79% conviction rate in the highest court of the Land, resulting in nearly 88 years of combined prison time.

Contrast this to the U.S. and U.K., where the approach (from the outside, at least) seems to be to go after small institutions and small fry within each. A cursory look down the online press releases of the SEC, the U.S. markets regulator, shows a lot of small-time scammers being stopped in their tracks. But hardly anything about the largest firms on Wall Street. It is the same in London. The number of post-2008 criminal fraud cases in each of these places is vastly smaller than in our tiny economy of Iceland.

But we had an advantage the Americans and Brits did not: the very largest banks in our economy had all crashed, and that gave us what turned out to be a very narrow window to sift through the wreckage and see what we could find. We had these banks frozen in amber in early October 2008, and we could take a microscope to their internal activities. What we found shocked us.

In Iceland, then, it was the opposite problem as in those much larger countries: the very top management did go to prison, but most

70   www.gagnsaei.is/wp-content/uploads/2017/12/Akaerur_og_domar_des2017.pdf

bank employees at middle management on down never really got touched. Our lack of resources saved them.

However, the top men did not go to prison for very long. The maximum sentences in most cases were only a handful of years. Nordic law is very light for these types of crimes, and it is not possible to charge multiple counts of the same crime. In addition, good behavior let most of them out of the Snæfellsnes country-club prison and back to their Reykjavík offices within months. With the bulk of their assets from the last decade safely stashed in Luxembourg, Switzerland, and other offshore destinations, some of these convicts are free to slowly repatriate the money, buying up hotels, real estate, and other assets in Iceland.

32

WHAT HAPPENED
TO THE CASES?[71]

Al-Thani

THE Al-Thani case was the first big 2008-related matter to go before
the Icelandic courts, as the prosecutor saw it as a test case for what
was to follow. Sheikh Al-Thani had lent his name to a 22 September
2008 deal to buy a 5.01% stake in Kaupþing for around $285m (25.6bn
ISK), with the bank in deep trouble just weeks before its ultimate
collapse.[72] But the Sheikh, a Qatari diplomat, didn't actually put up
any cash, and received a $50m fee for his participation in the deal. He
was not charged with a crime.

Remarkably, the defense teams of two of the accused quit at the
same time, days before the trial was initially set to take place in 2012,
a blatant stalling tactic. This had the effect of forcing the proceedings
to be postponed for nearly one full year. In its verdict, the district

---

71 Information on court verdicts, settlements, and other decisions is current to the best
of the author's knowledge as of 19 March 2021, when this book went to press.

72 www.prweb.com/releases/acquires/kaupthing/prweb1372414.htm

court took the unusual step of sanctioning the lawyers who had resigned for their unethical behavior, forcing them to pay a fine of one million ISK each, well under $10,000.[73]

Despite these delaying tactics, on 12 December 2013 the Reykjavík District Court convicted the two highest-ranking Kaupþing executives: Sigurður Einarsson, the executive chairman, and Hreiðar Már Sigurðsson, the CEO. In addition, the court convicted Magnús Guðmundsson, the CEO of Kaupthing Bank Luxembourg and a fourth man, Icelandic businessman and longtime Swiss resident Ólafur Ólafsson, the man who both introduced the Sheikh to the other Icelanders and flew in Elton John for his 50th birthday. Prison sentences ranged from three to five and a half years, and the Icelandic press considered this heavy time. The crimes were market manipulation and also *umboðssvik*: 'agency fraud', or using their positions in the bank for personal gain.

The convictions of the four criminals were upheld in the Icelandic Supreme Court on 12 February 2015, with even longer prison sentences handed down.[74] However, around this time (March 2016) a mysterious change of law enabled convicted white-collar criminals to spend less time behind bars and be transferred early to halfway houses. So these men spent only around one year in prison each, despite having earned much longer terms. Ólafur Ólafsson, for example, returned to his office to work starting in the middle of 2016.[75] He made the news shortly afterward when a thankfully non-fatal helicopter crash in the Icelandic lava revealed that he had been

---

73 Two of the defense attorneys submitted a claim to the European Court of Human Rights, which did not find in their favor. hudoc.echr.coe.int/eng?i=001-187476

74 *Hæstiréttur Íslands*, case number 498/2015.

According to a February 2021 article by Icelandic state television RÚV, the Icelandic state entered into a settlement agreement with Magnús Guðmundsson. The settlement includes the state's recognition that Magnús' right to a fair trial has been violated in both the Al-Thani and the larger Kaupþing market abuse case, the state's payment of €12,000, and recognition that Magnús can request that the two cases be reopened. These represent two of the three cases in which Magnús was convicted.

www.ruv.is/frett/2021/02/20/rikid-vidurkennir-brot-a-retti-magnusar

75 icelandmonitor.mbl.is/news/politics_and_society/2016/04/11/release_of_jailed_bankers_olafsson_returns_to_his_o

choppering around with foreign guests while still technically serving out his prison term.[76]

After the Al-Thani verdict, the defendants subsequently submitted a claim to the European Court of Human Rights, alleging "that in the criminal proceedings against them they had been denied full access to the file held by the prosecution, that insufficient efforts had been made to summon two key witnesses and that the Supreme Court had not been impartial on account of the positions held by family members of one of its judges". The Strasbourg court found indeed that there was a lack of impartiality on the part of one of the Icelandic Supreme Court judges, and dismissed the rest of the complaint. It awarded each defendant €2,000 to partially reimburse their court costs in Strasbourg.[77]

The Al-Thani case has a parallel in a case against Barclays executives in the UK. Qatar Holding, part of the sovereign wealth fund of Qatar, and Challenger, an investment vehicle of the former Qatari prime minister, invested around £4bn in Barclays in June and October 2008. This investment helped to keep the bank afloat, and kept it from having to seek emergency funding from the UK government.

However, the UK Serious Fraud Office accused then-CEO Varley of Barclays and three former colleagues of disguising £322m in kickbacks to Qatar in order to get this deal done. Varley was the only UK banking chief to face a criminal trial over his actions during the 2008 financial crash.

Former CEO Varley was acquitted in the first trial, and in a second trial the three remaining executives were acquitted in February 2020.[78]

This case rings a bell with the Al-Thani case: both seem to involve payments made to wealthy Qataris to get investment deals done as the Icelandic and British banks were failing in 2008. However, it seems that in the case of Barclays, real (and much-needed) Qatari capital did pour into the bank, whereas in the case of Kaupþing, the

76   www.mbl.is/frettir/innlent/2016/05/26/bretar_glottu_spurdir_um_thyrluflug
77   hudoc.echr.coe.int/fre?i=001-193494
78   www.theguardian.com/business/2020/feb/28/three-former-barclays-executives-found-not-guilty-of-fraud

only money that changed hands was the payment itself: Kaupþing never received any new investment at all.

The Icelandic media did a good job of covering the Al-Thani case and the other unfolding investigations. In 2010, for example, Icelandic State TV (*RÚV*) broadcast a series of three evening programs to explain how the market manipulation had worked at each bank, and how the Icelandic public had been deceived. They created animations to show how shares were purchased on the open market and then hidden domestically and offshore. They seemed to structure these documentaries on information from our FME criminal case referrals, and they were well put together.

The newspapers *Morgunblaðið* and *Fréttablaðið* followed the criminal cases as they developed. But conflicts of interest inherent in the ownership or control of each (the first the mouthpiece of the Independence Party, the nation's dominant political party, the second controlled by the same owner as the third-largest of the banks) meant that in-depth unbiased reporting was always unlikely. Later, *Kjarninn* launched as an independent website and provided much-needed investigative journalism for the Land, following up on stories such as the €500m 'emergency loan' that Davíð Oddson's central bank had made to Kaupþing in its dying moments. (More on this later.)

What was always missing in the coverage by the Icelandic media was a sense of international context. The criminal cases were treated very much as a matter of local interest ('our boys done bad'), rather than as the global dynasties of white collar crime they in fact were. One exception here would be the *Icelog* of UK-based journalist Sigrún Davíðsdóttir.[79]

The international media never really returned to the Land after 2009. To them, the Iceland story was done and dusted, when in fact it's never really been told. The criminal cases that played out over the next decade received almost zero coverage outside of Iceland.

It pays to be an insider

Friðfinnur Ragnar Sigurðsson was the deputy treasurer at Glitnir, the third biggest bank, and the head of interbank borrowing. Throughout

79 uti.is

2008, he attended a series of meetings and exchanged a high number of emails on the fast-worsening cash status of that institution. At the same time, he completed a string of trades to sell off his personal shares in Glitnir and was successful by the time of the bank's collapse in selling 100% of his ownership. His total proceeds on the trades were about $470,000. This was the highest-profile insider case to emerge from our investigation team.

The behavior pattern of this knowledgeable executive struck the team at the FME as particularly egregious and an investigation was opened in the autumn of 2010; the agency referred the case for prosecution in the spring of 2011. The Office of the Special Prosecutor conducted its own investigation that year, interviewing the accused plus five other witnesses. The prosecutor charged Friðfinnur for only five of the eight trades: the ones he completed in March, April, and September 2008. The indictment leaves out the three trades he completed in January, February, and May, somewhat amazingly as May comes after March and April.

In February 2013, the district court in Reykjanes heard the case. The court found Friðfinnur guilty of insider trading for these five trades. The judge sentenced him to 12 months in prison and to pay back the money (about 20M ISK or $260,000) he had made on the five.[80]

Friðfinnur appealed the conviction to the Icelandic Supreme Court, which rendered its verdict in December 2013. The top court knocked his prison sentence down to three months.[81] And it knocked back the profit calculation on the trades even more, determining that Friðfinnur had only profited by 7.1m ISK (around $90,000). The rest of the cash proceeds he was free to keep.[82]

---

80 www.mbl.is/greinasafn/grein/1458244
81 Nine months with six of those suspended. In most cases, the convicted served their time, but not all of them did and it has proven difficult to know for sure how long anyone actually spent in prison.
82 *Hæstiréttur Íslands*, case number 193/2013.

The big case:
market manipulation by Kaupþing

The indictment in the big Kaupþing market manipulation case was handed down in March 2013, around three and a half years after our team at FME sent the prosecution referral. The special prosecutor charged nine people in all. First came the same top Kaupþing executives as were charged in Al-Thani: Sigurður Einarsson, the executive chairman, Hreiðar Már, the group CEO, and Magnús Guðmundsson, the CEO of the Luxembourg private bank.

Added to those were the CEO of Icelandic operations, the head of proprietary trading, two proprietary traders, the head of credit, and a senior credit officer.

The indictment covered only the period of November 2007 to October 2008, roughly the last year of the bank's existence. The charges were in three parts: market abuse through real trades (the bank buying up its own shares on the market), market abuse through fictive trades (the bank unloading shares offshore through the back door), and breach of duty (executives acting against the best interests of shareholders by extending bad loans).[83]

The document itself contained some staggering statistics regarding

83 There were two separate market abuse charges and those stem from the EU Market Abuse Directive. And then there was a third major charge which is best translated from Icelandic as agency fraud, or breach of duty.

The first market abuse charge is called market abuse through real trades, and that is using actual buys and sells with the intention of moving a price around. The second type of market abuse, that done through fictive trades, means using trades where in fact the underlying ownership of the shares does not really change, but the trades are done for some manipulative purpose.

These European market abuse laws were designed for activity in only a few trades or within one day, so any one of these days on its own could constitute its own market abuse case. The law was apparently never written to imagine organized market abuse carried out by a large number of individuals acting in concert over a long period of time.

Agency fraud refers to the age-old principal-agent problem: if you are the agent for a principal and you abuse that agency, then this is agency fraud under Icelandic law. To take a more concrete example, if you are the manager of a company and you use that company to benefit yourself rather than to benefit the owner of the company, that could be charged as agency fraud.

market abuse through activity on the public stock exchanges. On the time period set out in the criminal charges, Kaupþing was directly responsible for buying up 42% of all volume in its own shares on the Icelandic stock market, and 31% of volume in the Swedish market, on which its shares also traded. These huge volumes were quite expensive for Kaupþing: the bank spent 94bn ISK (around $1bn) on manipulative share buying in Iceland and 2.5bn SEK (around $250m) on the same in Sweden, just in this final 11 months before it collapsed.

The Kaupþing managers spent these billions just in these two tiny Nordic markets buying up their own shares using their own money. The resulting high share price gave anyone watching (employees, shareholders, the Icelandic public, and present and potential creditors) the false impression that these shares were a thing of value. In fact, the market never supported that value. We cannot know what the true share price of the bank should have been during that time, because the market was so thoroughly distorted by this one-sided buying. In fact there may have been a healthy demand for the shares, or even a willing foreign buyer, just at a much lower price. We will never know.

Kaupþing's buying of its own shares made up a bigger and bigger percentage of the KAUP volume in Iceland, with for example a staggering 67% of exchange volume in August 2008 and 74% of volume in October 2008.[84] On many days of the 229 trading days carefully laid out in the indictment Kaupþing bought at least 25% (148 days), 50% (75 days) or even 75% (20 days) of all the shares traded for the session. Of course, Kaupþing management never once disclosed that they had effectively cornered the market for their own shares. Around the time of the indictment, Gylfi Magnússon, professor of economics at the University of Iceland, stated: "Icelandic bank share prices were in reality falsified. They didn't reflect reality or anything outside of what the top management of the banks were trying to create."

The development of the market price for all three Icelandic banks did not give a normal indication of a company in trouble, because the

---

84 And this may be understating the true size of the bank's purchases of its own shares, because the bank was likely also using other brokers and intermediaries in Iceland to purchase even more of its own shares through these parallel channels.

price in each case never dipped below its high 2006 level all the way until the October 2008 collapse, when it lost everything in one day. If one compares that to a normal company in trouble, as analysts and the media raise questions about the health of that company the share price slowly slides and if the company eventually goes under the final drop is from a level that's already close to 0.

As Kaupþing equity itself made up around 35% of the total market value of all Icelandic shares, this illegal buying had a massively distortionary effect on domestic and global perceptions of the health of the Icelandic market as a whole. There were around 30,000 Kaupþing shareholders, many of them just normal people in Iceland, and all of those 30,000 lost everything that they had invested because the share price went to zero. Those people thought they owned something quite valuable and in many cases had a lot of their savings entrusted there, only to wake up one day to find them evaporated.

Next the indictment lays out the 'fictive trades', the sales out the back door of manipulated shares to dummy companies. The prosecutors chose four of these from the dozens of potential examples: one BVI company (Holt Investment Limited), one Icelandic company (Mata ehf.), one Cypriot company (Desulo Trading Limited), and finally referenced the Sheikh Al-Thani case, to tie that one with this. These were all large trades with no real exchange of ownership. In the case of Holt, around $250m worth of shares 'sold' in just a handful of trades.

Finally, the indictment gave examples of breach of duty, via the extension of bogus loans to finance these deals. One example involved British businessman Kevin Stanford. The bank granted him a short-term money market loan for around $120m to buy Kaupþing shares offshore. When the loan came due after a few weeks, in early September 2008, the bank rolled the balance into a new loan two more times.

On 26 June 2015, the Reykjavík District Court convicted seven of the nine people charged and handed down prison terms between no time and four and a half years. The defendants appealed their case to the Icelandic Supreme Court and that court imposed an even stricter judgment: it found all nine defendants guilty in its ruling of 6 October 2016, though not all of them received punishment.[85]

We can look at one example of how the executives in the scam benefited personally, as cited in the case. The CEO, Hreiðar Már Sigurðsson, cashed out some of his stock options immediately as they vested on 6 August 2008. To do this he used a new company incorporated in Iceland. It is named after him: Hreiðar Már Sigurðsson ehf (like an LLC). The company exercised his options for him at the 'market' price (a price created out of thin air by the actions of him and his staff) and bought the shares from his personal account. How did a newly created company get the money to do this deal? It took a loan for 100% of the deal value from Kaupþing, of course.

Hreiðar's personal cash profit for this one-day transaction was about $3.25m. But his bank was out of business two months later. He kept the cash. The company bearing his name ended up with a bunch of worthless shares and a loan to Kaupþing that it could never repay.[86]

"If the owners of a solvent firm pay themselves a dollar today out of the firm, they diminish the amount they can distribute to themselves tomorrow by that dollar plus its earnings. So the owners of a solvent firm have no special incentive to take money out of it today.

"In contrast, if the owners of a bankrupt firm take an extra dollar out of their firm, they will sacrifice literally nothing tomorrow. Why? Because the bankrupt firm is already exhausting all of its assets ...

"Since there will be nothing left over for the owners, they have the same economic incentives as Genghis Khan's army, as

85 *Hæstiréttur Íslands*, case number 145/2014.
    In addition to the three executives Sigurður, Hreiðar Már, and Magnús, the high court found the CEO of Icelandic operations, the head of proprietary trading, two proprietary traders, the head of credit, and a senior credit officer all to be guilty in this case.
86 Hreiðar Már was charged separately in this case with insider trading and abuse of agency, and absolved at the appeals court level in 2020. *Landsréttur Íslands*, case number 917/2018.

it marched across Asia: what they do not take today, they will never see tomorrow. Their incentive is to loot."[87]

Market manipulation by Landsbanki

In the big Landsbanki market manipulation case, the CEO Sigurjón Árnason was convicted, alongside three employees of the Landsbanki proprietary trading desk, who bought up Landsbanki shares on the open market, day after day. The Supreme Court of Iceland upheld the decision in February 2016[88]; three of the four had been convicted at the district court level in November 2014.[89] All of the men maintain their innocence, despite the convictions, in a pattern very similar to that of the Kaupþing executives. Some of the defendants submitted a claim to the European Court of Human Rights, which announced in March 2021 that it had "struck the applications out of its list of cases after receiving friendly settlement declarations". In these, "the Icelandic state acknowledged violations of the applicants' right to a fair trial and undertook to pay them €12,000 each".[90]

Prison sentences for the big Landsbanki market manipulation case can be seen as light, but in the case of Sigurjón, his prison term

---

87 *Phishing for Phools: The Economics of Manipulation and Deception*, George Akerlof & Robert Shiller, 2015, p. 118

88 *Hæstiréttur Íslands*, case number 842/2014.

On 12 March 2021, Iceland's top court, Hæstiréttur Íslands, issued a new judgment for Sigurjón in the Landsbanki market manipulation case. It upheld his earlier conviction for market abuse, but restricted now to the trading days 29 September to 3 October 2008. It sentenced him to nine months in prison and suspended the sentence. The Court instructed the Icelandic state to pay the costs of his defense attorney for this reopened case, totaling 4.5m ISK or about $35,000. It further instructed the Icelandic state to pay his legal costs in its earlier verdict of 2016, 7.44m ISK or about $57,000.

Hæstiréttur Íslands, case number 35/2019.

89 kjarninn.is/frettir/2016-02-04-sigurjon-th-arnason-daemdur-fyrir-markadsmisnotkun-i-haestaretti

90 According to the declarations seen by the ECHR, "the applicants are free to apply for the reopening of their cases" hudoc.echr.coe.int/eng-press#{%22item id%22:[%22003-6954127-9356139%22]}

was added to a sentence handed down in the related 'Imon' case[91], which also snared two other senior Landsbanki executives, the head of corporate lending[92] and the head of the brokerage desk. Imon was a shell company created by Landsbanki to stuff full of worthless shares bought up on the open market.

The case of the offshore companies holding Landsbanki shares made its separate way to the highest court of Iceland. The bank had made use of ten different companies incorporated in Panama, the British Virgin Islands, and other tax havens to hold its own shares off balance sheet. The stated justification for these companies was so that the bank would have shares on hand for when its executives and employees exercised their share options in the future. This is, of course, preposterous: publicly listed companies routinely create new shares from scratch to fulfil employee option grants, they don't warehouse them offshore for years in expensive and secretive entities. And even when employees

91   kjarninn.is/frettir/sigurjon-th-arnason-daemdur-i-thriggja-og-halfs-ars-fangelsi-i-imon-malinu

92   After her conviction in the Imon case, one of the parties submitted a claim to the European Court of Human Rights, asking for €5m in damages from the Icelandic state. The court found partially in her favor, as one Icelandic supreme court justice had lost significantly on the collapse of Landsbanki yet not declared this, and awarded her €17,000. www.courthousenews.com/wp-content/uploads/2020/02/echr-iceland.pdf

On 12 March 2021, Iceland's top court, Hæstiréttur Íslands, issued its judgment in the reopened Imon case. The Court upheld its original decision that Sigurjón was guilty of market abuse and that this second party was also complicit. The Court reversed its earlier convictions for umboðssvik, or agency fraud.

The Court reduced Sigurjón's sentence to 12 months from three years and six months. The Court reduced the sentence of the second party to four months from 18 months. Both sentences were also suspended. The original sentences were handed down by the same court in case number 456/2014.

The Court instructed the Icelandic state to pay the defense costs for both parties in this reopened case, totaling 12m ISK, or about $93,000. In addition, the Court instructed the Icelandic state to pay all defense costs in the earlier verdict of case number 456/2014.

The second party served 16 months in prison, and will serve no more time. Sigurjón never began serving his sentence for either this or his conviction for the big Landsbanki case, and now will not serve any time, according to RÚV.

www.ruv.is/frett/2021/03/12/sigridur-elin-thegar-afplanad-16-manada-refsingu

Hæstiréttur Íslands, case number 456/2014.

Hæstiréttur Íslands, case number 34/2019.

did exercise their share options to buy 217m shares between 2004 and 2008, the share positions Landsbanki held offshore did not drop at all![93]

In addition, the offshore companies were effectively given free put options—that is, the right to 'put' the shares back to Landsbanki in case the share price fell. The oldest of these companies, LB Holding, was incorporated in 2000, when Landsbanki was still partially government owned. By 2008, these shady entities controlled 13.2% of all the shares in the bank, yet they were financed through 2006 by the bank's own cash, and afterwards indirectly so. On 10 March 2016 Hæstiréttur Íslands found the two defendants in this case not guilty.[94]

Market manipulation by Glitnir

In the case of Glitnir, the third largest bank, the special prosecutor charged five in the large market manipulation case, using bank funds to boost their share price, in March 2016. They include Lárus Welding, the CEO. Lárus was convicted in December 2017 in Reykjavík District Court in the related Stím case and reported to prison to begin serving a five-year sentence. Stím was an Icelandic company created to buy up shares in Glitnir and FL Group, the investment company. Also sentenced in the Stím case were a senior executive from Glitnir, as well as the head of Saga Capital, Þorvaldur Lúðvík Sigurjónsson, the CEO from the dawn raid.[95,96]

Also charged in the big Glitnir market manipulation case were the head of corporate banking and three traders on the proprietary

93 The third volume of *Aðdragandi og orsakir falls íslenku bankanna 2008 og tengdir atburðir*, the report of Iceland's Special Investigation Commission, pp. 60–72, features a wonderful section on these companies. Their saga is probably worthy of its own book, as is so much else in this story.

94 *Hæstiréttur Íslands*, case number 781/2014.

95 kjarninn.is/frettir/2017-12-21-larus-welding-faer-fimm-ara-dom-i-stim-malinu

96 In a strategy similar to Kaupþing and Al-Thani, the prosecutor started with a smaller Glitnir case as an appetizer before moving on to the main course of the grand-scale market abuse. Al-Thani and Stím had both gone earlier to him from FME, because they were easier for FME to investigate. And once they got to his desk, he decided to pursue them pending extended investigations of the bigger cases.

trading desk. (The names of these prop traders are the same ones we had so much trouble getting the Fixer to confirm to us.)

In contrast with Kaupþing and Landsbanki, which both made heavy use of offshore shell companies—for example, in the BVI—to hide their illegally purchased shares, Glitnir relied more on having its own employees buy the junk shares off its books. The indictment lays out for example a famous disgorgement of shares by the bank to 14 newly created shell companies on 15 and 16 May 2008. Each of the 14 companies, incorporated in Iceland, had as its listed owner a member of senior management or employee of the bank itself. And of course, the companies possessed no funds of their own: all of the money used in the deals came from loans made by the bank.[97] The total value of these free gifts to employees' bogus companies was worth around $90m at the time. This small amount was of course only a fraction of the size of the years-long share laundering scheme perpetrated by Glitnir. And as with Kaupþing, some pieces of this scheme (like Stím and another case called BK-44) were successfully prosecuted as separate cases before the big one came to court.

The five defendants in the big case were all found guilty by the Reykjavík District Court in March 2018. However, the CEO was given no additional prison time (he was already sentenced to prison time in other cases) and the three traders were given suspended sentences. The second executive received a 12-month sentence.[98] In December 2019, the new Icelandic appeals court completely cleared one of the prop desk traders in the case, Pétur Jónasson, and suspended the prison sentence for the head of corporate banking.[99] In its decision, the court pointed out that it had been nine years since FME referred the case to the special prosecutor, and in light of "great and unexplained" delays in bringing this case to trial suspending this man's prison time was "inevitable".[100]

97 kjarninn.is/skyring/2018-01-18-um-hvad-snyst-markadsmisnotkunarmal-glitnis
98 www.visir.is/g/2018180309767
99 *Landsréttur Íslands*, case number 332/2018.
100 kjarninn.is/frettir/2019-12-06-syknad-og-refsing-mildud-i-glitnismali

Marple and Lindsor

The Marple case went to trial in 2015. It was a cross-jurisdictional
investigation involving both Iceland and Luxembourg. The case
featured giant movements of money, including using mispriced bond
trades to funnel cash. It also featured the use of 'demand guarantees'
to move funds between countries, and from Kaupþing straight into
the pockets of one of its banner clients. This was the case that I
worked on in my spare time at the FME.

There were ultimately four charges to the Marple matter:
embezzlement (*fjárdráttur*), breach of duty (*umboðssvik*), collusion/
cover-up (*hylming*), and money laundering (*peningaþvætti*).

In 2007, the Bakkavör Brothers, big shareholders in Kaupþing,
wanted out of some of their holdings in the bank. They owned quite
a bit of stock in Exista, another publicly traded shell company created
more or less as a wrapper around Kaupþing shares, and they wanted
their money out of this investment. (According to the 2006 Merrill
Lynch report, their holding company Bakkabræður, for example,
owned around 60% of Exista BV, which in turn held around 20%
of the shares in Kaupþing. And they likely had other exposures to
Kaupþing through their tangled web of companies.)

So Kaupþing management found a 'buyer' for these unwanted
Exista shares, and that was wealthy investor Skúli Þorvaldson, through
his company Marple, a company incorporated in Luxembourg. (In
court, Skúli disputed that he was the true owner of this company,
saying he didn't even know it existed until after the banks collapsed
in 2008 and that Kaupþing management had foisted the whole thing
on him.)

Through a couple of large trades in 2007, this Marple bought out
some of the Bakkavör Brothers' huge position in Exista, to the tune
of 11.4bn ISK (around $190m at the time). Skúli's Marple wasn't a
true buyer, though, because the little company didn't have any funds
of its own. Kaupþing, through its Luxembourg private bank, loaned
cash into Marple to pay for the deal, as they had so often before.
"We're a bank; we make loans!"

The problem for Marple was that the deal was a dog. The Exista shares dropped like a rock, and Skúli's sad little company ended up with around 3bn ISK in losses by the end of 2007. That's real money for some people: around $50m at the time. Skúli's firm was technically on the hook for these losses.

Not a problem: the managers at Kaupþing in Iceland decided to make the man whole, and wired Marple the 3bn ISK in cash directly from their treasury on 19 December 2007. The only issue here: there wasn't any business reason for this cash wire of 50 million bucks. Everyone went home and had a good Christmas. But on 12 January 2008 they created and backdated an 'option agreement' to try to justify wiring the funds (it didn't justify the wire at all; such options have value in the financial world, and Marple never paid a dime for this one).

A few days later, on 31 January 2008, Kaupþing in Iceland created a 'demand guarantee' for Kaupthing Luxembourg. The parent bank guaranteed that it would cover a loan balance of up to €50m for any amount that Marple owed the Luxembourg private bank, where Skúli had been a client since the doors opened. Six months later, at the end of July, the Icelandic bank raised the guarantee amount to a whopping €140m. The guarantee was put in place to ensure that if Marple couldn't make good on its loans, Kaupþing would immediately disburse these large amounts to its daughter bank, Kaupthing Luxembourg, in cash.

Things continued to worsen for Marple because it was stuffed full of junky Exista shares, really themselves just wrappers around heavily manipulated worthless Kaupþing shares, and these all kept losing value. So to try to make Marple whole again, in May 2008 the Luxembourg bankers executed a series of up-and-down bond trades designed to funnel cash into the ailing company: they'd sell the company some securities and buy them back soon thereafter for inflated prices, leaving the cash behind in Marple. But Marple was a black hole of losses.

So again, at the end of June 2008, Kaupþing wired over another 3bn ISK in cash, directly into Marple. (This was around $38m at the time.) And finally, on the Friday before Kaupþing's collapse, 3 October 2008, the Icelandic bank transferred 10bn ISK to Marple (around $88m at that time). The internal justification for these giant money wires was the demand guarantees but these had been made between the two banks. Never mind that, the money went straight into Marple's account anyway. And straight out to someone's pocket: as Kaupþing was collapsing on 6 October, someone—I never found out who—withdrew £10.4m from the Marple accounts.

The verdict in the Marple case was handed down in Reykjavík District Court on 9 October 2015. The defendants were the Kaupþing CEO (Hreiðar Már), who received six additional months in prison, the Kaup Lux CEO (Magnús Guðmundsson), who received 18 additional months in prison, and the investor Skúli Þorvaldsson, who received six months in prison but was acquitted by the Icelandic appeals court[101,102] in 2019. The Kaupþing CFO was also acquitted. According to the judge, this chief financial officer of an entity 30% larger than Enron had no way to know that the contracts her boss asked her to execute were criminal and was merely acting in good faith in her role.

Funds totalling €46.75m had been frozen in Luxembourg on request of the special prosecutor in Iceland. Skúli or his companies were holding large sums of money in various pockets abroad. These were frozen on 3 June 2011.

Of those, €6.7m were returned to the Icelandic state in the Marple verdict, representing 14% of the total amount frozen. No funds were returned to the estate of Kaupþing.

The Lindsor investigations continue in the Grand Duchy of Luxembourg, where the case was referred to a prosecutor in 2020. According to an Icelandic news article, it is very likely that charges will be filed against some of the suspects in the case.[103]

101 kjarninn.is/frettir/2019-02-15-hreidar-mar-og-magnus-sekir-i-marple-malinu
102 Landsréttur Íslands, case number 90/2018.
103 kjarninn.is/skyring/2020-07-07-lindsor-rannsoknin-naer-til-nyrra-grunadra-og-ad-ljuka-fyrir-haustid

Nothing more to CLN here

In early 2008, the Kaupþing bosses had expressed their displeasure about the cost of the insurance premiums on their debts to their contacts at Deutsche Bank. The Kaupþing guys said their CDS spread was just too high and did not reflect a liquid market. By this they meant that if there were more parties willing to insure their debt, the added competition would bring the cost of this CDS insurance down to levels they deemed reasonable.

Deutsche Bank smelled an opportunity. It explained to the Icelanders that there were ways to add liquidity to the CDS market, such as through custom-tailored derivatives. The Deutsche team followed up with a memo in February 2008, titled: 'Why the CDS curve is where it is and what can we do to take it back to normal levels'.

And here is where the CLN—credit-linked note—comes in. Deutsche offered this product as their solution. (The Kaupþing bosses had by this point in fact already purchased around $70m in CLNs from Credit Suisse and stuffed them in their YFST portfolio— the ones we had come across already—so they knew the ropes of this kind of deal.)

Emails back and forth between the top executives of Kaupþing and a senior trader from Deutsche Bank throughout 2008 show how eager the Icelandic bankers were to get the CLN train moving. Improvement in their CDS spread was crucial to their survival. (And then, weeks after the Kaupþing collapse, Sigurður Einarsson, the executive chairman, sent his famous "Kæri vinir og vandamenn" email to try to justify the massive corrupt deal.)

With the CLN, Deutsche in effect proposed to Kaupþing: "Give us a pile of money today. We will pay you interest on that money each year. If you're still in business in five years, we'll give you the money back. Otherwise, we'll keep it."

Deutsche also implied that in the interim they would use the pile of money to issue new insurance to the market, bringing the Kaupþing CDS spread down to 'normal' levels—signaling to the world that Kaupþing wasn't in fact about to shut off the lights.

"Great, where do we sign?" said the Kaupþing bosses.

"Not so fast," said Deutsche. "If you do this trade directly with us it could look like you're trying to manipulate the key market for your debt. So, why not bring us some clients who want to do this trade instead?"[104] Wink, wink.

So, no stuffing of these shiny new Deutsche derivatives in the YFST slush fund after all. The bank would have to find, or create, clients to buy these derivatives. Discussions with London continued as the Icelanders put together the deal. The key executive for Deutsche discussed market timing in a classic email from June 2008, where he advised the Kaupþing bosses how to get the "most bang for the buck" as they attempted to bend the giant, global CDS market to their will.

By August 2008, the winter storms were starting in the Land, and everything was ready. Kaupþing had created a wedding cake of shell companies in the British Virgin Islands, through their Luxembourg private banking subsidiary.

The British Virgin Islands are a British Overseas Territory in the Caribbean. They carry the imprimatur of the Queen of England but are not technically a part of her United Kingdom. As such, they seem almost purpose-built as a tax haven. The capital Road Town has just under 10,000 people, but hundreds of thousands of companies with registered addresses. Among them, thousands established by Icelanders during the boom years.

Luxembourg has a lawyer (and likely more than one) who spends his days out at cafés smoking cigarettes or on the links perfecting his swing. Back in his rarely visited office he has a file cabinet full of shell companies he's already named and established in the British Virgin Islands. The Kaupþing Luxembourg guys call or email him and say, "We need another couple companies, boss." These Icelanders make good customers: ever in need of new shells.

Happy to oblige, the Gauloises-sucking lawyer puts down his café crème, picks up his Blackberry, and fires back a list of names: companies he has warmed up and ready to go. The emails reveal

104 Quotations are paraphrased.

a surprising amount of back and forth on which funny name best suits the crooked deal at hand. For this one, the ex-pat Icelandic bankers in Luxembourg choose Chesterfield and Partridge as the main vehicles, and for the next layer of the wedding cake, four more funny-sounding holding companies: Charbon Capital, Holly Beach, Trenvis, and Harlow. These companies, in turn, have real people as their listed owners—VIP clients of the bank: Antonious Yerolemou, Skúli Þorvaldson, Karen Millen, Kevin Stanford, and Ólafur Ólafsson.

Let's talk for a second about these BVI entities, like Chesterfield and Partridge. In effect, these are just names written on empty envelopes. There are a handful of sheets of paper outlining the founding of each, stuffed in drawers at law firms around the world. Even the government of the British Virgin Islands itself cannot tell us who owns a given firm, the same as the government of the U.S. state of Delaware (on which the BVI models its dubious system) cannot say who exactly is behind each of the companies it charters. In the case of the BVI, a local law firm called a registered agent is supposed to have this information. In practice, they often do not if the company changed hands abroad since its founding.[105]

The principal two shell companies in this case, Chesterfield and Partridge, contract directly with Deutsche Bank on buying the CLNs, thus moving a pile of money over to London, where Deutsche's derivatives desk is based. But of course Chesterfield and Partridge are just sheaves of paper and have no assets of their own: the money will have to come from Kaupþing in Iceland. And quite a pile: €510m in all.

The Kaupþing deal with Deutsche began to go forward in early August 2008, with the transfer of only half the total amount,

---

105 In fact, what gives these 'offshore'/Delaware companies any standing at all is not their scanty founding documents, but the willingness of 'onshore' banks in places like London, New York, and of course Reykjavík, to transact with them as though they are legitimate: to open bank accounts and trading accounts in their names. The dirty secret of offshore finance is that it's really onshore finance; it doesn't exist at all without the say-so of 'reputable' banks in major cities. The choice of the word 'offshore' itself is a smokescreen, a way to direct attention away from the big-city firms that always hold the funds. The money never leaves their accounts.

around €250m, plus fees. (The rest could be called on by Deutsche if market conditions worsened and insurance on Kaupþing got even more expensive.) The Icelandic bank transferred the funds out of its Luxembourg subsidiary in the names of the two shell companies Chesterfield and Partridge. Inside Kaupþing, top executives emailed back and forth with a combination of excitement and apprehension: finally the CDS market would be made to behave, and the world would be able to see how safe and secure was the largest Icelandic bank.

Unfortunately for Kaupþing, the CDS spread hardly seemed to move in their favor. And then it really did get moving—but in the wrong direction! The Icelanders couldn't believe it. Day by day it got worse: despite the big outflow of cash to offer up insurance on themselves, the market price of insurance showed an ever-riskier bank.

Things continued to worsen. And then, in early September, Deutsche made its first margin call: to keep the deal active, Kaupþing had to wire another €100m in cash, again funneled via Luxembourg. And then just days later, another €100m. Deutsche was bleeding the Icelandic bank dry to keep this deal open. The internal emails of Kaupþing show a combination of panic and hope as bank executives command their docile staff to set up gigantic money wires.

In early October, with the imminent collapse of Glitnir and Landsbanki, Kaupþing appealed to the central bank of Iceland. It said it needed exactly €500m to stave off disaster, the same amount it was losing in this massive deal with Deutsche. At the same time, Deutsche was hounding the Icelandic bank, loan-shark style, via ever more aggressive emails, to send them the final €50m.

On 6 October 2008, the same day as Glitnir went down, the Icelandic central bank turned over the full amount, exactly €500m, in cash, to Kaupþing. This was substantially all the foreign currency that the nation of Iceland possessed—a few thousand bucks from every man, woman, and child in the Land. And that day, Kaupþing made good the last €50m margin call.

Within three days Kaupþing was out of business.

Kaupþing executives say they had the assurance of Deutsche Bank that the new CDS insurance flowing from the €510m deal would be sold on the open market. But instead of issuing new CDS protection, the Deutsche Bank guys kept at least some of that insurance for themselves. They knew that the Icelandic bank was in trouble. And their bank had lent a lot to Kaupþing over the years—money that the German bank was in clear danger of losing. (Deutsche still held £4.8bn in claims on Kaupþing after the crash, according to The Guardian[106].) Did Deutsche concoct an elaborate scheme to get the Icelanders to sell insurance on themselves and place the German bank ahead of the other creditors in Kaupþing's inevitable bankruptcy? In effect Deutsche Bank obtained €510m in cash from its borrower, Kaupþing bank (and the Icelandic public), in the days leading up to the bank's collapse, cash it did not have to repay. The Icelandic central bank never recovered most of its emergency loan. (Without admitting wrongdoing, Deutsche Bank did, however, pay back €425m of the €510m to the two shell companies Chesterfield and Partridge in December 2016,[107] and most of this money would flow back to the estate of Kaupþing.)

Remember those employees in Luxembourg, the ones who took loans from their employer to buy hundreds of thousands of euros worth of Kaupþing junk bonds in their own names? Their buying seems to have coincided with the beginning of the CLN deal between Kaupþing and Deutsche. Did these employees of the Kaupþing Luxembourg private bank know the inside information that the bank was about to start manipulating its CDS spread in London and decide to profit personally by buying and holding Kaupþing bonds, pending completion of the deal with Deutsche? Perhaps they assumed that once the CDS spread manipulation went through, their bonds would jump in value and they would make big money.

If that was their plan, what these KauLux staffers didn't count on was that the traders at Deutsche would take the Icelanders for a ride, and issue very little CDS on the public market. So their junk bonds

106 www.theguardian.com/business/2010/jun/06/kaupthing-deutsch-bank-iceland
107 uti.is/2019/02/deutsche-bank-kaupthing-and-alleged-market-manipulation

ended up being worthless. Luckily, they could use stolen money (the €171m Lindsor wire) to bail them out of their failed attempt at insider trading.

The behavior of both Kaupþing and Deutsche in this sorry episode could remind one of the phrase: 'You can't con an honest man'—or maybe its contrapositive: 'If you want someone easy to defraud, look for another fraudster.' Kaupþing hired Deutsche to con the credit markets on its behalf, but Deutsche turned around and conned Kaupþing instead. I had already seen this principle in action: during the dotcom boom, I worked briefly for a shambolic San Francisco software company. Lacking a fully functional product, we nevertheless wrote user manuals in perfect English to describe features that did not yet and probably never would exist.[108] Juiced up on fat up-front commissions, our sales guys went out and sold $5m, $10m, or $30m software packages to unwitting customers in corporate America. Some of the biggest buyers of our junk software were Enron, WorldCom, HealthSouth, and Global Crossing. All four of these firms, which had seemed easy targets for our predatory sales force, were taken down shortly thereafter and in grand style by their own internal accounting frauds. The software firm itself mostly evaporated around the same time in waves of lawsuits from unhappy customers, but unfortunately not before it had its IPO on Nasdaq and earned both its founders and Goldman Sachs, its Wall Street bankers, big paydays.[109] The San Francisco saga came back to mind as I puzzled through the facts of the Deutsche-Kaupþing fiasco.

The special prosecutor charged the parties behind the Icelandic side of the CLN agreement with Deutsche Bank on 22 April 2014. These ended up being the same top three Kaupþing executives from earlier cases (Sigurður Einarsson, Hreiðar Már Sigurðsson, Magnús

---

108 A well-known practice in the often-shady world of Big Software, this is known as writing 'vaporware'.

109 In a parallel with my later departure from Landsbanki, I had become increasingly uncomfortable with the work environment. We were making substantial promises to our earnest midwestern client that we had no ability or internal will to deliver on, and I quit a few months before the IPO.

Guðmundsson). The case centers around the extension of bank loans to shell companies in BVI, whose beneficial owners were wealthy clients of the Luxembourg private bank. The prosecutor maintained these loans represented violations of the general criminal code of Iceland, specifically criminal breach of duty: they pumped the bank's own cash out the door in furtherance of this scheme.

The case went before the Reykjavík District Court in early December 2015, where the three defendants were subsequently found not guilty. The Icelandic supreme court then heard an appeal by the prosecutor and rendered its judgment on 19 October 2017, finding serious flaws in the reasoning of the lower court sending the case back to the lower court to be retried from scratch.[110]

However, the Reykjavík District Court dismissed the CLN case in September 2018, citing incomplete investigation by the prosecutor.[111] The court found that the prosecutor's team had not sought enough information from either Deutsche Bank or the liquidators of the two BVI shell companies Chesterfield and Partridge. In its verdict of 19 March 2021, the new Icelandic Court of Appeals found both Hreiðar Már and Magnús guilty, but did not confer additional punishment. The court confirmed that Sigurður was not guilty in this matter.[112] On the Deutsche Bank side—issuance of CDS on Kaupþing backed by monies from Kaupþing—there was never a legal determination.

Kevin Stanford, a VIP borrower from Kaupþing whose name was used to both hide shares offshore and as a front investor in the sham CLN deal with Deutsche Bank, had this to say in a 2019 open letter[113] to Kaupþing managers: "Whilst you live off the proceeds of your 'Kaupthinking' hidden in your Wives' Swiss Bank Accounts, we are forced to defend wrongful claims from the successors of Kaupthing … that use your deception to their benefit. It is ironic is [sic] that after you stole what amounts to the cost of new hospital (€171m) from the Icelandic people, today the government-owned banks, Landsbankinn

110 *Hæstiréttur Íslands*, case number 156/2016.
111 kjarninn.is/skyring/2018-09-11-heradsdomur-visar-fra-cln-mali-kaupthingsmanna
112 *Landsréttur Íslands*, case number 604/2019.
113 kjarninn.overcastcdn.com/documents/0.7_Hreidar_and_Magnus_open_letter_.pdf

and Islandsbanki provide you with funding for your hotel portfolio. What is also quite astonishing is that Stefnir hf a subsidiary owned by Arion Bank hf (formally Kaupthing hf) have invested in your hotel group. We invite you to refute our allegations, and if you cannot, it will appear that in this particular instance crime does pay in Iceland."

And there is yet another twist in the CLN story, never fully investigated. At the end of 2007 and beginning of 2008, Iceland's Housing Finance Fund (HFF / *Íbúðalánasjóðurinn*), the government vehicle that issues mortgages and sponsors home ownership throughout the Land, and the same entity with whom the banks couldn't compete in part I of this book, also bought seven different CLNs referencing Kaupþing Bank! The issuer of the notes in this case was not Deutsche Bank but two other Icelandic banks, Glitnir and Straumur. With the collapse of Kaupþing a few months later, the Housing Finance Fund (and thus the people of Iceland) stood to lose a total of 9.4bn ISK (about $160m pre-crisis, $80m post-crisis) on these trades. However, the Fund entered a further complex series of trades at this point with a cash-starved Straumur (Iceland's fourth-biggest bank) to try to reduce the immediate loss it had to take onto its books: it let Straumur buy back the CLNs at full face value, and simultaneously gifted Straumur valuable Icelandic mortgage bonds at half price. The HFF kept all the money it received on these deals at a cash savings account with Straumur that paid below-market interest rates. A few months later, Straumur itself collapsed, taking this slush-fund savings account with it.

But why did this government agency initially gamble Icelandic taxpayer money betting on the continued health of Iceland's biggest private bank, Kaupþing? Was such a giant gamble even allowed under the agency's charter? Who oversaw these trades, what was the rationale for them, and what was the process by which the agency approved them? And who approved the shady series of cover-up trades with Straumur after the crisis?[114] These questions remain unanswered.

114 www.rna.is/ibudalanasjodur/skyrsla-nefndarinnar/bindi-3/
kafli14/?CacheRefresh=1#footnote-61440-22
www.mbl.is/greinasafn/grein/1471672

33

POLITICAL FALLOUT

The Landsdómur and Geir Haarde

THE parliamentary Special Investigation Commission report of 2010 recommended prosecution of some senior politicians for their role in the crisis. A special committee of the parliament decided in September 2010 to push forward a case against four government ministers named in the report. Later that month, the full *Alþingi* (parliament) decided to charge only Geir Haarde, the prime minister during the 2008 financial collapse. This kicked off a process called *Landsdómur*. Iceland convened a special national court for the first time in its history. This particular constitutional remedy had never been used. The prosecutor for the parliament led off his 2011 indictment of Geir Haarde with "intentional delinquency or sensational negligence in his official duties as prime minister".[115]

The former top politician was found guilty on one of the charges against him in April 2012.[116] He was found "grossly negligent" (*af*

---

115 www.mbl.is/media/34/3034.pdf

116 upload.wikimedia.org/wikipedia/commons/a/a2/Dómur_Landsdóms_nr._3-2011.
pdf, judgment in section XIII

stórfelldu gáleysi) in failing to address the problems that Icelandic banks were facing or their potential consequences for Iceland's economy at his cabinet meetings, thereby keeping other ministers in the dark.[117] In this, he is the only Icelander in history to be convicted of a high crime by this special national court.[118] He was, however, not sentenced to any prison time or other sanctions on the grounds that he was (1) 61 years old, and (2) had no previous criminal record. Subsequently, he was appointed Ambassador to the United States, arguably the most prestigious Icelandic ambassadorship among one of only a handful of foreign missions maintained by the Land.

Pals in Panama

After public unrest and endless public demonstrations ('the pots and pans revolution') in winter 2008–09,[119] Iceland finally had new elections, resulting in a new government: a coalition between center-left and green parties to replace the big two—Sjálfstæðisflokkur or Independence (fishermen) and Framsóknarflokkur or Progressive (farmers)—that had dominated Icelandic politics for decades. In early 2009 the Office of Special Prosecutor was established to coincide with the intensification of investigations into the collapse of the banks at FME. But by the end of 2011, FME was winding down the investigation teams, despite a huge backlog of open cases.

The years 2009–13 were very difficult for the Icelandic public. Much of daily life became a struggle. People lost most or all of the equity they had in their homes. Their salaries barely covered basic

117 He was found not guilty on the other charges against him: (i) not taking action in his capacity as Prime Minister to avert a national catastrophe, (ii) not conducting a risk analysis of the banking sector, (iii) not ensuring the 2006 Consultative Group on Financial Stability and Preparedness worked effectively, (iv) neglecting to actively reduce the size of the banking sector, and (v) not taking an active role in transfer of the Landsbanki Icesave accounts to a UK entity.
118 After his conviction, Geir submitted a claim to the European Court of Human Rights, which did not find in his favor. The decision is here: hudoc.echr.coe.int/eng?i=001-178700.
119 This populist revolt in a tiny country torn apart by political and financial corruption perhaps augured the rise of populism elsewhere in the West, during the decade to come.

necessities. Only the social safety net kept daily life from complete collapse.

The big two parties successfully tarred the new coalition government as responsible for the poor economic conditions in the country, conditions they themselves had created in the botched privatization of the banks, followed by the cheerleading and zero-regulation policies of the boom years that allowed the banks to grow quickly into criminal enterprises.

In the 2013 elections, these political parties got back into power, promising a return to the good times of 2007. The big accomplishment of this new government was large write-downs on high-value home mortgages, to benefit the wealthy voters who had put them back in power.

In December of 2015, this government closed down the office of the special prosecutor, but created a new district prosecutor to take over all the open cases—with a fraction of the headcount and budget. That year, a record number of Icelanders with college degrees moved away from the country. There was nowhere to work and nowhere to live: few good jobs to match education levels. With a university education, one could expect to take home only around $2,650 per month. And the post-crisis tourist boom had converted whole neighborhoods to Airbnbs, pushing families into desolate and undesirable exurbs. Even now, families who manage to purchase a home with a mortgage cannot get ahead, as the monthly inflation adjustment robs them of the equity they work so hard to establish.

In this context, the Panama Papers hit the presses in April 2016. It turned out that the head of each of the big two political parties was hiding both offshore wealth and onshore conflicts of interest from the Icelandic public.

Most egregiously, Sigmundur Davíð, the then-prime minister and head of the Progressive Party, had an offshore firm called Wintris Inc. It was stuffed with tens of millions of euros worth of assets held by Credit Suisse, money that came from his wife's sale of the valuable Toyota franchise in Iceland. As prime minister, Sigmundur

Davíð was negotiating with the creditors of the collapsed banks for final resolution of their bankrupt estates. However, hidden in his own firm offshore were €3.6m in claims on those same banks. The prime minister himself was personally a large creditor to the failed banks—so was he negotiating on behalf of the Icelandic public or his own wallet?

Sigmundur was forced to step down after a humiliating interview by a Swedish journalist came to light. The journalist asked him about Wintris on camera; he stuttered and stammered, finally ripping off the mic and walking out of the room. Today he remains in parliament and head of his own breakaway party, the Middle Party.

The head of the second party in government—the most powerful political party in Icelandic history—was also named in the Panama Papers. Bjarni Benediktsson appears to have owned a Seychelles company called Falson & Co via bearer share certificates, and maintained power of attorney for the firm. He claimed that Falson was set up to invest in real estate in Dubai, but that the investments were sold at a loss.[120] He received a cash payment out of the firm to a Swiss bank account. When questioned, he claimed he thought that his undeclared offshore firm was actually registered in Luxembourg, not the Seychelles. Bjarni took over as prime minister in 2016, with the resignation of Sigmundur Davíð. Bjarni denies wrongdoing in the Falson matter.[121]

Seðlabanki and the emergency loan

As soon as I dug into it, I had wanted to further investigate the €500m emergency loan that Seðlabanki, the central bank of Iceland, made to Kaupþing on 6 October 2008. But my superiors at FME told me that it was not clear if the agency had any jurisdiction over the more prestigious and independent central bank of Iceland. (I argued unsuccessfully that it was worth a try: the central bank was after all a bank, and FME was the regulator of banks.[122])

The former Prime Minister, Davíð Oddsson, the same one who

120 offshoreleaks.icij.org/stories/bjarni-benediktsson
121 www.youtube.com/watch?v=WP-Zaidoylw, stundin.is/grein/5562
122 FME and the central bank merged at the beginning of 2020.

oversaw the botched privatizations of the banks, had somewhat unbelievably become the loose-lipped central banker of Iceland, a post he served through the 2008 crisis. The central bank, under his control, pumped out a round sum of exactly €500m to Kaupþing just three days before its collapse. This was nearly all the foreign currency reserves of Iceland—the equivalent of the country placing all of its last chips on red only to watch the wheel come up black.

In exchange for all the cash, Kaupþing gave the central bank its equity shares in a Danish bank called FIH as collateral. It was likely forbidden under the charter of the Icelandic central bank to even receive an equity stake in another institution, but Davíð and his team took it on anyway. The Danish bank turned out to be mainly a vehicle for holding U.S. subprime mortgage junk, so it had little value. The central bank would have had no way to know this; they did not perform any due diligence on the Danish bank. They simply had no time.

How this sale was agreed and who approved the loan is still a mystery today. A November 2018 news article in Kjarninn states that there was never a loan application from Kaupþing, no approval by the board of the central bank for this loan, and no restrictions on how Kaupþing could use the funds.[123]

We can't pin down exactly how Kaupþing made use of the Seðlabanki loan proceeds, because money is fungible and there was lots of it sloshing around in those final hours. The amount, €500m, is roughly the same amount that Kaupþing lost to Deutsche Bank in its failed attempt to manipulate its own credit spreads. Also, on the same day as the emergency loan was granted, Kaupþing granted €171m to Kaupþing Luxembourg in the Lindsor deal. That money was used to buy up worthless bonds, bailing out Marple, five employees in Luxembourg, and as well as the bank's own trading desk. These parties had tried to personally profit on their inside knowledge of the Deutsche CLN deal, but failed. Now Icelandic central bank largesse helped to wallpaper over their bad actions.

123 kjarninn.is/frettir/2018-11-15-hvernig-var-neydarlanid-veitt-og-hvernig-var-thvi-eytt

34

RECOMMENDATIONS

S O, how could any of this have been different? Well, none of it
is really rocket science. Mostly it comes down to allocating the
right resources to enforce laws and regulations we already have. More
concrete recommendations follow.

For the Land

Most evidently to me, the FME or its successor needs to come in line
with international best practice and establish an enforcement division,
with a permanent staff of six to eight, and a mandate for investigating
potential criminal cases in the Icelandic financial sector. (To my
knowledge, they have no plans to do so at present.) This group would
report directly to the board of directors, or to a special enforcement
board, and would work directly with police and prosecutors. The staff
of this team would necessarily maintain complete independence from
the day-to-day activities carried out by the regulator. They would
pursue cases of insider trading and manipulation on the Icelandic
markets, as well as corruption in the banking sector (illegitimate
loans, conflicts of interest) and Ponzi/pyramid schemes, of which
there are dozens active at any given time in Iceland. Having been

wholly subsumed by Seðlabanki, the central bank, (as FME was at the beginning of 2020) could make this necessary independence all the more difficult. It has lost its visibility as a separate entity.

The independence of this new enforcement division from the rest of the activities of financial regulation will be key. Those who keep in daily contact with regulated entities must maintain good relations with their counterparts at banks and other financial firms. Those investigating potential cases of civil or criminal wrongdoing require a different skillset—and a different relationship with them. If Iceland is large enough to have its own financial sector, it is large enough to have its own enforcers. Without a well-staffed and serious enforcement capacity, a repeat of 2008 is nearly certain.

A decade after the collapse, Iceland still needs to right-size its banking sector. Currently, the three banks are still too big for the economy they serve. Having one of the three as a subsidiary of a bigger Nordic or mainland bank could also confer an advantage in much-needed knowledge and capital. Iceland could make an interesting test market for some of the innovative ideas for general reform of the financial sector, like limited purpose banking, which would transform financial corporations into mutual fund holding companies subject to full and real-time disclosure.

Finally, Iceland needs to phase out inflation-indexed (and foreign currency) home mortgages and other loans. This phenomenon is a forward-feedback loop that builds inflation (and hence instability) into the fabric of the economy. The negative-amortization loans themselves, with the next month's payments unknowable at any time during the loan's lifetime, behave as complicated derivatives and are likely not even legal to provide to retail customers under European law.

For legislators and voters everywhere

Today we stand at an equilibrium point: securities markets all over the world are full of bad actors and corrupt trades, yet no national regulator wants to seriously go after these criminals because to do so would disadvantage their market *vis-a-vis* all of the other markets. No country wants to lose market share! So the cancer continues to eat away at markets across the globe. When I describe the high level of illicit transactions in the markets of the world, some are surprised that there are so many trying to gain a little advantage by breaking laws and regulations. But those same people are not surprised by drivers who speed past them on the highway, trying to get home a little faster. In every area of human endeavor, there are those who seek to profit by skirting the law.

The losers in this culture of pervasive securities crimes are us: the public, who, if we are lucky, have pension or retirement fund money invested in these rotten markets. The value of our investments gets slowly siphoned off by inside traders and market manipulators, but we never really see or feel these losses. And the perpetrators of these scams talk about victimless crimes. Perhaps they are right: after all, if I break into your house at night and steal your television set, you get upset and call the police. You demand the authorities catch the thief. But if I break into your retirement fund and steal the value of your new car, you never notice.

A further detriment to proper policing of the securities markets in many countries comes from those who choose to believe in the fantasy of these markets as immaculate conceptions—conceived without sin. These law and order types suddenly seem to lose their sheriff hats when confronted with the question of how much markets should be monitored. The idea that any crime at all could be committed in these markets is anathema to a whole worldview, and therefore entirely unwelcome. Don't seek, and ye shall never find.

Make sure your financial regulator has an enforcement capability. Look at the size and types of cases they have brought down recently. Are these serious cases or window dressing? Are they naming the parties in these cases or hiding them from view?

At work and in life, we respond to incentives. What are the incentives for a financial regulator to oversee a truly well-regulated market? Spoiler alert: there aren't so many. How many 'page turners' might there be—men and women who flip through legal books until they can justify taking another coffee break? Thousands. As societies, what incentives have we created for these staff to dive deep into their work and really do a great job? We have created incentives to create ever longer lists of legal and regulatory codes, yes. But we reward these people with nothing, or even with losing their jobs, when they try to take necessary action against conmen who poison the well for us all.

On the other hand, what are the incentives for a market participant to cut a corner, to cheat to make an extra million or two? Well, an extra million or two is the answer. Who has the stronger incentive to take action, the regulatory lawyer who collects his paycheck either way, or the small-time fraudster who pockets millions on a couple of inside trades?

The financial sector grows huge, fueled by the bonus culture. But those supposed to oversee this sector are not similarly rewarded for doing great work. Their rewards are the same day in, day out.

If we as a global society really want to clean up the dirty world of finance, we can 1) ensure our regulators are compensated as well as they would be in the private sector, ensuring the best pool of talent, 2) tie part of the pay of the regulators we hire to the size and severity of the successful civil and criminal cases they bring in. This would encourage some of the best and brightest minds in the financial world to become regulators, and it would seriously reduce the incidence of page-turning paralegals looking for an excuse to take no action. A nice side benefit would be the fascinating headlines as a never-before-seen batch of criminals are brought to justice.

If we continue to ignore these problems and let widespread illegal behavior in markets fester, we risk a COVID-like infection of the world financial system—if it is not already present. To quote journalist Spencer Ackerman: "Impunity is wildfire. Impunity never stays in one place."[124]

124 theintercept.com/2020/01/29/john-and-the-giant-impeachment

For management

If you're a corporate executive and want to make a little money for yourself by skirting the law or playing in grey areas, don't. If you want to justify your insider trading with 'nobody got hurt' rather than saying the truth: 'I stole from everyone else in the market that day', don't. If you spend $5m of your own money manipulating a share price to save you $50m in an M&A deal a month later, you also stole from everyone else. Just because you can't see them or name them all, doesn't make your action any less thievery.

Why not admit to yourself what you really are when you steal from others: a criminal. If you make this difficult admission, you'll have one clear advantage: you'll take better precautions. Seasoned criminals— for example, international drug traffickers—have no illusions about who they are. They don't hide behind rationalizations. Instead they work hard to hide the trail of their activities, and they know the law is always out to get them. (And maybe that's the difference here: today, at least, there's no competent and fearsome cop coming after the criminals of the markets, in any place that I know of.) So if you want to commit crimes, come clean about it. It'll be much easier to carry it out successfully. Or maybe just stick to the securities markets, where nobody seems to care.

35

CONCLUSION

THE CEOs and other top executives at each of the three giant Icelandic banks—Kaupþing, Landsbanki, and Glitnir—were convicted of serious felonies and did serve at least some time in Iceland's spectacular white-collar prison at Kvíabryggja. However, through changes in the law, already short sentences became comically short—and within mere months they were back to flying helicopters and dining out with their spouses at the best restaurants in Reykjavík. The deterrent effect of these sentences would seem to a layman to be insignificant.

The three banks continued business as usual under new ID numbers and kept most of their workforce. Kaupþing changed its name to Arion; Glitnir changed its name back to Íslandsbanki, in Spinal-Tap-esque rebranding efforts.

Really, the only savior for Iceland in this—the only reason Iceland is doing even half decently today—is that the *króna* lost more than half of its value during the crisis and has never recovered its pre-crisis strength. Iceland suddenly became a lot cheaper. Foreign money flowed into the country again—this time via tourism.

But that drop in the currency carried a tremendous cost for the average Icelander, who lost half his buying power. Effectively everybody in the country took a 50% pay cut during those years. Iceland today is Swiss prices on Polish salaries, or Manhattan living on Wisconsin money.

By 2019, Airbnbs had taken over all the formerly charming neighborhoods of the capital Reykjavík. Most of the classic cafés and restaurants and bookshops that made Iceland's only city charming were replaced by schlock shops selling stuffed-animal puffins. To handle the surge of tourists (ten times the country's population in visitors each year), Iceland imported foreign workers. So even the Icelandic language has disappeared downtown. The crash in the currency meant a surge in budget tourism, and the cyclone wrecked the city. "All I saw in Iceland were other tourists," an American friend confided to me.

But far worse is the breakdown in social norms since 2008. One friend tells me that the crisis tore the fabric of Icelandic society in two. Now Icelanders yell out their angry views. No one seems to care about the effects of their actions. Everyone is worried about being swindled by everyone else. There's a widespread nihilistic attitude towards relationships and society.

In November 2018, five parliamentarians—among them, former prime minister and Panama Papers celebrity Sigmundur Davíð—were caught in an audio recording at a bar near the parliament building. According to other patrons in the bar, they were speaking in loud voices and could be easily heard as they slagged off the disabled, gays, as well as their own female colleagues in parliament by name. A new low for the Land.

It would be a grievous mistake to write off the Icelandic financial crisis as not more broadly relevant: Iceland is in many ways the world writ small. It is a petri dish for what can happen everywhere. The popular press abroad holds up Iceland as a success story, but this naïve view of things is nothing more than a sugar coating: empty calories designed to make a worried public feel as though cleanup and reconciliation are possible. Yet despite the devastating events of 2008, the dragon of deeply corrupt financial markets has still not been slain, in Iceland or anywhere else. Iceland in 2004–08 is a preview of coming attractions for the world's big markets. Today we find ourselves back in the equivalent of the 1930s, thinking the Great War is over and done with. We naïvely refer to 2008 as the Global Financial Crisis, as if there will only ever be one, when GFC II almost certainly looms on the horizon. We are sitting on a time bomb.

Economic markets can do good work for societies, but they are always and everywhere human creations. The temptation to twist and abuse markets, to lie and cheat by using these imperfect human creations in the service of personal enrichment, will never disappear. We would do well to remember this and structure our markets accordingly. In the words of Justin Rockefeller: "Everything we do with money has moral implications."[125]

White-collar crime is the true crime of the world, accounting for a much more significant chunk of the global economy than its poor blue sibling. But its effects are usually distributed, abstract, and hard to pin down. Unfortunately, the public in all but the most obviously corrupt countries does not perceive crimes committed by politicians and professionals as a serious problem. Societies put a disproportionate amount of resources into combating blue-collar street crime—and by comparison hardly anything into white-collar crime, the crime that keeps us all poor.

Don't get smug about how your own country might stack up against Iceland. The only way we know any of the stories in this book is that our whole economy collapsed, and with that we had a gift: a brief opportunity to try to find some truth among the rubble. We were able to see the banks, frozen mid-crime. The window for our investigative work was narrow because vested interests closed it only a few years after the crisis. Some version of this same story is most likely playing out in your own country right now. Maybe not as extreme as in Iceland (few things are), but it is there.

My aim in going after the biggest fraud I could find was not to stand out. I sat anonymous and alone at an empty desk as I dug through those early trades. I pushed this case hard because I thought that once

125 swiss.cfa/private-equity-investing-for-generations

those around me (and later the nation) realized the magnitude of the financial crime, we would gain the momentum and resources to help us carry out a proper and complete investigation of the run-up to 2008. My strategy worked for a handful of months. Then our own agency closed down our hard-won investigation teams after we had covered less than 10% of the total cases. Looking back, it feels like a whole power structure was against the effort. After all, most of the criminal beneficiaries of the Icelandic boom walked away scot free, and we will never know their stories.

Seen another way, as they oversaw vast conspiracies to set the share prices of their own institutions, the executives at Iceland's overgrown banks were merely responding to incentives. What incentives did we give them, other than to take in as much personal profit for themselves as they could? What incentives did we give the stock exchange and regulator to sniff out and put a stop to this behavior? Human beings respond to incentives. But as human societies we do not often think explicitly of what incentives we create: we prefer to think in laws and regulations, imagining that once these are in place they will function as perfect machines. In reality, following the law is always optional, as is enforcing it. Hard-won experience has shown me that all prosecutions are political: from the wide range of cases a well-resourced prosecutor can take forward, political considerations determine what will hit the docket and what will be filed away. The prosecutor's incentive, after all, is to further the prosecutions that lessen political pressure on her, and to ignore those that increase it. Are we all caught in a game we shouldn't even be playing?

Every language has a word for corruption. But speakers of the language apply that word only to stuff that happens somewhere else. For the corruption that happens right around them in plain view, people tend to have a milder phrase or expression. In Icelandic, corruption is literally *spilling*, a nice word. It means the same as it does in English, like spilling a bit of wine from one glass to another. But in my experience spilling is only ever used to describe activity in places Icelanders look down on, like countries in the east of Europe. Domestically, Icelanders use the verb *redda* (like fix) to signal corrupt activity. So we get *við reddum þessu* (we'll fix it) or *þetta reddast* (it'll fix itself). These expressions nearly always indicate corrupt behavior: how things get fixed is usually through personal connection, line-cutting, rule-bending, or other forms of favoritism.[126]

Transparency International, the watchdog on such matters, routinely classifies Iceland as one of the least corrupt places in the world. That is because their surveys measure the *perception* of corruption. The idea of 'fixing' things is so deeply embedded in the Icelandic psyche that very few Icelanders surveyed would link that concept with corruption. Also, cash bribes probably won't get you very far in the Land. Cash is a relatively recent phenomenon in an economy long dominated by barter. In Iceland you are far more likely to talk your way out of a speeding ticket by having worked on the same farm as the cop's cousin; he would take serious offense at any attempt to slip him a few bills. The United Nations, however, has a broader and more suitable definition of bribery: the conferral of an undue advantage, and by this definition the 'Hey, say hi to your cousin for me' exchange definitely fits the bill.

In the United States, of course, the word corruption is also generally applied to things that happen 'overseas' as Americans like to say. But right there at home America has ingrained corruption by other names. 'Campaign finance' is one.

Through this experience, I learned that without sustained public interest and public pressure, the pervasive corruption in our financial markets will fester and grow. Today, the rapid heating of our planet presents the biggest challenge we have ever known as a species, and there are some interesting market-based proposals that might help to reduce carbon dioxide emissions. But without clean markets to underpin our economic system, how can we expect to have clean air?

126 This idea, of things fixing themselves, is seen as a very positive feature within Icelandic society. Most Icelanders do not recognize the idea that the fixing might harm someone else or the collective. The fixing is seen as a way to get around some cumbersome and unnecessary rule or process. As an example, think back to our favorite compliance officer who called himself Reddari, literally the Fixer. Not so much an enforcer of the rules, he was one who could find ways to fix things so that they would appear to be in compliance.

That public pressure starts with you. Demand of your elected officials that they dedicate commensurate resources to fighting corporate crime as they do to street crime. And pay to support good journalism. Smart and properly incentivized journalists are often our only financial regulators.

ACKNOWLEDGMENTS

THIS book was a real labor of love, and I would like to thank anyone who believed in it during the long years of its creation. For making it possible at all, I would like to thank Mathilde Farine for the brilliant structure and threading of personal and professional, Haig Simonian for his rough-hewn English encouragement, Dominic Büttner for his photographic fluidity, and Christopher Parker and the staff at Harriman House.

On a personal note I would like to thank br. Chân Pháp Lai, br. Bảo Tạng, br. Đạo Kiên, Anita Desai, Meire Yamaguchi Chesney, Russell Napier, Katja Reuther, Bob "Father Chez" Sanchez, Prof. David Trumper, Bethany McLean, Brentie Smalls, Seehallen Kaffeerösterei of Horgen, Good & Pure Coffee of Huế, Kavárna Kolonial of Jindřichův Hradec, and everyone who asked when the book was coming out. I would like to extend extra gratitude to those who gave me the freedom to really pursue this project: you know who you are!

Að lokum vil ég þakka öllu Glitnis-, Kaupþings-, Landsbankastarfsfólki, Framsóknar-, Samfylkingar- og Sjálfstæðisfólki, saksóknurum og öllum öðrum persónum sögunnar. Við skrifin áttaði ég mig á því að við erum öll í sama liðinu. Ef við vinnum saman getum við tryggt að það sem gerðist á Íslandi árið 2008 mun aldrei endurtaka sig, hvorki hér á landi né annarsstaðar í heiminum. Það er mín æðsta ósk.

Endilega verið í sambandi.